Arming Mother Nature

Arming
Mother Nature

*The Birth of Catastrophic
Environmentalism*

JACOB DARWIN HAMBLIN

OXFORD
UNIVERSITY PRESS

OXFORD
UNIVERSITY PRESS

Oxford University Press is a department of the University of Oxford.
It furthers the University's objective of excellence in research,
scholarship, and education by publishing worldwide.

Oxford   New York

Auckland   Cape Town   Dar es Salaam   Hong Kong   Karachi
Kuala Lumpur   Madrid   Melbourne   Mexico City   Nairobi
New Delhi   Shanghai   Taipei   Toronto

With offices in

Argentina   Austria   Brazil   Chile   Czech Republic   France   Greece
Guatemala   Hungary   Italy   Japan   Poland   Portugal   Singapore
South Korea   Switzerland   Thailand   Turkey   Ukraine   Vietnam

Oxford is a registered trade mark of Oxford University Press
in the UK and certain other countries.

Published in the United States of America by
Oxford University Press
198 Madison Avenue, New York, NY 10016

© Oxford University Press 2013

Library of Congress Cataloging-in-Publication Data
Hamblin, Jacob Darwin.
Arming Mother Nature : the birth of catastrophic environmentalism /
Jacob Darwin Hamblin.
pages cm
Includes bibliographical references and index.
ISBN 978-0-19-974005-5 (acid-free paper)
1. Environmental policy—United States—History—20th century.
2. Environmentalism—Political aspects—United States—History—20th century.
3. Environmental sciences—Political aspects—United States—History—20th century.
4. Disasters—Environmental aspects—United States—History—20th century.
5. War—Environmental aspects—History—20th century.
6. Military planning—United States—History—20th century.
7. United States—Military policy.
8. Cold War—Environmental aspects—History—20th century.
9. Nature—Effect of human beings on—History—20th century.
10. Global environmental change—History—20th century. I. Title.
GE180.H35   2013
363.340973—dc23   2012045618

1 3 5 7 9 8 6 4 2

Printed in the United States of America
on acid-free paper

To Cathy and Paul Goldberg
for all they made

Contents

Acknowledgments

I FIRST BEGAN thinking about this project while writing my book, *Ocean-ographers and the Cold War* (2005), which brought me into contact with numerous intriguing sources about the uses of the oceans and the air during the Cold War. I subsequently was drawn into the subject of environmental contamination while writing *Poison in the Well: Radioactive Waste in the Oceans at the Dawn of the Nuclear Age* (2008). As that book went into production, I decided to pursue the idea of "environmental warfare," and I promised a paper on that topic to John McNeill and Corinna Unger, who were organizing a conference at the German Historical Institute in Washington, DC, on the environmental history of the Cold War. I thought I would write primarily about weather control and atmospheric modification, but my sources drew me deeper into military thinking about fighting a third world war, and I ended up producing a chapter on early planning for biological and radiological warfare. By then I was hooked onto a subject that, over the past several years, has been exhilarating, enlightening, and often sobering.

I happened to walk by the Oxford table at the annual meeting for the Society for Historians of American Foreign Relations some years ago. There I met Susan Ferber for the first time, and we had a brief conversation about my idea for a book called "Arming Mother Nature." I'm thankful to Susan for following up, putting the book under contract, and serving as an extraordinarily responsive, diligent, and patient editor.

The research for this book was made possible through the generous financial support of several institutions and the continued cooperation of archivists and staff at libraries and archives in several countries. I acknowledge the assistance of the National Science Foundation, which offered a generous Scholars Award (project # 0738377). I thank Clemson University for its institutional support from 2006 to 2009, and Oregon State

University ever since then. I especially thank Jens Boel (UNESCO Archives), Anne-Marie Smith (NATO Archives), Giuliano Fregoli (FAO Archives), and numerous specialists at the World Health Organization, United Kingdom National Archives, and United States National Archives and Records Administration.

I would like to thank a number of scholars. I am especially grateful for the encouragement I have received over the years from fellow Gauchos Anita Guerrini, Andy Johns, Fred Logevall, Patrick McCray, Peter Neushul, Mike Osborne, Ken Osgood, Zuoyue Wang, and Ben Zulueta. In addition, I extend my thanks to specific people who helped in this work, either by reading portions of it, providing commentary, talking with me about it, or inspiring it in substantial ways. They include Keith Benson, Lisa Brady, Soraya Boudia, James Burns, Mark Carey, Erik Conway, Angela Creager, Soraya de Chadarevian, Sam Deese, Roger Eardley-Pryor, Ron Doel, Kurk Dorsey, Carmel Finley, Jim Fleming, Greg Good, Michael Gordin, Kristine Harper, Gabrielle Hecht, Toshihiro Higuchi, Joshua Howe, Jeff Hughes, David Kaiser, John Krige, Roy MacLeod, Pam Mack, Steve Marks, John McNeill, Erika Milam, Ben Mutschler, Naomi Oreskes, Jahnavi Phalkey, Ron Rainger, Linda Richards, Peder Roberts, Tom Robertson, Adam Rome, Helen Rozwadowski, Lisa Sarasohn, Richard Tucker, Simone Turchetti, Alex Wellerstein, and Audra Wolfe.

On a personal note, I thank my family, especially the women in my life: my wife, Sara, and my daughters, Sophia and Harper. I also thank my parents, Sharon and Les Hamblin, and my sister Sara, not only for their support but also for their perspectives: I would not think the way that I do had I not grown up as an Air Force "brat." I also am grateful to my in-laws, Cathy and Paul Goldberg, for their constant stream of positive energy.

Finally, I would like to acknowledge the enormous intellectual debt I owe to my late mentor Larry Badash (1934–2010), who first introduced me to the history of science when I was 19 years old, with his course on "The Atomic Age." Thanks, Larry.

Arming Mother Nature

Introduction

Total War and Catastrophic Environmentalism

IN MAY 1960 the people of Chile faced the most profound human disaster in their history. A seismic event sent several earthquakes rippling along the length of western South America. The quakes shattered buildings, trapping families in their homes, killing and injuring thousands of people in the rubble. The largest convulsion was so intense—a stunning magnitude 9.5—that it threatened life many thousands of miles away. The shifting ocean floor lifted up a tremendous wall of water nearly 30 feet high that smashed against the Chilean coast, drowning villages and towns. The waves fanned away from the coast, moving at 450 miles per hour, sending 35-foot waves to strike Hilo, Hawaii, and 18-foot waves to the shores of Japan, killing dozens. Tsunamis crashed into the Philippines, Australia, the western coast of the United States, and many Pacific islands. By all accounts, it was the largest earthquake in recorded history.[1]

The grisly scenes made some commentators remark that Mother Nature had a way of putting matters into perspective. Despite scientists' conquest of deadly diseases and taming the power of the atom, humans were extraordinarily vulnerable to the slightest whims of nature. It was time to lay aside petty disagreements and show one's humanity in the face of catastrophe, a lesson some took to heart. Strikers went back to work and donated their wages to relief efforts, and blood plasma was flown in from Argentina. After many residents of the coastal city of Concepcion fled to the woods to escape their crumbling homes, the army mobilized to put families in tents; the navy brought in medicine, food, and clothes; and American planes from the Panama Canal delivered supplies.[2]

In Paris, then the headquarters of the North Atlantic Treaty Organization (NATO), scientists and military officers drew a different lesson from the disaster. They saw the Chilean earthquake as a shining example of what

Americans might soon implement against the Soviet Union. If scientists could identify areas of strain and instability in the earth's crust, a well-placed hydrogen bomb might unleash just the kind of power that had wrought so much destruction in the Pacific. "Environmental warfare" NATO called it. It was a newly conceived class of weapons that utilized human knowledge of the natural environment to fight a global war, and to make America and its allies less vulnerable to catastrophic change.

Arming nature, by harnessing its physical forces and exploiting its biological pathways, fit with the methods American scientists and military leaders expected to use to fight a war against the Soviet Union. Aside from earthquakes, scientists in the decades after World War II worked on radiological contamination, biological weapons, weather control, and several other projects that united scientific knowledge of the natural environment with the strategic goal of killing large numbers of people. Vannevar Bush, the American engineer who dominated government scientific research in the 1940s, once wrote that humans avoided such extremes, not wanting to poison or spread diseases among humans, livestock, or crops. Even Adolf Hitler had refrained from it, Bush said in his 1949 book *Modern Arms and Free Men*. Whatever the reason, he wrote, "somewhere deep in the race there is an ancient motivation that makes men draw back when a means of warfare of this sort is proposed." Bush was thinking of biological and radiological warfare, both of which promised to harm one's enemies indirectly through contaminated land, water, or entire ecosystems. He was intimately familiar with the latest developments on them, having served as chairman of the National Military Establishment's Research and Development Board, which liaised with the Joint Chiefs of Staff (JCS) on military matters related to science and technology. Publicly, he suggested that military men did not take such weapons seriously, that little money was spent on them, and that scientists shied away from research on them.

Subsequent history showed how wrong Vannevar Bush was. As his book went to press, the US government was in the process of stepping up, not scaling back, research and production of weapons designed to harm civilians through disease, starvation, and physical destruction. In the public sphere, revulsion toward these weapons, and any kind of modification of the environment for purposes of war, has been reinforced by international conventions—including the Geneva Protocol of 1925 (finally ratified by the United States in 1975), the Biological and Toxin Weapons Convention of 1972, and the Environmental Modification Convention of 1977. But the United States and its allies pursued scientific research on biological and radiological warfare vigorously after World War II. Other studies to harness the forces of nature in war—for example, to change the course of ocean currents, to manipulate the weather, and to melt polar ice caps—also found a receptive audience among powerful patrons throughout the Cold War. When catastrophes struck innocent people—as in the case of Chile in 1960—scientists and their military partners perceived such events as the future face of war.

As American General Curtis LeMay sent bombers over Japan in the closing months of World War II, he and his statisticians calculated that they had killed between 50 percent and 90 percent of the people in nearly 70 cities prior to dropping atomic bombs. He later confided to a colleague that had the United States lost the war, he would have been tried as a war criminal.[3] His goal had not been to win battles but to kill as many people on the ground as possible. The widespread death of humans, armed or otherwise, became an end in itself. Likewise, in the earliest days of the Cold War, scientists refined their expertise at maximizing human death by arming Mother Nature. They conducted intensive investigations of nature's centuries-old diseases to find out how to create epidemics in humans, animals, and crops. They found military uses for radioactive waste as weapons of large-scale contamination. They also began to experiment with weather control. If war were to break out against the Soviet Union, they knew it would be another world war. That meant another total war, making civilians, factories, and fields legitimate targets.

American strategic planners, particularly the Joint Chiefs of Staff, conceived of a war with the Soviet Union as one that would require mobilizing all industrial and human strength. Imagining future weapons systems, Admiral William Leahy pointed out candidly that civilians would be drawn into a third world war even more than they had been in the second. He and other officers recognized that industrial capacity and human life could not be separated, and they expected to target human population centers.[4] Yet the small number of deliverable atomic bombs (and the lack of them in the Soviet Union) indicated that a war in the near future would be a prolonged conflict in which atomic bombs might not be decisive. This invited research opportunities in other fields targeting entire ecosystems.

Scientific research became a tool to extend "total war" thinking to the natural environment. Top scientists began to imagine contamination on a city and regional scale as an important line of research. For example, scientists at the University of California, Berkeley, knew from wartime work on human patients that internally absorbed radioisotopes could cause severe health damage without being detected easily. They also discovered that plants readily absorbed radioactivity and that radioactive soil was nearly impossible to decontaminate. Radioactive debris, they concluded, could turn a nation's staple crops into fields of poisonous weeds or poison the water supplies of whole cities. At the height of the Korean War, Congressman Al Gore Sr. even recommended dumping radioactive waste all along the border separating North and South Korea. Given the abundance of this troubling radioactive waste available at American nuclear production facilities, he and others reasoned, why not adapt these plants to situations in which contamination was a desired outcome?

Vannevar Bush had been uncomfortable with weapons whose sole purpose was to cause widespread death, yet the United States and United Kingdom pursued many lines of research on exploiting environmental vulnerabilities for this very aim, as did the Soviet Union and its allies. Scientists helped their governments to push the frontiers of human mastery over nature's processes, and by the 1950s they began seriously to contemplate the control of large-scale geophysical forces. Mathematician John von Neumann wrote in 1955 that scientists and the military were taking global climate control quite seriously, attempting to manage solar radiation. Even as he encouraged the US government in this direction, he marveled at it. Could humans survive their own technology, he wondered, as scientists in one country gained the knowledge to alter the climates of others?[5] The intractable diplomatic problems presented by weapons of environmental modification convinced countries of the two Cold War blocs to ban them in the late 1970s, but scientific research on these weapons continued. Even as diplomats negotiated limits on specific weapons, the expectation of a total war never disappeared.

The Cold War has been over for more than two decades, and formerly classified materials document the kind of future that scientists and military planners expected—a future of global war, of planetary contamination, and of epic struggles to survive in a post-apocalypse world. These documents highlight scientists' and policy makers' learning processes about man's place in nature, his startling ability to make drastic and harmful alterations to the globe, and his inability to control them. In the early 1960s, for example, NATO convened a scientific committee, chaired by famous aeronautics expert Theodore von Kármán, to identify the next decade's most probable military developments. One of the committee's conclusions was that man's ability to harness the forces of nature would soon reach a point at which he could interfere drastically with the environment of the enemy. Defense establishments in Europe scrambled to confront a future of environmental warfare by consulting leading oceanographers, meteorologists, and ecologists. Some ideas were spectacular in scope: detonations of nuclear weapons to clear the polar ice caps for easy naval passage, to raise the mean sea level and drown coastal cities, or to create artificial tsunamis. Others were no less extreme: setting fire to huge expanses of vegetation, changing local climates, or using biological agents to target vital links in ecological chains in the enemy's homeland. The goal would be the same as it had been in the strategic bombing deployed during World War II—to maximize the number of humans killed.

Although the Cold War era is sometimes characterized as the "nuclear age," all weapons of widespread human death assumed legitimacy in the immediate postwar years. Atomic bombs, made from the fission of uranium or plutonium, soon gave way to thermonuclear bombs, made from the fusion of hydrogen atoms. In the late 1940s, when confronted with the question of whether to build hydrogen bombs, President Truman's scientific advisors—including celebrated atomic scientists J. Robert Oppenheimer and Enrico Fermi—argued that there were no conceivable military targets that could justify a hydrogen bomb. A hydrogen bomb could be the size of a thousand Hiroshimas. To develop hydrogen bombs would be a decision to make a weapon of genocide, they told Truman. Nonetheless the United States, the Soviet Union, and other countries proceeded to develop them.[6] These weapons of genocide stood at the foundation of American and Soviet geopolitical strategy until the collapse of the USSR in 1991.

Nuclear weapons have so dominated strategic thought that it is easy to forget how scientists tried to exploit the pathways and forces of nature in other ways. US Secretary of State John Foster Dulles complained in 1953 about the growing difficulty with nuclear weapons: "Somehow or other we must manage to remove the taboo from the use of these weapons."[7] Likewise, when in 1951 China and North Korea began to accuse the United States of waging biological warfare in Korea, Secretary of Defense Robert Lovett exhorted subordinates to resist using the term "weapon of mass destruction" to describe America's biological weapons arsenal. Doing so made it difficult to explain why they existed in the arsenal at all. In truth, these were all weapons of total war. Scientific research in the service of total warfare asked such questions as what did the enemy eat, where were his water sources, what epidemic diseases had his population already been exposed to? In the late 1940s, that was the kind of war that American military planners anticipated fighting soon. That expectation lasted for nearly five decades.

ENVIRONMENTAL APOCALYPSE. The planet in peril. Earth in the balance. These familiar phrases about human impacts on the global environment have been popularized in books, television shows, and newspapers. Given recent discussions of climate change, it is easy to assume that scientists' discovery of global warming led them to believe humans were running headlong toward environmental Armageddon. In fact, the catastrophic mode of discussing climate change is a reflection of other environmental crises that date back many decades, among them acid rain, ozone depletion, pesticides, radioactive waste, and nuclear fallout. The common denominator for all these issues was catastrophe on a vast scale.

This catastrophic brand of environmental thinking is typically attributed to two powerful causes. One is the rise of environmental consciousness, as economic development and population growth made countries seem smaller and nature more vulnerable to man's influence, and the other is the rise of environmental science. Efforts to preserve wilderness, to conserve natural resources, to combat pollution, and to mitigate the effects of environmental degradation date back at least to the nineteenth century. After World War II, "the environment" became a global issue, as countries around the world debated the ecological effects of pesticides, the impacts of oil spills or toxic waste in the oceans, and the consequences of emissions on the atmosphere. The United Nations created a special Environment Programme and sponsored "earth summits" in order to call attention to the transnational nature of the issue. Along with that global consciousness came fears of global catastrophe and the pressing need to act together.[8]

The language of the Cold War's global crisis and that of environmental crisis are strikingly similar. That has left room for alternative views about the causes of environmental thought, challenging the prevailing view that postwar affluence, dissatisfaction with pollution, and a new understanding of environmental hazards were the most important factors.[9] For example, sociologist Joseph Masco has argued that the global reach of the nuclear crisis enabled new visions of planetary threats, allowing global warming to take on, in public discourse, the dire characteristics of nuclear war. Long ago ecologist turned environmental activist Barry Commoner said that he dated his "environmental" thinking to the first hydrogen bomb tests. Others have probed further the ways that nuclear issues shaped notions of ecological relationships and environmental risks.[10] Nuclear weapons were only the most far-reaching and destructive product of an approach to warfare that was total in scope, and of an ongoing scientific project to understand humans' vulnerabilities and the earth's susceptibility to manipulation.

The other known cause of catastrophic environmental thought is the growth of modern science after World War II, particularly the massive expansion of the environmental sciences. Oceanography, meteorology, and ecology were among the many disciplines that underwent unprecedented growth in the postwar decades. Many governments increased their budget allocations to subsidize scientific research, with the United States leading the way. Not only were there more scientists doing research, there was also more international coordination, more data collection around the world, and with the advent of digital computing, more powerful tools for crunching data. International groups of experts could draw from the expertise of many nations. With considerable confidence, they could make broad claims about the earth's vulnerability and man's role in it.[11]

Scientific growth after World War II owes its greatest debt to the US armed services, which paid the lion's share of the bill. Indeed, the discovery of global warming would have been impossible without scientific projects funded by the American military.[12] The same can be said of countless subfields of science and technology. But Cold War–funded science is only one part of the story. Especially in the environmental sciences, the Army, Navy, and Air Force routinely asked scientists to help them define their missions and to build the world's most technologically savvy organizations.[13] These armed services explored all possible uses for, manipulations of, and effects upon the global environment. They routinely thought about total war and human fragility and tried to integrate these issues into national security.

Explanations for catastrophic environmental thought typically overlook the historical actors who tried to bring such catastrophes about and who, in planning for a total war, attempted to understand how vulnerable humans were to hostile manipulations of the natural world. This book squarely focuses upon them, on the collaborative activities of scientists and military partners, and on the roots of today's concerns about environmental catastrophe in the geopolitics of the Cold War. It explores the development of weapons of massive death, the contamination of large areas of land, the poisoning of crops, the harnessing of geotectonic forces, the steering of storms, and, most important of all, the vulnerability of man to large-scale environmental changes of his own making.

These perspectives on the natural environment, especially those that are global in scope and predict dire consequences for humans, have firm roots in the plans for a war that never happened: World War III. Military questions and the environmental questions were often identical and pursued by the same people. Boundaries were hazy: as scientists, military leaders, and diplomats tried to figure out how realistic environmental weapons were, in what context they could be used, and how politically acceptable they might be, they also fundamentally shaped conversations about peacetime changes to the environment. For example, in the United Kingdom, the same Oxford botanists who published on ecology were consulting on agricultural defense at home, as well as advising British military commanders in Malaya how to protect rubber trees and kill enemy crops. In the United States, the National Academy of Sciences anticipated environmentalists' arguments when it warned the Air Force that Americans' reliance on technology had made them more susceptible to disease and starvation, vulnerabilities easily exploited by the Soviet Union. NATO advisors such as Edward Teller and William Nierenberg, who in the 1960s tried and failed to find easy ways to harness vast geophysical forces, became leading skeptics of environmental predictions. The same computer modeler who helped develop defense systems for the entire northern hemisphere in the 1950s, Jay Forrester, was one of the first to publish quantitative predictions of environmental doomsday in the early 1970s. Several of the biologists, oceanographers, and atmospheric scientists who advised governments on the 1977 treaty to ban military uses of environmental modification—the ENMOD convention—were enlisted to craft the first major reports on anthropogenic climate change. The two worldviews went hand in hand, both attempting projections of catastrophic environmental consequences on a massive scale.

Arming Mother Nature consists of three main sections that are both thematic and loosely chronological. These divisions are partly a reflection of the changing subject emphases of scientists working with military partners, as they moved away from biological and ecological questions and focused increasingly on the opportunities and threats raised by hydrogen bombs, and then as they began explicitly to confront the politically charged questions about large-scale alterations to the natural world. They also reflect a gradual change in emphasis, from military questions of maximizing human death toward environmental questions about human-caused cataclysm. Throughout the book, strategic issues predominate, from the 1940s decision to pursue biological weapons to the 1980s Central

Intelligence Agency (CIA) analyses of the effects of climate change on Soviet crop yields. The first part, "Pathways of Nature," discusses the unpredictable migrations of organisms, research on biological and radiological warfare, the threat of epidemic disease, and political clashes between the United States and the Soviet Union—including accusations of clandestine use of biological weapons in Korea, Czechoslovakia, and East Germany. The next part, "Forces of Nature," treats the thermonuclear era beginning in the 1950s, when it became clear that nuclear warfare with hydrogen bombs would dominate any conflict between the superpowers. It shows the government efforts to envision post-apocalypse survival, to understand the effects of fallout, and to channel geophysical forces such as oceans and winds to develop weapons on a vast scale. Finally, "Gatekeepers of Nature" tells the story of diplomats' efforts to ban weapons of environmental modification in the 1970s, ties the science of the environmental movement to this military research, and reveals how deeply these ideas informed environmental thought and protection efforts at the international level. This section also reveals how deeply the Cold War conflict shaped responses to the environmental challenges of the 1980s—from the droughts in Africa to the global acquired immune deficiency syndrome (AIDS) epidemic and the science of climate change.

In attempting to narrate the interplay of science in the Cold War and the history of environmental thought, this book makes three arguments. One is that the collaboration between scientists and the armed services created a scientific worldview obsessed with environmental change, manipulation, and vulnerability. Scientists extended "total war" thinking to the natural world, believing that human population centers would be the most important targets in the coming war, and the entire earth would be the battleground. In part this meant research on what NATO called environmental warfare. It also meant geophysical studies of the earth, which would provide the information necessary to allow bombers to fly over the poles to deliver nuclear bombs to their targets, to measure the shape and gravity of the earth to enable guidance of intercontinental ballistic missiles, and to detect radioactivity from enemy nuclear tests. In addition, it encouraged ecological studies of how vulnerable Americans and their allies were to scorched landscapes, destroyed crops, contaminated fish and livestock, and epidemic diseases. These were not merely scientific projects that pushed the frontiers of their disciplines; rather, they asked questions about vulnerability and manipulability on a vast scale.

The second contention is that such scientific research, much of it secret but some quite open, encouraged the belief that large-scale human-induced changes already were within the power of American and Soviet scientists. Accusations of natural manipulations flew both ways across the Iron Curtain many times in the postwar decades. The United States stood accused of waging biological warfare in Korea and of spreading potato bugs in Eastern Europe to cripple its economy. Both the British and Americans actually did engage in crop destruction in Southeast Asia, and the Americans tampered with the weather in Vietnam. The Soviet Union denounced the United States for having concocted the AIDS epidemic in its biological weapons laboratories, and Americans suspected that some outbreaks of disease in the Soviet Union were really experiments gone awry. Nuclear weapons tests often had unexpected effects, as when Japanese fishermen were blanketed with radioactive debris in 1954 or some of Hawaii's electrical grid was inadvertently shut down by an electromagnetic pulse in 1962. Scientists reported that, with the aid of nuclear detonations, they had created artificial radiation belts surrounding the earth. These experts working with the armed forces seemed quite willing to tamper with the earth, the oceans, and the atmosphere. "We know how we can modify the ionosophere," nuclear physicist Edward Teller once proudly stated. "We have already done it."[14]

The third argument is that Cold War geopolitics fundamentally shaped how scientists, economists, military leaders, and politicians responded to the scientific evidence of large-scale harm from human actions. Perhaps one of the surprises of this book is not how little was known about environmental change, but rather how much. During most of the Cold War, change was not as much denied as it was justified. Large-scale environmental change could be justified in national security terms, as in the case of worldwide nuclear fallout from nuclear tests. It could be justified in strategic terms, as when Herman Kahn insisted that global contamination from a full-scale thermonuclear war was survivable. It could be justified in economic terms, as when free-market economists preferred mass migrations to socialist-sounding suggestions to curb economic growth. It could be justified in military terms, as in the case of chemical spraying in Malaya and Vietnam. It could be justified in terms of Soviet intransigence, as in the case of carbon emissions. And it could even be justified in scientific terms, as when American scientists argued that humans could not hope to compete with the forces of nature, making even large-scale changes seem ephemeral in the grand sweep of natural history. In these and many other ways, American and allied responses to environmental issues depended on their perceptions of the global contest with the Soviet bloc.

The philosopher Alfred North Whitehead once said that the progress of civilization has not been a uniform drift toward better things. His cynicism may have stemmed from watching respected colleagues turn their knowledge of nature into the lethal poisons used in the trenches of World War I. During the Cold War scientists gained an extraordinary amount of knowledge about the global environment, the earth's dynamics, its natural resources, and the biological web of life. This was knowledge of human vulnerability on a global scale, serious research motivated by military concerns. When scientists learned about the environment during the Cold War, they were asking questions, drawing conclusions, and learning about change and vulnerability. This book is a step toward understanding how fully the experience of the Cold War transformed thinking about humanity, the vulnerabilities of the earth, and the poisoned fruits of human labor—bestowing the idea that, as President Richard Nixon once claimed, man holds in his hands too many of the seeds of his own destruction.

PART ONE

Pathways of Nature

I

The Natural Vulnerability
of Civilizations

It is the mass conscience of mankind—the dominance
of the moral or the amoral—which determines whether
research is to be used for life or death.
—US Surgeon General THOMAS PARRAN, 1946

This is not a prediction of horrors to come. These weapons
exist.
—US Navy Rear Admiral ELLIS M. ZACHARIAS, 1947

IN JULY 1945, dozens of distinguished American and European professors gathered to condemn German scientists for their part in the heinous crimes perpetrated by the Nazis against civilians. Scientists, they proclaimed, had "contributed, actively or passively, to the prostitution of science for the purposes of total warfare."[1] A month later, a mere two atomic bombs, built by American and European scientists, laid waste Hiroshima and Nagasaki, killing or wounding a quarter of a million Japanese people. When World War II ended, no amount of sanctimonious condemnations could hide the reality that total war had come, and civilians had become acceptable targets. Scientists on all sides of the conflict had become experts at maximizing human death.

This extraordinary moral shift toward civilian death altered not only strategic thought but also the role of scientists after the war. No longer were they charged merely with developing war-winning weapons. They also thought earnestly about ways to use natural scourges to fight in the next war. They began to ask how people lived—what sustained them, what protected them, and how the natural world could be used against them. Some scientists joined new international agencies to find ways to make humans more secure and to prevent future war. Others began to plan for the conflict to come, joining national research establishments designed to exploit human susceptibility to hunger and disease.

How vulnerable were the peoples of the world in the first full month of peace, September of 1945? Japan had surrendered to the Americans in August, and the Nazi hold over Europe had collapsed the previous May. Already the alliance against Hitler showed signs of splintering, with the future of democracy in Eastern Europe uncertain and a growing pall of gloom about a world with atomic bombs. In Asia, the fighting was not really over. The Chinese Civil War, stalled by years of Japanese imperialism and the Soviet occupation of Manchuria, would resume in less than a year's time. Yet the Cold War between the United States and the Soviet Union had not truly begun. For a brief moment in history, peace had come.

The sheer scale of death in the Second World War is difficult to contemplate. More than 60 million people died. A small fraction of these— less than half a million people—were Americans. About 25 million were Soviets—some 14 percent of the Soviet Union's prewar population. In China, between 10 and 20 million people were killed, a huge range that suggests how little is known about what happened in Asia under Japanese rule. Estimates of Germans killed range between 4 and 8 million, and of Poles slightly less than 6 million. The rest were citizens of scores of countries around the world. The Nazi regime massacred nearly 6 million people in the Holocaust. Roughly two-thirds of the war's casualties were civilians, not soldiers. Some resulted from acts of genocide, slaughter, and the indiscriminate bombing of cities. Others were consequences of malnourishment, starvation, and disease, the byproducts of all wars.[2]

For governments at war's end, one immediate task was to prevent further human disasters. The war itself had entailed the wide-ranging movements of people—as refugees, as migrants, and as soldiers. The coming of peace brought more of the same, threatening to spread disease even further. During the war, syphilis had debilitated entire armies—a problem solved by the Allies when the Americans began to mass produce penicillin. In China, military commanders had come to expect the cycles of epidemic disease that inevitably broke out among troops, but after the war, these problems did not dissipate. The soldiers returning home took their diseases with them. Occupying forces continued to impose their will on local people, particularly women. The problem of rape in the Soviet zone of Germany was an especially severe one, but given the level of pain and ruin that Germany had inflicted on the Soviet people, officials were reluctant to clamp down on the soldiers except for public health reasons.[3]

Public health officials were well aware of the disruptive effects of the movement of people, plants, and animals. At the onset of war in Europe in September 1939, the British government had enacted a major evacuation of London in order to limit casualties from German bombers. In the autumn of 1939 nearly 1.3 million inhabitants relocated, making it the largest migration in England since the city's Great Fire of 1665. Those who did not leave had to pack themselves in bomb shelters during air raids. Public health authorities in England and elsewhere justifiably feared new outbreaks of the world's scourges: plague, cholera, typhus, smallpox, tuberculosis, dysentery.[4] In some parts of the world, where public health services already had been weak, the war left millions to die of disease. Just one month after the Japanese surrender, *The Times* of London reported staggering figures for death by communicable disease in India. On average during the war, cholera took some 145,000 lives per year, smallpox killed 70,000, and tuberculosis claimed half a million. Another 3.6 million died each year from some form of "fever." The country had one doctor for every 10,000 people.[5] Even in places with good medical care, pathogens rather than bombs often were the real killers.

The prospect of peace was no more heartening. Once the peoples of the world would be able to travel safely again, they would spread diseases over even larger areas. Public health officials braced for impact. A former medical director in the League of Nations, Frank G. Boudreau, warned in 1945 that epidemic disease would be the most acute problem in Europe and Asia immediately after the war. "The stage has been set," he proclaimed, "for epidemics of typhus fever, dysentery, and cholera." He urged national health services to enact strong control measures and, most important, to work together across national lines. The peoples of the world had never been more vulnerable to wide-ranging, uncontrollable plagues.[6]

The war's victors tried to stem the tide of disease. In 1946 a returning officer of the Royal Army Medical Corps unwittingly initiated a smallpox outbreak in Essex, precipitating a string of quarantine policies by local authorities throughout England.[7] Across their occupation zones American and British forces de-loused people with the synthetic pesticide DDT to control outbreaks of typhus. The Soviets saw louse-borne typhus outbreaks in Slovakia, Hungary, Romania, Poland, and parts of Russia. Around the Mediterranean, spraying marshlands with DDT was the only effective way to halt malaria. There were plentiful cases of typhus, diphtheria, and typhoid fever throughout Europe—in Germany, cases of typhoid fever rose to 30 times their normal levels. Exacerbated by the problem of rape in the occupied zone, the cases of syphilis rose between three- and ninefold in most of Europe—20-fold in Germany. "Progress made in twenty years of venereal disease control has been virtually wiped out by war years in Europe," one United Nations report lamented.[8]

The persistence of regional conflict after the war only intensified human vulnerability to disease. In China, the withdrawal of Japanese and Soviet forces by 1946 opened the path for renewed fighting between the Nationalists under Chiang Kai-Shek and the communists under Mao Zedong. Mao's promises of land reform helped to mobilize millions of peasants against Chiang, but that meant millions of people gathering together to march long distances without much medical care—falling ill, dying, and spreading pathogens. In India, Hindus and Muslims fought intermittently in the Punjab region after Britain's creation of Pakistan in 1947 and soon entered full-scale war over Kashmir. Refugee camps began to fill up, and the cases of cholera infection began to mount.[9]

Such diseases were the most significant ones to attack in human populations at mid-century. Even without humans fighting each other, harmful pathogens followed nature's pathways through water supplies, food chains, air, and the human touch. The threat was global in scope, and public health officials readily called to mind the fact that the greatest epidemic in history—the Spanish Influenza of 1918–1920—had occurred toward the end of the First World War. By war's end, the flu had become a global pandemic. All forms of crisis, such as famine or war, increased the odds of spreading infectious disease. Epidemics were effective killers within armies, aboard ship, and in cities, towns, and villages. That is why in 1946 public health scientists and officials of several governments banded together and signed what US Surgeon General Thomas Parran called "a Magna Carta for Health," outlining the goals of the future World Health Organization. It would disseminate drugs to combat disease, find ways to keep water supplies free from contamination, and, above all, promote cooperation between nations. Peace and security would be impossible, Parran and others argued, without health and well-being for all people. They would target the "ancient human plagues," such as malaria, cholera, tuberculosis, and syphilis.

Essential to the spirit of all the United Nations' (UN's) specialized agencies at their founding was a plea for an end to war. The first agencies explicitly addressed the causes of war: disease, starvation, and morality. These required agencies focusing not only on health but also on food (the Food and Agriculture Organization). Morality was trickier to pinpoint, but the UN started by mixing those elements of society that shaped the mind, creating the UN Educational, Scientific, and Cultural Organization (UNESCO). Within their speeches and writings, these organizations' leaders spoke in terms of hope and desperation: the slaughter was over, but it might begin anew at a moment's notice. This must not be allowed to happen, they urged. In Parran's words, "Never again can our world disintegrate into the insanity of another total war."

The shadow of such future insanity haunted these founders, especially because of the ambiguous role of modern science. Scientific understanding would help to fight disease, as it had in the case of penicillin, but scientists also had conducted gruesome experiments in Nazi death camps and had created the weapons used on Hiroshima and Nagasaki. Parran spoke of science in the starkest moral terms. In his view:

> Public health experts realize that science may be used either to save life or to destroy civilization. Whether science is to be used for good or for evil is not determined by scientists themselves. The same type of research worker may discover penicillin or atomic fission. It is the mass conscience of mankind—the dominance of the moral or the amoral—which determines whether research is to be used for life or death.[10]

The founders of these organizations took up, rather ambitiously, the role of guiding the work of scientists toward acts of goodness. Yet already it seemed that many scientists had chosen a different path.

The scientific centers of the world—the United States, Europe, the Soviet Union—symbolized not merely hope and progress, but also power and destruction. The atomic bomb and the public disagreements about the international control of atomic energy in the postwar world highlighted how scientists had mastered nature's power for the benefit of their governments. But the presence of the atomic bomb, the result of a massive investment of money, scientific manpower, and industrial capacity, provoked questions about government-sponsored weapons research in other arenas. If diseases were the principal scourge of the postwar years, did scientists have the ability to cause and stop diseases from breaking out?

Britain was among the first countries to face the accusation of using knowledge of disease to ensure control of strategic areas after the war. Few countries were more occupied by the global problem of epidemic disease—after all, Britain faced the daunting task of resuming control of a far-flung empire despite having its economy shattered by the world war. The death toll from disease in key colonial possessions such as India and Egypt had always been high. During and after World War II, bubonic plague was rampant in the Middle East and North Africa. The protection of the Suez Canal and Port Said deeply worried colonial administrators. Especially problematic was the Hajj, the massive annual Muslim pilgrimage to Mecca. One of the Five Pillars of Islam, making the trek to the holy city was an obligation of faith, but for the British who dominated the region, it was a public health nightmare. By international agreement dating back to 1926, pilgrims were to be vaccinated against smallpox and inoculated against cholera and plague prior to leaving home. Most of these pilgrims then passed through the Canal and then across the Red Sea to Jeddah, near the holy city. Once in Mecca, they interacted with other Muslims from around the world. Before returning through the Canal and into Port Said, pilgrims had to stop for five days of medical monitoring at a quarantine station at El Tor to prevent the British-controlled Canal Zone from becoming a global epicenter of disease.[11]

But the system was far from fail-safe. The origins of all major cholera epidemics in Egypt in the first half of the twentieth century had been traced back to the annual pilgrimage to Mecca. In 1947 the system again broke down, and new cases of cholera began to appear.[12] It turned into the first major postwar cholera epidemic, claiming at its height hundreds of lives every day even after DDT was sprayed throughout Cairo to control excrement-carrying flies. Egyptian officials began to accuse the British government of sending ineffective serums and of mishandling quarantine procedures in the Canal Zone. The Muslim Brotherhood newspaper *Ikhwari el Muslimin* printed an article claiming the British had resolved to poison the Egyptian people and were withholding the real serum. With the Egyptian and British governments engaged in contentious disputes about Egypt's national sovereignty, newspapers accused Britain of using its knowledge of science to ensure its control over the region.[13]

The British government scoffed at the notion that responsible men of science would willfully contribute to the indiscriminate slaughter of thousands of Egyptians and blamed an unreliable black market filled with false serums. Unfortunately for Britain, many Egyptians believed that the British were capable, scientifically and morally, of doing it. Articles in *The Times* complained about the willingness of the Egyptian government to allow such claims to go "unbridled" or "unchecked." In its zeal to defend the British government, *The Times* went so far as to deny any links to the

Canal Zone. Actually the claims were checked—Egyptian Under-Secretary for Health Abdel Khalek Bey was dismissed from his post for making the same allegation about the British. Nevertheless, the fiercely anti-British Muslim Brotherhood continued to disseminate the idea. Some Egyptians abandoned modern science altogether and relied on the ancient technique of cutting the air with wooden scissors. Only after a few months, millions of inoculations, and widespread spraying of DDT did the crisis end.[14]

The 1947 Cairo cholera epidemic, laced with political conflict and anti-imperial accusations, raised the question of whether a great power might have the scientific capability—and the will—to deliberately spread rampant disease. Could the observations and experiments conducted to protect people also be used to harm them?

The Soviet Union gave this question widespread public attention in late 1949, when it put several Japanese military leaders on trial for war crimes. The Japanese stood accused of preparing to wage bacteriological warfare against the Soviet Union, of actually waging it against China, and of engaging in human experimentation on American, Korean, and Chinese prisoners of war. At the trials, the former commander of the Kwantung Army, General Otozo Yamada, revealed that he had personally approved the use of "Ishii bombs," fragile porcelain containers holding germs of typhus and bubonic plague. Yamada acknowledged that such weapons had been designed for use against civilian populations. According to the Soviets, one Japanese military leader claimed that Emperor Hirohito had signed an order to prepare to wage bacteriological warfare against the Soviet Union.[15]

Japanese scientists captured by American forces had not endured similar war crimes trials, and at the time there was little evidence in the public domain that the Japanese had thought seriously about waging biological warfare. The American-led War Crimes Tribunal in Tokyo in 1948 sentenced prominent Japanese leaders to death and imprisonment, including General Hideki Tojo and other high-ranking figures, for directing or allowing the murders, rapes, forced labor, death marches, and horrific prison conditions during the war. But the bacteriologists named by the Soviets had not been tried at all. The Soviet government demanded not only that Shiro Ishii, the microbiologist who headed the bacteriological warfare unit (Unit 731) of the Japanese Imperial Army, be put on trial, but that Emperoro Hirohito be tried as well.[16]

The United States did neither. By the time of the Soviets' demand, the war had been over nearly half a decade and neither the United States nor

Japan seriously considered putting Hirohito on trial. Newspapers dismissed the Soviet action as an Asian propaganda move. The *New York Times* reported, "Allied headquarters has been able to find no evidence either that there were bacteria plans in Japan during the war or that Hirohito would have had sufficient knowledge to participate."[17] The fact that the Soviets had been at war with Japan only a matter of days prior to the surrender added little to the moral urgency.

The Japanese did have such a program, it was later revealed, but the experimenters at Unit 731 never saw a courtroom because they cut a deal. In return for amnesty from war crimes prosecution, they provided their American interlocutors with data. Like the Japanese, American scientists had been researching bacteriological warfare, as had the British. In fact one of the scientists who studied the Cairo epidemic, Bruce White, had played a leading role in such research during World War II. With the deal, American epidemiologists and bacteriologists gained extensive information about experiments on humans. At first, Japanese scientists kept quiet, but once they realized that talking about their secret wartime research would prevent them from being tried for war crimes, they spoke up. Scientists from Camp Detrick, Maryland—the headquarters of the American biological warfare program—gathered information from several of the Japanese participants, including Ishii, who had worked for years trying to find effective ways to spread the scourges of humanity—cholera, plague, smallpox, and other diseases. After providing this information, Ishii and his collaborators went free.[18]

This research did not become public knowledge in 1949, but the Soviet trials of the Japanese served as a grim reminder that modern warfare had taken a decisive turn, with human death as an end in itself. Even leaving aside biological weapons, the war had involved civilian deaths on a massive scale. Several prominent Americans, including Air Corps pilot Chuck Yeager and future Secretary of Defense Robert McNamara, acknowledged long after the war that their bombing of civilian targets probably qualified as atrocities. Yeager was under orders to shoot anything that moved, on the grounds that even German farmers toiling in the fields were helping the war effort by feeding soldiers. The same argument applied to all strategic bombing, which targeted centers of industry but could not easily be separated from the schools, churches, and houses nearby. McNamara assisted General Curtis LeMay's strategic bombing of Japanese cities by applying statistical analysis to mission plans in order to maximize civilian death. When planning the atomic bombings, the only special consideration affecting target choice was a city's cultural value; Secretary of War Henry Stimson refused to bomb Kyoto because of its historical buildings and believed this civilized decision would be praised after the war.[19]

This was the kind of "total war" that Thomas Parran feared would recur should the nations of the world fail to cooperate in healing and feeding themselves. Yet despite his lofty goal to ensure that the powers of modern science were turned toward saving lives, researchers in all major combatant countries continued to work on weapons of civilian death. Although today it is commonplace to use the term "weapons of mass destruction" to describe nuclear, biological, and chemical weapons, it is a misleading term. Some of these weapons were designed specifically to bring about biological death rather than physical destruction, and scientists led the way in helping their governments acquire them.

The United States government had pursued biological weapons research secretly during the war, but in 1946 it issued a public report by George W. Merck, the president of the American pharmaceutical giant Merck and Company, who had headed the work. Bacteriologist Theodor Rosebury and his colleagues subsequently summarized some of their pre-war work in an article in the *Journal of Immunology*, which was later expanded into the 1949 book *Peace or Pestilence*.[20]

Scientists did not yet know whether it was feasible for humans to tap into nature's pathways on a large scale, letting natural processes do the deadly work, but they were hopeful. The United States and United Kingdom established robust chemical and biological warfare research centers at Camp Detrick and Porton (near Salisbury, not far from Stonehenge), respectively. Over the years these centers would have independent programs, but they also kept up lines of communication and cooperation with each other. The British were very enthusiastic about biological warfare's potential to transform warfare. At a 1946 meeting on defense policy research, an Air Ministry official recalled:

> I stressed very strongly at the meeting that Biological Warfare was likely to be as important as Atomic Warfare, but by subtracting one percent from Atomic Warfare costs we could increase Biological Warfare by one hundred percent, and therefore Biological Warfare should really have first preference on account of the relative cheapness, and also the fact that it was not in such a forward state as Atomic Warfare.[21]

With such support, Porton's staff expanded considerably in the late 1940s to accommodate biological warfare's perceived importance in the coming conflict.

One of the early public introductions to the subject of biological warfare in the United States was on the pages of *Life* magazine. A 1946 article with the title "BW" led with a photograph of a worker in a protective suit, carrying his own oxygen tank. The opening sentence intoned "Biological warfare, using scourges of disease and famine as weapons, is as dreadful as the atomic bomb and far more difficult to control." The author, Gerard Piel, included photographs of specific toxins, bacteria, and viruses causing anthrax, botulism, undulant fever, typhus, and bubonic plague. He discussed a full range of offensive and defensive work being done at Camp Detrick and compared the workers there to those who built the atomic bomb at Los Alamos. He also pointed out the advances in modern medicine that could emerge from the research. But he painted the subject in stark moral terms, as part of the "equation of good and evil." Scientists were once members of a true world society, he wrote, but were now divided into working for nation-states, as "the frontiers of the public domain have been staked out in the name of military secrecy."[22]

Bringing the *Life* article to print proved an ordeal for Piel and for those managing biological warfare research. Piel had interviewed a number of high-level officials for the article, including Major General Alden Waitt, chief of the US Army Chemical Corps. After reading a draft of the article, Waitt was enraged: he had thought Piel would focus on the defensive side and the positive good that might come from the research, rather than to enumerate actual offensive weapons. He told Piel that the article would damage both American national security and international relations, so gave him a lengthy list of corrections—often of passages that provided too much inflammatory detail, such as specific pathogens and locations of proving grounds. For instance, Piel revealed that the United States had planned to attack the 1945 Japanese rice crop. Waitt objected strenuously, writing that this "is on a matter that I asked you not to say anything about." Piel initially had pulled few punches about American capability during the war: "As the first nation to drop an atomic bomb, the United States was also prepared to give a major biological weapon its first field trial in an active theater of war." Waitt objected adamantly to this. "This policy had never been enunciated or established," he wrote. "None of us know whether the weapon ever would have been used."[23]

Piel made several changes and eliminated specific references to American plans during World War II, but Waitt was still not satisfied and harangued Piel and the editor of *Life*. Others, including Vannevar Bush, also called Piel to persuade him to alter the grim tone of the article. Eventually Waitt visited Piel and his editor in person and was finally able to convince them to omit most of the objectionable passages. As the article was about to come out in late November 1946, Waitt wrote the American embassy in London to pass on to colleagues at Porton that the article was not based on a security breach. "I did my best to suppress it," he wrote, "and did succeed in eliminating a number of things that would have been disturbing."[24]

Even as they tried to control media discussion, American military leaders themselves still struggled to understand the radical changes in warfare brought about by new scientific capabilities. Much of their thinking was distilled in a 1947 classified paper by the Joint Chiefs of Staff entitled "Estimate of the Effect on the Nature of War of Future Technical Developments in Weapons." The document projected a future in which rockets would deliver atomic bombs, submarines would not need to resurface for air, tanks and infantry would be more mobile and possess more reliable equipment, and fighter planes would break the speed of sound. But the document also warned of the tendency to jump too far into the future, without diligent attention to present capabilities. After all, "we must not allow ourselves to think that the era of 'push-button' or 'Buck Rogers' warfare has arrived or that it is likely to arrive in the next ten years." The United States should not devote so many resources to future weapons, the document warned, that it finds itself incapable of fighting an unexpected war.[25]

What would such a war entail? As in World War II, the Joint Chiefs expected the next war to be a global *total war*, requiring the participation of every life and drawing upon the nation's industries running at full capacity. Total war meant that every person was a combatant, soldier and civilian alike, each a participant in the clash of whole societies, not merely the clash of armies. Total war enlisted all the industrial, human, and technological power of one civilization against another.[26] Weapons of biological annihilation embodied such thinking, because they implicitly targeted civilians.[27] "The civil population of the United States," the Joint Chiefs wrote, "will be drawn much more closely into war of the future than ever before." Their underlying assumption was that "the most profitable targets for attack by new weapons" would be the vital areas of industry, military power, communication, and population. Direct attacks on the American industrial system and population—that is, cities—should be expected.[28] Therefore, the methods of warfare that maximized the death of large numbers of people would prove most decisive.

Referencing Buck Rogers, the comic book character who piloted spacecraft and battled aliens in the distant future, was the Navy's way of taking a shot at the empire-building of the newly formed Air Force. Over the next couple of years the Navy would be fighting the efforts of the Air Force to focus on strategic bombing as the cornerstone of American military strategy. The head of the Joint Chiefs at this time, Admiral William D. Leahy, downplayed the importance of strategic atomic bombing in the future, stating that no other nation was likely to have more than a few atomic bombs available for use in the next 10 years. Yet the Joint Chiefs did try to make the Navy seem relevant, pointing out that enemy submarine-launched rockets could attack American coasts and, if loaded with radioactive materials, disperse lethal doses into American cities without needing a bomb at all. The Joint Chiefs named biological weapons second after atomic bombs as most likely to have an impact on the nature of war. The full potential of such weapons was not known, but "the possibility and, in fact, the probability of biological warfare being extremely effective cannot be ruled out."[29]

Outside government, civilians were left to wonder about the line between reality and fantasy. On the one hand, it seemed unbelievable that the US or Soviet militaries might be able to start epidemic diseases at will. On the other hand, the atomic bomb had trained people to expect the unexpected. The US government policy of silence only heightened the mystery and intensified the anxiety. Theodor Rosebury's article and subsequent book on biological weapons, for example, intensified suspicions of the government. One chapter of *Peace or Pestilence* was tantalizingly entitled "How Much Can Be Told?," clearly implying that the United States continued to work on such subjects and was not revealing all.[30] So the policy of silence turned into a ridiculous source of embarrassment. Robert W. Berry, assistant to the secretary of defense, pointed out to the Joint Chiefs in 1948 that "the subject gets frequent and not always judicious discussion in the press," and he suggested that some public statements might help to exert greater control over how journalists treated it.[31]

Such "injudicious" treatments usually pointed out the vulnerability of the world's peoples to sickness and disease and to the possibility that both the Americans and Soviets were capable of unleashing ruin on the world.

One such view appeared toward the end of 1947 in the magazine *United Nations World*. The author of "Absolute Weapons . . . More Deadly than the Atom," retired US Navy Rear Admiral Ellis M. Zacharias, pointed out that even the disavowal and prohibition of atomic bombs would leave weapons in the arsenal that could wipe out mankind. These weapons he called chemical, biological, and "climatological," capable of exterminating not just humans but all vestiges of animal and human life. He emphasized: "This is not a prediction of horrors to come. *These weapons exist.*" Rumor had it, he wrote, that the United States had not only three major secret weapons projects (atomic, biological, and radiological), but perhaps four or five. Zacharias's sensational article observed that the Soviets were not idle in the face of American successes. In addition to exploring rocket technology, they were pressing forward with an intensive project on the military applications of cosmic rays.[32]

For Zacharias, the distinctive character of these new "absolute weapons," when coupled with rocket technology, was that they would permit the waging of an intercontinental "push-button" war. The war's tactical nuances would be insignificant, he said, compared to the strategic goal of destroying lives and property on a massive scale. If the future indeed held this kind of conflict, even seemingly modern armaments like aircraft carriers, long-range bombers, incendiary bombs, and automatic heavy artillery "represent an era of warfare which will never again return." The wars of the future would be enormously destructive, targeting human lives, with the landscape continuing to kill trespassing life long after the war itself. The postwar world would be one of quarantine, keeping healthy people out of contaminated areas and keeping infected people within them, with futile attempts to do the same with animals, insects, and vegetation. Zacharias's solution was to take the matter to the United Nations and to demand it abolish these "absolute weapons."[33]

Were Americans already capable of unleashing a massive wave of ruin upon the world? The World Health Organization's director-general, Canadian psychiatrist Brock Chisholm, thought so. In a September 1948 address at the annual meeting of the American Psychological Association, Chisholm mentioned that the old notion of competitive survival, long aided by science and technology, "has become synonymous with race suicide." His speech, published in the journal *Science*, emphasized the importance of developing a consciousness of belonging to humanity, rather than to any individual nation.[34] The term "race suicide" had been employed for years by eugenicists worried about disproportionate breeding between

Anglo-Saxon and other ethnic populations, but Chisholm used the term in reference to the entire human race, believing that the risk of damaging it severely or wiping it out completely was quite real. Chisholm and others coupled the fear of fantastic new weapons with a "one world government" solution.

Casting these weapons in the language of global contamination—as a menace to all humankind, animals, and vegetation—deeply troubled some of the influential American scientists who thus far had dominated the nexus between science and the state. One of these was Harvard president James Conant, a chemist who had helped organize wartime scientific work, including the atomic bomb project, and had had the displeasure of hearing one of Chisholm's speeches in 1948. He found what Chisholm said "truly alarming," and the next day he wrote as much to his friend Vannevar Bush, who headed the US military's Research and Development Board. Chisholm had made a categorical statement that there was no way that defensive warfare could catch up to the destructive possibilities already existing in offensive warfare; thus the next war could mean the suicide of the human race. Conant was especially disturbed by Chisholm's decision to single out biological weapons as the culprit:

> The conclusions he drew in terms of education, cooperation, one world, etc. are not to the point. What disturbed me was his categoric statement about bacteriological warfare. It developed that it was not the atomic bomb, which he more or less pooh-poohed, but bacteriological warfare on which he based all his arguments.

Conant saw the political implications clearly when Chisholm's statement, that no one should be elected to office except on the issue of survival of the human race, was met with loud applause by some 1,200 people in the audience.[35]

Chisholm's statements were powerful evidence of a widely held view among even the best informed people: that the US government had the ability to tap the power of nature and to instigate outbreaks of epidemic disease. Here was Chisholm openly explaining what total war would mean in a world that possessed biological weapons. Conant, never enamored of biological weapons but a firm believer in the importance of the atomic bomb in deterring Stalin, felt that the US government should make a statement playing down biological weapons. The public ought to know, he felt, that these weapons were not yet as significant as Chisholm imagined.

It was the government's responsibility, Conant believed, to tell the American people whether Chisholm was right or wrong, rather than just allow speculation and fear to dominate. He urged Vannevar Bush to use his influence to organize a civilian panel to tell the truth to the American people. "To do otherwise is to play directly into the hands of Stalin and Molotov," he wrote. "Dr. Chisholm's arguments are worth a fifty-group air force to the Soviet rulers!"[36]

In fact no national policy about biological weapons existed at all. The Joint Chiefs of Staff had not resolved their own reservations and internal conflicts about the weapons' importance, and they wanted to make a thorough comparison of the three kinds of contamination-based warfare, namely, biological, radiological, and chemical. All three, as Captain W. G. Lalor put it, "had a similar potential in that they would be employed to contaminate areas for neutralization or mass casualty effect without material destruction."[37] Admiral Leahy, who headed the Joint Chiefs, supported studies on biological warfare, protection against attack, and coordination of intelligence about other countries' activities.[38] But all the armed services still were haggling about responsibilities, technological systems, and other implications. Thus far they had deferred judgment and certainly were not ready for a national policy on their use.[39]

Even in the absence of a policy, however, few doubted that weapons of contamination would be used in a war with the Soviet Union. This was not just true of biological weapons but also radiological ones, the use of deadly radioactive byproducts of nuclear reactors, usually called radioactive waste. Was it possible to simply contaminate the countryside rather than occupy it with troops? During World War II the Allies expected greater use of this kind of contamination than occurred. In 1944, as Allied troops stood waiting for the tides to shift to enable the long-awaited invasion of Normandy, a few of them carried a peculiar device called a Victoreen Model 247A. It was a hastily manufactured portable ion chamber, designed to detect radioactivity. Few of the soldiers landing on the beaches on June 6, 1944, could have comprehended its purpose. But General Leslie Groves, the military head of the Manhattan Project, understood that the Germans had started their own atomic bomb project long before the Americans had and feared that the Germans might have radiological weapons. Groves was afraid that the Nazis might contaminate the landscape as they retreated, leaving the Allied troops to march into a radioactive wasteland. The portable ion chambers, ready to detect radioactivity, were designed to alert military commanders to any such strategy by the enemy.

That the Germans did not in fact contaminate the land as they retreated was a genuine surprise to American scientists and military commanders. Vannevar Bush later wrote that there must be something in man stopping him from poisoning other humans through animals and crops—even as he willingly killed in more direct ways. Even Hitler had chosen not to use radiological weapons.[40] That did not stop scientists after the war from preparing for their use, however.

A number of scientists who had worked on military projects during World War II came to see radiological warfare as the environmental weapon of the future. To them, it seemed like the ultimate weapon of interdiction: what troops would risk entering a vast contamination zone? One of the scientists who believed this was Joseph G. Hamilton, a researcher at the Radiation Laboratory at the University of California, Berkeley, who had conducted experiments on humans—including injections of plutonium—without their consent while under contract with the Manhattan Project.[41] Such experiments continued during the Cold War on schoolchildren, pregnant women, and hospital patients and went unacknowledged by the US government until the 1990s. By pushing these ethical boundaries, American scientists led the world in knowledge of radiation's toxicity to humans.

After the war, two of Hamilton's colleagues, soil chemist Roy Overstreet and plant biochemist Louis Jacobson, saw the potential to reach such toxic levels through plants. They wrote to him in November 1946 about their "belief that one very ominous phase of atomic warfare has not been fully anticipated and has not been given the thorough investigation it requires." Based on some small-scale experiments conducted at Berkeley, they predicted that fission products could likely be used to make agricultural land barren.[42] They poured solutions of radioactive elements into soil columns and discovered that most of the radioactivity remained in the first few millimeters. These upper layers held the radioactive material so tenaciously that it would not sink down by water leaching—and indeed even efforts to remove the radioactive elements efficiently with chemical reagents failed. However, barley plant roots absorbed them quite easily. After a certain degree of concentration, this process proved toxic to the plant.[43]

This seemed an extremely promising way to interfere with an enemy's agriculture. After dropping radioactive material onto soil, the fission products would be taken up by plant roots. Even if the plants themselves were not killed, the amount of radioactive cesium and strontium in them would transform life-giving, economy-sustaining staple crops into fields of poisonous weeds. The beauty of this weapon was that the necessary material already existed. Operations at America's plutonium plant at Hanford, Washington, produced many megacuries of long-lived radioactive waste, which presently had to be collected and stored safely. "This takes on an added significance," the scientists pointed out, "when one reflects that the widespread distribution of one megacurie of long-lived activity such as Sr^{90} or Cs^{137} may be ample for the destruction of some 250,000 acres of agricultural land for a period of years."[44] It seemed possible to create a powerful weapon cheaply simply by taking out the trash—converting radioactive waste into radiological weapons.

It did not take long to consider even more direct effects on humans. Hamilton took news of these experiments to Colonel Kenneth Nichols at the Manhattan Engineering District, writing of the promising use of "radioactive warfare" against large concentrations of people. Radioactive agents seemed novel in several respects. They could be used in small quantities; they could not be detected by touch, smell, or taste. Damage was both acute and chronic, killing some immediately while contributing to the decline of others over time. Effects could be long-lasting, with decontamination nearly impossible. In addition, the creation of lethal topsoil could prove a "most ominous complication" for humans. Rain and melting snow would wash away some of it, transporting it into creeks and rivers, and then possibly on to major population centers built around major waterways.[45] Hamilton strongly urged the armed services to study "the full potentiality of such an agent," as a protection against its possible use by an enemy.[46]

Partly because of the wartime human radiation experiments, Hamilton had a fair grasp of the effects of fission products both inside and outside of the body, and he had already developed some estimates about how this kind of warfare could target cities. He guessed that if radioactive materials could be spread efficiently, they would create large zones that killed people by damaging their bones and lungs. Already the technology existed to make this happen. Radioactive aerosols were used in experiments on the respiratory effects of inhalation by animals. These could be combined with the military's smoke-producing agents designed to obscure ships and troop movements. "Such a type of preparation would appear well adapted," Hamilton wrote, "for producing fission product aerosols to subject urban populations to fission product poisoning by inhalation." Once accomplished, as scientists had learned during Operation Crossroads, a 1946

Pacific Ocean atomic test, exposed structures would be impossible to decontaminate.[47]

This kind of experimentation suggested startling possibilities for the
future. Any bridge, canal, road, or even a mountain pass could be targeted
for radioactive saturation, barring the effective movements of armies.
Aerosol sprays might render a military base inaccessible or unusable without firing a shot. The economic strength of a nation could be sapped by
the contamination of railways, shipyards, docks, power plants, factories,
and mills. If the right mixture of fission products could be selected, with
short half-lives, this would allow for economically important areas to be
taken over without having to blow up the infrastructure.[48]

Some military figures did not require much convincing. The chief of
the Army Chemical Corps, Major General Alden H. Waitt, recommended
to the War Department in early 1947 that it start working on radiological
warfare right away.[49] Waitt had few illusions about whether an enemy
might develop them; from his headquarters in Camp Detrick, he was
about to send another mission to Japan to interrogate the scientists he
correctly suspected of holding back information on biological weapons
experiments. Maximizing American capabilities in radiological warfare
seemed an obvious course of action. As waste, fission materials were trou-
blesome; as war materials, they were "potentially far more toxic than most
of the agents which have heretofore been developed." Waitt was intrigued
by a line in the Smyth Report—the official history of the atomic bomb
project published less than a week after the bombings of Hiroshima and
Nagasaki, written by Henry DeWolf Smyth. The line read: "the fission
products produced in one day's run of a 100,000 kw chain-reacting pile
might be sufficient to make a large area uninhabitable." Waitt wanted
some programs in place "for obtaining such results."[50]

In fact, both the Atomic Energy Commission (AEC) and the short-lived
Armed Forces Special Weapons Project (AFSWP, a joint undertaking of
the Army and Navy) initiated research projects on military uses of radioactive material toward the end of 1947. Influential civilian scientists reinforced these decisions. The eminent mathematician John von Neumann
advised the AEC in 1947 on the advantages of radioactive weapons, emphasizing that they could be fashioned to any size, unlike atomic bombs. "In a
continuing war," he pointed out during one meeting, "a country which has
solved the problem of making plutonium but not the atomic bomb has at
that time a military potential . . . not very different from one who cannot
only make plutonium but can also produce a nuclear explosion." In Von

Neumann's opinion, a strong nation needed reactors but not necessarily bombs. He calculated that the materials generated from making the Nagasaki bomb could lethally contaminate 6.4 square miles, whereas the bomb itself had only produced an "important damage area" of about three square miles. This difference could be increased if more attention were paid to putting waste products to efficient use. All of this would be especially pertinent in a long-term war because stockpiling such weapons, with their short half-lives, would not be effective.[51]

Was this really how wars would be fought in the future? The military establishment agonized over this question, and many disagreed with Von Neumann. A series of secret scientist-military panels in 1948 stated that radiological weapons would not revolutionize war. Contamination of an area to prevent troop movements was not feasible; a death rate of at least 50 percent would be needed for psychological effect. Offensive capabilities were at least two years away, and this would mean careful selection of just a few targets.[52] As for biological weapons, Secretary of Defense Forrestal had heeded Conant's advice to downplay their importance. He issued a public statement in March 1949 saying that most public discussion had overestimated the catastrophic nature of biological weapons. There were some specific impressions Forrestal hoped to correct:

> For example, it has been stated that a single plane with a small bomb filled with a biological agent would be capable of wiping out the population of an entire city with a single blow. . . . [I]n a recent article it was stated that one ounce of a particular biological material would be sufficient to kill 200,000,000 people. . . . One article stated that biological warfare makes it possible to kill the inhabitants of an entire continent very quickly. . . . Such claims are fantastic and have no basis in fact.

Forrestal went on to say that it would be folly to underestimate the potential of biological weapons, but presently there was no reason to make extravagant claims about the use of super-weapons to spread diseases at will.[53]

If Forrestal's statement had a calming effect at all, it evaporated quickly. In half a year's time, the Soviet Union shocked the world by detonating its own atomic bomb, years in advance of most experts' predictions. US president Harry Truman informed the world that American scientists had detected evidence of a blast somewhere in Siberia, and the Soviets did not deny it. The atomic monopoly had been broken; now the Soviets seemed to have just as much control of nature as the Americans. Just days later, on October 1, 1949, Mao Zedong declared a communist victory in the Chinese Civil War, announcing the creation of the People's Republic of China. In the global struggle of the Cold War, more than half a billion people had to be moved to the "communist" side of the ledger. Western politicians scrambled to explain it, trying to find a scapegoat for "Who lost China?"[54]

Whatever optimism existed about the prospects for peace was tempered by a strong dose of pragmatism about the catastrophic nature of future conflict. In a new global war there was little reason to think that the combatants would limit their options for ensuring victory. Armies would clash, civilians would toil, and cities would be fair game. Added to that the ideological conflict would be between a capitalistic liberal democracy and a communist totalitarian society—a true clash of civilizations. Both sides of the Cold War saw this future coming and tried to plan accordingly. Even if the general public had been kept in the dark, leading military figures knew that the Japanese had indeed conducted biological weapons trials in China. Perhaps the Allies might have explained this atrocity with cultural stereotypes about Japanese racism and cruelty. But the inherent cruelty of these weapons could be ignored quite easily by any culture. Heinous acts against civilians could be justified by the concept of "total war." Special weapons like biological and radiological ones could be justified by discussing their strategic significance, and they easily assumed legitimacy as objects of scientific research.

By the end of the decade, questions about the vulnerability of the world's peoples shifted to include not only the scourge of age-old diseases but also the prospect of scientists and governments deliberately initiating plagues. The development of the atomic bomb—and the actual bombing of Hiroshima and Nagasaki—made it seem not only possible but probable that humans would again bring about catastrophic consequences for humankind. It was not merely a matter of colonial peoples mistrusting their rulers—as the Egyptians living near Suez did. Even the best-informed people, such as the leaders of the World Health Organization, spoke out about the real probability of race suicide at the hands of the superpowers. While some would have doubted the will, few doubted the way. Despite efforts by the US government to downplay its capabilities, nagging concerns lingered that the Americans and Soviets could contaminate broad swathes of land with radioactivity, or that they could initiate a waves of disease over huge expanses of territory. It seemed only a matter of time before the unstable relations between the two countries exploded into a bona fide armed conflict using nature itself as a weapon.

2

Bacteria, Radiation, and Crop Destruction in War Planning

Official information which reaches the American public should, whenever possible, try to allay exaggerated fear. . . . There should be no moral implications expressed concerning these possible weapons. Use of the term "weapon of mass destruction" and "unconventional weapons" shall be avoided.
—US Department of Defense Directive, 1951

The peoples of Korea and China have indeed been the objective of bacteriological weapons. These have been employed by units of the U.S.A. armed forces, using a great variety of different methods for the purpose, some of which seem to be developments of those applied by the Japanese army during the second world war.
—British biochemist JOSEPH NEEDHAM, 1952

IN THE SPRING of 1951, North Korean Foreign Minister Pak Hun Yung announced that the Americans had brought smallpox to his people. An epidemic among the Korean and Chinese troops could be traced, he claimed, to areas where American planes had flown. Soon the accusation widened to include other diseases, including bubonic plague. In the midst of a strategic stalemate during the Korean War, the Americans apparently had used biological weapons to weaken the enemy. The US government denied it, and a full-blown international controversy ensued. In the months that followed, the Americans confronted what they considered a propaganda blitz from the Communist world, and at the same time tried to puzzle out what the controversy meant for their mounting arsenal of biological weapons. Were these weapons illegitimate manipulations of the natural world, bent on human destruction, or were they normal applications of scientific knowledge in the service of national security? The US Department of Defense recognized that many people were torn on this issue, but it had no intention of stopping research on them and tried to make them seem less abhorrent. It issued a directive: "Official information which reaches the American public should, whenever possible, try to allay exaggerated fear. . . . There should be no moral implications expressed concerning these possible weapons. Use of the term 'weapon of mass destruction' and 'unconventional weapons' shall be avoided."[1]

Despite their effort to downplay biological weapons, by that time scientists and their military partners had made several significant decisions about them. They had agreed that in a total war, disease pathogens could be effective instruments of human death, even more so than atomic bombs. They had chosen which pathogens to focus on, had begun field trials, and had built production facilities for the ones likely to cause widespread human death most efficiently. They also understood that diseases, once unleashed, would be impossible for American military commanders to control. But because the Soviet Union would be working on such weapons too, the US Joint Chiefs of Staff and its scientific advisors believed American forces had to be ready and willing to integrate them into their arsenal.

Whether or not the weapons were used during the Korean War, the United States military had acquired a capability in them, in cooperation with American scientists, and it was consistent with the US military establishment's outlook about how a third world war would be fought. The goal was to maximize human death. The creation of biological and radiological warfare capabilities reflected a learning process among scientists and military planners about human vulnerability that went beyond funding scientific studies of diseases. It entailed comprehensive assessments to match diseases to environments and different strategic situations. Despite the diseases' uncontrollability, the US government pursued them as weapons of total war against the Soviet Union—though not necessarily the Koreans. Meanwhile, the controversy inflamed critics and fueled the belief that the United States and the Soviet Union already were capable of harnessing nature's power, even to the point of spreading infectious diseases on an epidemic scale.

The mere existence of the research centers at Camp Detrick and Porton suggested to outsiders the reality of actual scientific capabilities of destroying crops and spreading disease. The *Journal of Bacteriology* published dozens of articles in the 1940s explicitly mentioning Camp Detrick as the authors' affiliation or source of sponsorship. The authors typically made feeble attempts to whitewash the purpose of Camp Detrick's scientific work. For example, in his study of the production problems of *Brucella suis* (the pathogen causing brucellosis, or Mediterranean fever), Army Lieutenant Philipp Gerhardt explained innocently that it "was undertaken to devise a laboratory process for continuous culture of the organism that might be translated to the production of larger quantities for chemical and immunological studies."[2] Another study using egg yolks to cultivate *Bacterium tularense* (the pathogen causing deerfly fever) focused on the ultimate development of a better vaccine for the disease.[3] Yet another analyzed problems in the cultivation and viability of malleomyces (variants of which caused the diseases glanders and melioidosis), despite the fact that "the disease has been almost eradicated in most civilized countries from its natural equine hosts."[4] Anyone paying attention could have easily discerned that this was all research on biological warfare.

Secretary of Defense Forrestal had attempted to address this embarrassing situation by publicly dispelling fantastical rumors about biological weapons. But his statement had the effect within government of piquing the interest of those who believed that the rumors would not be so far off the mark, with a bit more scientific research. A few days after making this statement in 1949, Forrestal appointed his own ad hoc committee, chaired by entomologist Caryl Haskins, to examine the whole problem of biological warfare. The committee included leading civilian and military figures, including Camp Detrick's General Alden H. Waitt. Forrestal originally had planned to limit their task to unconventional uses, such as sabotage; however, Forrestal wrote to Haskins, "I now believe that we should avail ourselves of this opportunity to undertake a full examination of all the technical and strategic possibilities of biological warfare." He encouraged the committee to be "highly imaginative" yet realistic, taking into account all political, economic, and strategic implications.[5] The surprise Soviet test of an atomic bomb later that year gave this study even greater urgency.

As a result, in the year prior to the Korean War, the United States rethought its entire posture with regard to strategic weapons targeting humans. When Forrestal's successor, Louis Johnson, received the report, he found that a new concept had been created. Under Haskins's leadership, the committee had determined that all of these new weapons— unlike atomic bombs—had one thing in common; namely, their primary goal was disease in, and/or death of, living organisms. "Radiological weapons and some of the newer chemical weapons," the committee reported, "are essentially 'biological' in effect and closely resemble biological weapons in the importance of their future capabilities and in respect to strategic employment, defensive requirements, and public relations." The committee thus invented a unitary concept—CEBAR—that blended chemical, biological, and radiological warfare "as a new entity in national defense planning." These were the "silent" weapons, directed exclusively against man—directly as a biological entity or indirectly by diminishing his food and other living resources.[6]

These scientists and military officers believed biological weapons to be revolutionary. The biological and medical fields, they said, were on the threshold of great advances comparable to atomic fission in physics, including the ability to spread epidemics "or other biological 'chain-reactions.'" This term was employed to reflect a parallel to atomic bombs, to be sure, but it also hinted at ecologic vulnerability—indirect causes and effects through the food chain. The power to direct human epidemics was currently beyond their grasp, but they explicitly stated that creating epidemics was already quite possible in plants and animals, and the United States or the Soviet Union might begin doing it at a moment's notice. The usefulness of such weapons in military operations, foreign affairs, economic policies, psychological warfare, "and perhaps even other more subtle applications of national power, can be as important as bold and imaginative planning sees fit to make it."[7]

What was the best way to target humans? Evidence suggested that crop destruction, rather than disease, might prove most logical. Haskins had visited the United Kingdom a few months earlier and concluded that both countries had insufficient knowledge to tell whether epidemic human diseases could be started and controlled at will. The only relevant experience, the great influenza epidemic of 1918–20, suggested that the damage from epidemics would likely be worldwide in scope. Only with more research on immunizing against these diseases could offensive warfare against humans be realistically contemplated. By contrast, anti-livestock and anti-crop weapons seemed logical. These would have less of an effect on the United States because of its wide variety of foods and its surpluses of grains, but against countries like India or China, with their large populations and high reliance on single crops, anti-crop agents could prove devastating.[8]

The real enemy, of course, was the Soviet Union. All government advisors believed the Soviet Union was developing these same kinds of weapons. But it was not clear whether the Americans or Russians were more vulnerable to biological attack. Haskins's committee guessed that American knowledge lagged behind because the Soviets might have engaged in human experimentation. The Central Intelligence Agency asserted that the Soviets might view non-conforming communist satellites such as Yugoslavia as human testing grounds.[9] Haskins urged human experiments as well, to keep pace with Soviet scientists. This would require human volunteers and the use of publicly acceptable methods of experimentation, along with a vigilant awareness of public relations. Even if the dangers to these volunteers were great, they deemed the risk necessary: "In no other way can the needed knowledge be obtained."[10] Given the catastrophic potential of war, such choices seemed morally justifiable to these men.

Today there is considerable controversy about these discussions, because the United States was accused soon after of actually using biological weapons during the Korean War. After Haskins gave this advice, the secretary of defense continued to seek others' counsel about them. Another group, headed by Earl P. Stevenson, recommended that the Department of Defense and the Joint Chiefs abandon the "retaliation only" policy held by the United States. He and his panel firmly believed that the United States should consider using biological weapons whether the enemy had done so or not. Stevenson agreed that biological and radiological weapons posed a provocative question about the nature of modern war, the "so-called 'larger problem' of determining the total effect on a nation's war effort of large-scale personnel destruction (such as might be potentially possible by BW) as opposed to the presently accepted method of material destruction." Like Haskins, Stevenson saw great potential in spreading diseases in humans and crops, and he urged that bureaucratic barriers to research and production be removed.[11]

Did the activities of these committees mean that the United States was getting ready to use biological weapons? Yes. The Joint Chiefs were trying to integrate them into war plans, unsure how it ought to be done. They agreed that the United States needed a strong program of development at the proving grounds in Dugway, Utah, in order to obtain planning data. In addition, they ordered the construction of production facilities.[12]

But does that mean they had decided to use them? Some suggest that the US government's debate in the early 1950s about its "retaliation only" policy might have meant it was preparing to use such weapons in Korea. But the archival documents of the Joint Chiefs of Staff tell a somewhat different story. The Army, Navy, and Air Force disagreed among themselves about whether to change the policy. The Army and Air Force argued that the "retaliation only" policy hampered both offensive and defensive research, relegating it to a low priority and stifling American efforts for war readiness. In their view, the policy encouraged indecision and insufficient financial support of scientific research.[13]

Plenty of high-ranking officials in the US military establishment disagreed with this view, and officially the Navy opposed it. This was not due to any moral stand. Rather, the Navy said that abandoning the "retaliation only" policy would horrify the American public and American allies, making the United States an easy propaganda target. But the Navy also favored a strong program in research and development.[14] Admiral Forrest P. Sherman, the chief of Naval Operations, pointed out that trying to change the policy secretly would probably prove impossible, and in any event the question would get bogged down in the National Security Council, further impeding rather than increasing readiness. He wrote: "The current theme of the Soviet propaganda program . . . is aimed at proving that the USSR is the champion of peace and of the outlawing of weapons of mass destruction, while the United States is an imperialist nation, bent on conquering the world, and is preparing as rapidly as possible to use the most cruel, diabolical weapons of mass destruction to accomplish its purpose." With this in mind, changing the policy would be counterproductive for the United States.[15]

As the United States went into the Korean War, the Navy's view—particularly because of its sensitivity to political ramifications—won the day. The chairman of the Joint Chiefs, Army General Omar Bradley, tried to address the problem by emphasizing that a high priority should be given to continuing robust research and development programs, and Secretary of Defense George C. Marshall made it a directive.[16]

If they were not going to be used in Korea, why develop these weapons at all? They were meant for use in a future global conflict—a total war—against the Soviet Union. Not only did the government start to build production facilities and conduct extensive field tests of biological agents but it also attempted to coordinate doctrines and plans among the armed services. The United States needed extensive knowledge of biological weapons in strategic, operational, and emergency planning. All this was to be carried out "as rapidly as necessary engineering and design studies will permit, in order that actual readiness can be achieved at the earliest practical time."[17]

The US military took very seriously this task to learn everything it could about human, animal, and plant vulnerability. The Chemical Corps's Biological Department at Camp Detrick had already conducted field tests of a variety of plant killers. For example, in late 1950 it determined that birds would make good biological warfare agents because their feathers could be dusted with cereal rust spores in order to infect oat crops over a wide area. One such test, using homing pigeons, showed that birds had the potential to initiate an infection from up to a hundred miles away. In another test, conducted at St. Thomas, Virgin Islands, dusted pigeons were dropped from aircraft to see if aerial attacks might be effective. Of four different test plots of oats about a half-mile apart, all of them showed heavy infection.[18]

The key findings of these particular tests were not necessarily that rust spores ought to be prioritized but rather that bird feathers—which retained the spores over long periods of time—might be an ideal vehicle for transmitting infections. Perhaps instead of using the birds themselves—which might prove unpredictable—one could simply pack feathers into the same airborne devices used sometimes to distribute leaflets. Placing feathers into an M16A1 cluster adapter—designed to release leaflets rather than detonate a bomb—would allow the spores to fall over a wide area of enemy territory. At Pine Camp, in upstate New York, the Army conducted a much larger field test using these devices, dropping them over 16 half-acre plots of oats. They were dropped about a mile upwind of the plots, at various altitudes. This allowed the researchers at Camp Detrick to hone the technique considerably, concluding that releasing such containers "1300 to 1800 feet above ground level will carry sufficient numbers of spores to initiate a cereal rust epidemic." The scientists guessed that the yields of enemy oat crops thus infected would be decreased by at least 30 percent.[19]

Scientists did not have to invent these weapons because nature had already created the best killers. This was especially true of human diseases. The pathogens that had plagued mankind for centuries now had major production centers. The only difficulty was in choosing which scourge to mass produce. What was the most efficient, cost-effective way to arm nature? The answer depended on the environment of the targeted humans. By early 1951 the US Research and Development Board, under the chairmanship of William Webster, initiated a combined military and scientific evaluation of biological warfare agents. Webster wanted to prioritize which to test first, so that he could encourage research along those lines.[20] Seven months later, he had his answer. The Joint Chiefs ranked them in order of priority, mixing pathogen names with diseases, with maximum emphasis to be given to the first five:

Pestis
Brucella melitensis
Malleomyces
Tularense
Brucella suis
Burnetii
Anthrax
Psittacosis
Botulinum toxin

All of the agents were rated as superior or inferior to *Brucella suis*, the standard biological agent at that time.

This intensive inquiry into ranking diseases yielded useful data about human vulnerability in a variety of scenarios. Rather than protecting human life, scientists furnished recommendations on the best pathogens to harm them, based on costs, logistical considerations, incubation period, and the specific effects on humans as they died. Rather than just spreading disease effectively in humans or crops over time, they also wanted agents promising "rapidity of incapacitation" in support of actual ground combat. The Joint Chiefs recognized that any agent with an incubation period longer than a few hours would be useful only as a weapon of attrition or interdiction—both strategic uses. Botulinum toxin was the only one that seemed capable of being truly useful in combat, if a way could be found to deliver it in extremely heavy doses. Unfortunately, the cost of botulinum toxin at such concentrations was estimated to be about a million times as high as the cost of the other agents.[21] That made tactical uses hard to justify. It also meant that the main target of biological weapons would be centers of civilian population.

What kinds of characteristics did the US military want in a mass-produced pathogen? Like botulinum toxin, the other agents in the bottom four of the list had significant drawbacks. Burnetii, for example, was the only agent for which most target populations likely would have fairly low susceptibility, because of natural immunities. On the other hand, it had an extremely high casualty rate in those it did infect. By contrast, the agents causing anthrax and psittacosis (like botulinum toxin) did not imperil as many per pound, which meant that far greater quantities would be required to ensure adequate casualty rates.

High fatality rates were not always identified as optimal. In some military situations, one could argue that long-term incapacitation (requiring the diversion of food and medical supplies) was a far more intelligent goal. The Joint Chiefs wanted to have some agents that kept people sick for longer periods.

At the top of the list was *Yersinia pestis*, better known as plague. It was the only one of the diseases to promise a "bonus effect" of epidemic disease beyond the target area. More important, it could be produced in the same low-cost facility as the other vegetative agents, namely, malleomyces, tularense, and both varieties of brucella. A different facility would be required for anthrax and botulinum toxin, and still another for psittacosis and burnetii. The facilities construction cost per pound of the vegetative agents would be about $500, whereas all the others were in the thousands (with botulinum toxin a whopping $70,000).

These figures, the convenience of concentrating them in a single facility, combined with numerous other advantages, helped the Joint Chiefs of Staff to prioritize the vegetative agents. Brucella was a bacterium that caused Malta fever, so called because British soldiers stationed in Malta were known to die of it after a period of high fever, night sweats, fatigue, and even anorexia. The disease, called brucellosis, was first associated with specific bacteria in the late nineteenth century. *Brucella miletensis* primarily was found in goats and sheep, whereas *Brucella suis* was found in pigs. Malleomyces caused glanders, the respiratory disease sometimes afflicting horses and donkeys. *Bacterium tularense* was a cause for rabbit fever, sometimes called deerfly fever because deerflies and ticks were the typical vectors of the disease (see Table 2.1).

In several ways the Korean War would have been a perfect time and place in which to try out biological weapons (or as they were known at the time, bacteriological weapons). Some of the diseases identified by the Joint Chiefs were common to the region, so it might have been difficult to detect an artificial epidemic. Much of the knowledge from Japanese experiments in World War II was specifically geared toward the region—Unit 731 had been based in Manchuria, right across the border from Korea. And the Japanese had experimented on Chinese and Korean prisoners. Dehumanizing racial attitudes toward Asians left over from World War II might also have made it easier for Americans to attack North Korea or China with weapons causing debilitating and fatal diseases. If the pressing desire of Americans to "contain" communism, with its imagery of hordes of irreligious and rabidly Marxist-Leninist-Stalinist-Maoist ideologues, is added, using biological weapons in the Korean War does not seem beyond the imagination.

Table 2.1 Relative Advantages Accorded to Pathogens by the Joint Chiefs of Staff

Pathogen	Diseases	Advantages	Disadvantages
Yersinia pestis	Bubonic Plague, Pneumonic Plague	Short incubation; high fatality rate*; low facilities cost; epidemic "bonus effect"	
Brucella melitensis	Brucellosis/Malta Fever/ Mediterranean Fever	High effective doses per pound; low fatality rate*; extended disability period; low facilities cost	Very long incubation
Malleomyces mallei and *Malleomyces pseudomallei*	Glanders/Farcy, Melioidosis	Short incubation; high fatality rate*; extended disability period; low facilities cost	
Bacterium tularense	Tularemia/Rabbit Fever/ Deerfly Fever	Short incubation; low fatality rate*; high effective doses per pound; low facilities cost	
Brucella suis	Brucellosis/Malta Fever/ Mediterranean Fever	Low fatality rate*; low facilities cost	Very long incubation
Coxiella burnetii	Q Fever	Low fatality rate*; very high effective doses per pound	Very long incubation; low susceptibility; dissemination problems as bomb

Bacillus anthracis	Anthrax	Easily disseminated as bomb or aerosol	Long incubation; very low effective doses per pound; very long persistency**; high facilities cost; high munitions requirement
Chlamydophila psittaci	Psittacosis (Parrot Disease/Parrot Fever/Ornithosis)		Long incubation; very low effective doses per pound; dissemination problems as bomb; high munitions requirement
Botulinum toxin	Botulism	Very short incubation (tactical value); high fatality rate*	Very low effective doses per pound; dissemination problems as bomb; high facilities cost; high munitions requirement

*The Joint Chiefs of Staff wanted some pathogens with high fatality rates and some with low fatality rates. Particularly low fatality rates with long periods of disability could be advantageous, leading to long-term drains on enemy resources.

**Although long persistency might be a strategic advantage in time of war, extremely long persistency would create postwar problems.

Note: These sources do not always correctly distinguish between pathogens and diseases. For example, Psittacosis is routinely cited as a pathogen, though it is the ailment caused by *Chlamydophila psittaci*. Source: W. G. Lalor, Memorandum for the Chairman, Research and Development Board, September 13, 1951, NARA RG 218, Central Decimal File, 1951–53, Box 152, Folder CCS 385.2 (12-17-43) Sec. 12.

There also were powerful strategic arguments in favor of attempting to spread disease in North Korea and China. The United Nations troops, led by the United States, were locked in a stalemate, with no good options for victory, and faced an enemy with far greater stores of manpower. Despite beating back a summer 1950 North Korean invasion of South Korea, UN forces under the command of General Douglas MacArthur suffered a series of reverses as winter approached, when newly communist China sent equipment and men to reinforce the North Korean lines. Calling it an "entirely new war," MacArthur dismally observed that the hopes of a quick victory had been dashed when Chinese forces crossed the frozen Yalu River, which divided North Korea from China. As one observer from an airplane wrote, the Chinese were swarming "like locusts along every road, every gully, and every ridgeline." The war had entered a new phase, and the Americans began a hasty retreat southward.[22]

Over the next year, diplomats attempted without success to negotiate an armistice. Neither side of the conflict achieved decisive gains, despite fierce fighting. From the UN perspective, the North Koreans and Chinese seemed to have an endless supply of human resources, giving them a distinct advantage in a war of attrition. The imagery of swarming locusts suggested the same kind of solution when dealing with insects: extermination. American leaders struggled to identify new strategies. An obvious candidate was the atomic bomb. It is often thought that President Dwight Eisenhower's ability to achieve an armistice in 1953 was due to his threat to use atomic bombs against China. In reality, atomic bombs had never been off the table, and President Truman had already considered using them after the Chinese intervened in the war. But he and his military advisors believed that this was a step to be taken only in desperation, should the UN forces face annihilation, or should the Soviet Union enter the conflict.[23]

Others tried to convince the president to transform the landscape into a contaminated dead zone that would kill any humans who set foot in it. In an article entitled "Atomic Death Belt Urged for Korea," the *New York Times* pointed out in 1951 that Congressman Albert Gore had advised President Truman to "dehumanize" a belt across the Korean peninsula. The dangerous wastes from plutonium processing could be put to good use, he said, and the president could avoid the political repercussions of using an atomic bomb:

Just before this is accomplished, broadcast the fact to the enemy, with ample and particular notice that entrance into the belt would mean certain death or slow deformity to all foot soldiers; that all vehicles, weapons, food and apparel entering the belt would become poisoned with radioactivity, and, further, that the belt would be regularly re-contaminated until such time as a satisfactory solution to the whole Korean problem shall have been reached. This would differ from the use of the atomic bomb in several ways and would be, I believe, morally justifiable under the circumstances.[24]

Creating a kind of Maginot line across Korea had the advantage of not widening the war by bombing Chinese soil, and it might not scare allies as much as an atomic bomb would.

Gore's idea did not come to fruition, however, because radiological weapons simply could not be as effective as he suggested. Some applauded the idea: an Army publication emphasized the humaneness of radiological weapons, based on the fact that people could choose to avoid the accumulation of harmful radiation simply by evacuating the target areas. Thus wars might be won without killing people at all, simply by arming the countryside itself.[25] But Senator Brien McMahon, chairman of Congress's Joint Committee on Atomic Energy, pointed out the tactical limitations. Although a radioactive belt might be deadly, the physiological effects would take hold long after soldiers had crossed it. McMahon and others believed that such delays in harm were unlikely to stop Chinese military commanders from ordering their men into battle.[26]

For these reasons, atomic bombs and radiological warfare seemed unlikely to bring about an armistice or break the stalemate. It is true that General MacArthur openly advocated widening the war to include targets in China, and he firmly believed that escalation would lead to victory. But his strategic outlook openly contradicted the president's, leading Truman to relieve him of his command in April 1951. The war stayed confined to Korea, with indecisive action along a slow-moving front stretching across the peninsula. In the fall of 1951, the Americans scored a "victory" in the weeks-long Battle of Bloody Ridge, only to see enemy forces take up a new position just 1,500 yards away. This led to the even more destructive month-long Battle of Heartbreak Ridge, which left over 30,000 American and French casualties and 25,000 North Korean and Chinese casualties. Although ultimately the UN forces took the ridge, the cost in human life seemed appalling given the tiny amount of territory gained. The United States was not prepared to do something as politically costly as drop an atomic bomb. But would it secretly engage in biological warfare to cut into the enemy's human resources, willfully spreading disease behind enemy lines?

In February and March of 1951, Communist Chinese radio stations announced measures to control the spread of epidemic disease in the spring. They were concerned about smallpox, diphtheria, bubonic plague, typhus, and other diseases endemic to the region. The North Korean government in Pyongyang reported its own efforts to reduce the risk of such diseases spreading, including importation of medicines and vaccines from East Germany. Then, when those long-expected diseases did break out, they blamed the Americans. In May 1951, North Korean foreign minister Pak Hun Yung formally protested to the United Nations "the employment of smallpox germs by the American interventionists against the Korean people." By the winter of 1951/52, epidemic diseases were rampant in Korea and the neighboring Chinese province of Manchuria. In late February, the governments of both countries crafted a detailed accusation, blaming widespread illness on American planes dropping diseased insects behind enemy lines.[27]

Fortunately for the United States, its UN allies did not believe the accusation. UN Secretary General Trygve Lie declared it "utterly false."[28] Throughout the war the endemic diseases had struck hard, bringing smallpox, bubonic plague, and pneumonic plague. Conditions for their spread were ideal in the north, particularly with large, heavily concentrated armies living in squalor. Compared to the UN forces, the North Koreans and Chinese did not have decent sanitation or medical services. The fact that the accusation had been so broad in scope, mentioning a range of diseases and carriers—including flies, spiders, and grasshoppers—only deepened the allies' certainty that the "frantic charges" were quite false.[29]

The United States and its allies identified numerous reasons for China and Korea to mount such a campaign. First, blaming the Americans might split the West and enlist Asian sympathy. Second, it could help extract more medical aid from the Soviet Union. Third, it might distract public attention from the incompetence and corruption of the Chinese and North Korean governments. At the very least, it had the potential to discourage further bombing, because of the threat to treat captured airmen as war criminals.[30]

The accusation was easy to ridicule, especially because the epidemics had struck in winter, when temperatures throughout Korea were quite cold and not amenable to the insect vectors named. As one British reporter put it, the North Koreans "can hardly hope that anyone will be fool enough to believe that United Nations scientists have mass produced individual insulation jackets for each insect." One reporter suggested that the communists must subscribe to Hitler's thesis that if the lie is big enough and repeated loudly enough and often enough it will numb the listener's ability to think.[31]

What was at stake was the willingness of people around the world to believe the Americans had the will and the capability to harness these natural scourges. The bacteriological warfare charge did not disappear. US Secretary of State Dean Acheson asked China and North Korea to allow an impartial group to investigate. But China refused to allow the International Red Cross, on the grounds that the organization had not spoken out against the Holocaust during World War II and probably would not now stand up to the United States. China also refused to invite experts from the World Health Organization, on the grounds that a UN agency was unlikely to criticize UN troops. Instead it chose communist organizations, which did not serve to increase Chinese credibility in the West.

A few scientists lent support to the accusations. The highest-profile Westerners to endorse the Chinese accusations were the French physicist Frèdèric Joliot-Curie and the British microbiologist Joseph Needham. A Nobel Prize–winning scientist and husband of co-Prize winner Irène Curie, Joliot-Curie was the son-in-law of the world-famous scientist Marie Curie. A national hero, he had fought against the Nazis while in the Resistance and was instrumental in setting up an atomic energy commission in France after the war to help his country join the nuclear club. He also was, quite openly, a committed communist. Despite his fame and accomplishments, he had been pushed out of the corridors of power in the French nuclear world. He then helped to create the World Council of Peace, which became a mouthpiece of pro-communist information.

When Chinese writer Kuo Mo-Jo, vice-president of the World Council of Peace, contacted Joliot-Curie to tell him about the American use of biological weapons, Joliot-Curie immediately accepted it as truth. Kuo Mo-Jo sent him a mountain of corroborating evidence, including confessions of captured airman and photographs of various insects, laboratory scientists, and leaflet canisters with which the Americans were accused of dropping the insects. He included a timeline of events in which he claimed American planes dropped flies, fleas, mosquitoes, locusts, spiders, centipedes, ants, crickets, grasshoppers, beetles, ticks, midges, lice, and "another kind of black insect"—as well as chicken feathers and a variety of unidentified crystals, powders, and sticky substances.[32]

The information sent to Joliot-Curie was disarmingly specific.[33] In making the case, the Chinese drew heavily upon evidence from the slim public record of biological weapons. In addition to references to the Merck report, Rosebury's 1947 paper and 1949 book, and statements by US Defense Secretary Forrestal, there were numerous newspaper clippings—from the *New York Times* and other major papers, to military papers like *Stars and Stripes*, to communist-friendly venues such as *The Daily Worker*. All reported on research centers, projects, efforts to incorporate biological weapons into war plans, and the postwar use of Nazi and Japanese scientists by the United States.[34]

Most entomologists and bacteriologists in the West did not know quite what to make of this evidence. If indeed the Americans had done it, it had been a shoddy operation. It did not look like the product of a specific plan to spread a particular epidemic. It looked like the Americans, hoping to spread some kind of disease, had tried to drop everything but the kitchen sink on China and Korea.[35]

Joliot-Curie organized a team of scientists, under the auspices of his World Council of Peace, to visit sites in China and to investigate the accusations. These scientists soon published a lengthy report confirming that the UN forces had in fact engaged in biological warfare.[36] Because the members of the scientific team were all sympathetic to communism, the conclusion convinced few skeptics. The London *Times* quoted British diplomat Selwyn Lloyd saying "never had so much been written by such confirmed fellow-travelers to prove so little."[37] Several prominent American physicists, including Isidor Rabi and Robert Millikan, wrote to Joliot-Curie personally, calling on him to temper his views. But to Joliot-Curie, a government that could lay waste Hiroshima and Nagasaki was perfectly capable of launching biological attacks.[38] Joliot-Curie issued a public statement, calling the American action "a sequel to the no less monstrous crime of the destruction of hundreds of thousands of civilians in a few seconds by the atom bomb at Hiroshima and Nagasaki."[39]

From Britain, Joseph Needham proved a reluctant participant in the scientific team sent to China, but he returned with a renewed conviction that the Americans were guilty.[40] Other members of the team included a Swede, two Italians, a Frenchman, a Brazilian, and a Russian, all of whom exchanged outraged letters with each other after the American POWs retracted their statements in 1953.[41] Their outrage was not one of embarrassment but rather continued abhorrence of what they considered an atrocity by the Americans, in their view being covered up with, as Italian microbiologist Franco Graziosi put it, "ridiculous retractions."[42]

In one press conference, Joseph Needham recalled that he had been in China during World War II and had seen firsthand the evidence proffered by Chinese officials that Japan was using fleas to disseminate bubonic plague. One of his motivations for participating in the World Council of Peace team was that he "was naturally curious to enquire into what seemed to be further developments of their methods." He said that, as far as he knew, none of the scientists other than the Soviet one were members of the Communist Party. As part of their investigation, Needham reported, they heard evidence from intelligence agents and captured airmen, as well as witnesses from all walks of life in China and North Korea. While Needham acknowledged that they had to depend on Chinese and Korean documentation and witnesses, he said "their testimonies were too simple, too concordant, and too independent, to be subject to doubt." In Needham's view, there could be no doubt that the Koreans and Chinese had been attacked with bacteriological weapons, for which the American armed forces were to blame. The trail of abnormal disease outbreaks always led back to American air activity. As for casualties, Needham was not in a position to give precise figures, and even if he had such information, he would not provide it because the Americans undoubtedly were hoping for such data.[43]

Needham was far more problematic a figure for the British government than Joliot-Curie was for the French. Needham held no position of power but was greatly esteemed by his scientific colleagues and was a respected member of the Royal Society, the most prestigious scientific body in the country. "Biochemists of the quality of Dr. Needham," the Foreign Office lamented, "are most unlikely to give their imprimatur to evidence which can easily be proved false." Thus the government needed to "stiffen public resistance in this country to any new evidence that Dr. Needham may produce," internal Foreign Office documents stated. "An early and authoritative demonstration of the scientific fatuity of the charges that have so far been made would be invaluable."

The problem was that almost no scientists in the UK wanted to do it. Officials had attempted "to induce reputable scientific bodies like the Medical Research Council and the London School of Tropical Medicine to make a public and systematic refutation of the charges, but all with one accord have made excuses."[44] Trying to contradict Needham would have presumed that the charges were truly ridiculous. But they were not.

The Foreign Office next proposed sending a persuasive man on a private visit to the leadership of the Royal Society. The purpose would be "to

draw the attention of these eminent men to the difficulties which the re-
fusal of reputable scientific bodies in this country to become involved in
political matters causes us, and may even . . . suggest to their minds that,
in the present state of the world, circumstances may arise in which even
bodies like the Royal Society cannot indefinitely remain aloof."[45] But the
Royal Society still refused to take an official stand. However, two members, ex-presidents Sir Henry Dale and Sir Robert Robinson, argued in *The
Times* that Needham's achievements in biochemistry, which formed the
basis of his elevation to the Royal Society, had no bearing on his compe-
tence to give an impartial verdict.[46] Several other Royal Society members
wrote to *The Times* to defend Needham's scientific qualifications. Bacteriological warfare, they wrote, was a direct application of scientific knowledge.[47] Once Needham had returned with his report, the Royal Society
again was under pressure to denounce it, but did not.[48]

One important consequence of the Korean debacle was that it served as
an unintended test case of international public opinion about the Allies'
research on these new "absolute" weapons. The US Department of State
contacted Britain's Foreign Office to coordinate their estimates of the controversy's impact on the rest of the world. Britain's view was particularly
valuable because of its extensive contacts throughout its empire and the
British Commonwealth. The United States wanted to know how the controversy had altered public opinion in key strategic areas where the allies
competed with the Soviet Union for influence: Southeast Asia, India, and
the Middle East.[49]

The British saw that many believed the United States and its allies had
already crossed the line and were capable of extraordinary manipulations
of the natural world. In places like India, they feared, there were strong
pacifist traditions and an ignorance of the supposed subtleties of modern
warfare. These people tended to "blur the distinction between, say, strategic bombing and the use of bacteriological weapons." Other countries ravaged by war in the last decade might not have due appreciation for such
distinctions either, they said. The British tried to caution American colleagues that there was a long-standing, fundamental resentment of Westerners waging warfare against Asian peoples. The British Foreign Office
urged emphasizing the threat to civilians from disease and showing com-
passion for the victims.[50]

American diplomats were more concerned that the accusation was a
clever ruse by the Soviets to establish America's "first use," in case they
wanted to use their own biological weapons. At a private meeting in Paris,

US Secretary of State Dean Acheson met with British diplomat Pierson Dixon to discuss the disturbing intensity of the propaganda campaign. Acheson observed that recently some 28 percent of Soviet press was devoted to the subject, a figure American intelligence officials worried was unusual for any particular propaganda subject. Dixon agreed that there was probably some other objective that the "Big Lie" was intended to complement—or perhaps it was a distraction. Dixon concluded gloomily: "The Americans were, in fact, wondering whether the bacteriological warfare campaign might not be a build-up for something sinister."[51] Was a large-scale biological conflict looming?

Examining this evidence today, it is difficult to understand how it could have appeared as anything but staged. It is a hodge-podge of circumstantial evidence, buttressed by confessions of captured American airmen who retracted their statements when they returned home. The sheer number of pathogens and vectors mentioned defied belief and, more important, defied attempt at disproof. Still, if the Chinese fabricated the evidence, why do it so poorly? One possible answer is that its propaganda value was in the fear and outrage at American scientific power. Merely publicizing the research and planting the seed of suspicion was enough. Indeed the documents sent to Joliot-Curie, one scholar has argued, were compiled in typical Soviet propaganda fashion, designed as a narrative of mounting corroborating evidence leading the reader toward intense suspicion and distrust of the United States.[52]

But there is a difference between suspicion and evidence. One might just as easily accept that biological warfare had enormous propaganda value, precisely because the Americans seemed so capable of manipulating nature. And indeed, the US government already had admitted to conducting research on biological warfare. What is remarkable about the response to these accusations is that while many rushed to exonerate the Americans, few doubted that it could be done. And if it could, how vulnerable was the rest of the world to attack?

3

Ecological Invasions and Convulsions

> *We must make no mistake: we are seeing one of the great*
> *historical convulsions in the world's flora and fauna.*
> —CHARLES ELTON, *The Ecology of Invasions by Plants*
> *and Animals* (1958)

WHILE SOME SCIENTISTS were identifying pathogens for mass production, others imagined themselves digging in behind heavy fortifications. Was it possible to defend against an enemy who used nature as a weapon? After all, the Soviets had scientists who would be thinking about epidemics and crop destruction too. This question sharpened ecological ideas among scientists and military planners alike, as they worried about each country's vulnerability to attack. The scientific discipline of ecology focused on how organisms interacted with each other and with their natural surroundings. Ecologists routinely thought about the interdependence of humans, animals, plants, and nutrients. In a total war, ecological thinking would be paramount—for offense and defense alike. Questions of vulnerability loomed: which commodities could an enemy target successfully, crippling the economy? What was the best way to fend off insect infestations or plant blights? If a full-scale war should break out, what elements of the biological web of life would be crucial for post-nuclear survival? This chapter is about the quests to find answers to these worrisome questions.

What emerged by the late 1950s in the United States and Britain was a deep appreciation by military establishments of a couple of principles. One was based on ecologists' obsession with vulnerability. Biological diversity was the best defense in a total war, ecologists argued, meaning that a nation should not rely too much on any given crop. The vast breadbasket of wheat in the United States was vulnerable to rust blights, just as Britain's rich plantations of rubber trees in Malaya stood under constant threat of sabotage. The other principle was a silver lining on this dark cloud. Despite its disturbing weaknesses, especially in colonial holdings that focused on single commodities, the West appeared better equipped to deal with crop destruction or biological warfare than the Soviet Union and its allies. Here the difference in political and economic ideologies between the superpowers determined how the United States and Britain chose to act upon their own perceived vulnerabilities. After years of trying to find the right commodities to stockpile for a catastrophic war, defense planners eventually hoped to rely on Western market mechanisms to ensure their survival. These, they believed, would encourage variety in time of peace, so that clandestine biological attacks of the homeland probably would not be crippling. Should a nuclear war occur, the commodities provided by an open market at the commencement of hostilities would be far more diverse than any government stockpile could be.

Concern about ecological vulnerability sowed seeds of tension between East and West early in the Cold War. For example, throughout 1949 nervous Czech farmers patrolled their southwest frontier, looking for invaders from Bavaria. Only four years after soldiers had pushed the Nazis back across the border, the Czechs faced devastation of a different sort from a tiny, unstoppable enemy: the Colorado beetle. Near the Bavarian city of Regensburg, West German plant protection specialists launched a campaign of insecticide spraying, spurred on by international groups wanting to promote pest control across borders. Despite efforts by the European Organization for the Protection of Plants to involve them, Czech scientists and farmers remained aloof. By the end of the year, the bugs could not be stopped from crossing the proverbial Iron Curtain between West and East. West German efforts to keep their beetles out of Czechoslovakia were hampered by lack of access to machine parts and an unreliable system of transportation—using horse-drawn sprayers rather than motorcycles—near the frontier.[1]

Despite these spraying efforts, the insect invasion from the west continued. Colorado beetle infestations grew so intense by the summer of 1950 that the governments of both Czechoslovakia and East Germany began to call it intentional, as if it were the opening salvo against the communist world by the imperialist, capitalist West. The Czech government issued a proclamation to its people in late June 1950 comparing the beetle attack to the Nazi use of poison gas and the Japanese use of biological weapons. "It is a criminal attempt of capitalist exploiters," the proclamation went on, "who are systematically lowering living standards of their working people, to imperil [the] process of rising prosperity of working people of Czechoslovakia." The government called on its people to organize large-scale

beetle search days and offered rewards to individuals who showed dili-
gence in combating the pest.[2]

In response, the Americans observed that the potato bug was hardly an
effective instrument of national policy. Moreover, the United States doubted
"whether the potato bug even in its most voracious phase could nibble
effectively at the fabric of friendship uniting the Czechoslovak and
American peoples." Appalled at what appeared to be an absurd accusation—as well as at the Americans' willingness to engage with it—British
diplomats agreed that it seemed "to call for ridicule by the BBC, rather than
for diplomatic notes."[3]

The Czechs did not find it absurd at all. According to their complaint
lodged at the American embassy, beetles had begun to appear all at once
in the most unnatural places along the western and southwestern frontier.
Colorado beetles appeared not just in fields but also on roads, in towns,
and packed in bottles and boxes. Over the next week, the Czech government protested the violation of its airspace by American military aircraft,
saying they were armed with crates of beetles. Soon East Germany made
the same accusation, claiming violations of airspace and strange accumu-
lations of beetles in areas adjacent to the American occupation zone. The
Czechs also pointed out that American newspapers had reported the US
military's research on how to destroy an enemy's agriculture. The end goal
of that research, the government claimed, had become a reality in Czechoslovakia and East Germany.[4]

Just days later, the two communist countries signed a cooperative
agreement to control the pest and reiterated the charge that American
planes were responsible. The Americans and British guessed that the
Czechoslovakian and East German governments were attempting to kill
three birds with one stone: mobilize farmers to be more vigilant with
spraying, relieve themselves of any responsibility, and harp on the ex-
ploitive nature of capitalist societies. As one Brit put it, "the satellites are
determined to flog this horse (or beetle) to death." But some worried about
a darker possibility: that "tales of this kind might be used at a later stage as
'justification' for similar trials actually practiced by the USSR—e.g. bacteriological warfare."[5]

In fact, the Colorado beetle, *Doryphora decemlineata*, had been a pest in
Europe for many years. As the name suggests, it originally came from the
US state of Colorado, where for generations it fed only on that region's
indigenous plants. Once intrepid American farmers began to plant potatoes in the nineteenth century, however, the beetle found a new favorite

food and began to trek eastward, following potatoes wherever they might be grown. Its progress could be traced by panicked announcements in local newspapers. Europeans followed the news with dread, knowing that once the beetles reached New York City, they would find their way to Europe. In 1876 the beetle was firmly entrenched on the Atlantic seaboard, prompting most Europeans to curb imports of potatoes from the United States and Canada. But to no avail. In short time beetles were terrorizing farmers in Germany, France, Britain, and wherever else potatoes were grown. After World War II, the problem was compounded by the inadequate control measures during the war. When beetles were found in England in 1947, having been transported aboard the S.S. *Whitstable*, one sympathetic newspaper editorial injected some levity: "As likely as not our poor beetle, having little knowledge of geography, thought that the *Whitstable* would take him straight to his home state. It's a long, long way to Colorado, but its innocent heart was right there."[6]

Although the Americans insisted that they had not dropped beetles on Czech or East German farms, doing so would have been fairly simple. It would have required little effort and no sophisticated equipment. And the Czechs were right about one thing: the Americans and British were in fact engaged in research on crop destruction. For the most part this research involved synthetic chemicals, not insects. During World War II, scientists believed that chemical weapons could be used to destroy food supplies just as easily as to harm humans directly. They conducted experiments to test the viability of wide variety of crops—wheat, barley, kale, grass, beets, and potatoes—to conventional chemical weapons such as mustard gas and Lewisite (arsenic).[7]

Agricultural defense already played a major role in British scientific circles, because of the perceived vulnerability of the empire's crops around the world. In late 1949, a secret "Crop Committee" of Britain's Advisory Council on Scientific Research and Technical Development debated the possibility of an enemy introducing diseases to the British Isles, either into crops or livestock. The members of this committee worried that a saboteur could secretly initiate diseases such as rinderpest among cattle. Once it took hold, rinderpest would spread quickly.[8]

The Czechs and East Germans were not the only ones worried about tiny soldiers. Leading entomologists were only too aware that insects posed enormous threats to crops, and they often were vectors of epidemic disease in humans. Using insects, humans were capable of instigating long-term ecological changes. One such bug expert was a University of

London professor of medical entomology, Patrick A. Buxton, who had made his scientific name tracing the pathways of fleas and lice among humans. After an intensive study of isolated Pacific islands, he and a colleague observed in 1927, "The placid natives of Aitutaki, observing that the little creatures were constantly restless and inquisitive, and even at times irritating, drew the reasonable inference that they were the souls of deceased white men."[9] In the postwar era he wrote a textbook on the louse and fretted about entomological uses of biological warfare. He implored military leaders and scientists at Porton not to underestimate the destructive power of insects, not simply as destroyers but as vectors of disease.[10]

In the late 1940s, scientists envisioned two possible means of disseminating insect-borne diseases. The first was to breed millions of flies, infect them somehow, and drop them over enemy territory. This proved complex even to contemplate: what would the survival rates be? What temperatures would have to be maintained while airborne? How would the flies be mass produced? How could they be contained? It seemed far easier to take the second choice, which was to drop contaminated bait from aircraft and allow native flies to feast upon it. American, British, and Canadian scientists conducted field trials with this in mind during and after World War II. Sometimes houseflies were used, while at other times the classic experimental tiny fly, *Drosophila*, proved most useful. Scientists reasoned that it was a hardy, wide-ranging insect that was not very picky about its breeding areas—ripe fruit and excrement were equally suitable—and they were easily attracted to bait. During the war, Canadian researchers demonstrated the ability of *Drosophila* to pick up, retain, and pass on infections. Separately, American researchers conducted field trials on Horn Island, Mississippi, demonstrating that houseflies and *Drosophila* could pass on microorganisms and toxins responsible for diarrhea, enteritis, and botulism.[11]

The Americans and the British worried about different kinds of diseases. While Americans typically tried to imagine the impacts of biological attacks on major cities in the United States and Europe, British scientists' concerns stretched globally because of the varied conditions of the British empire. Buxton warned that experimenting on the classic pathogens in biological warfare research laboratories was short-sighted, focusing only on conflict between major powers in the northern hemisphere. He guessed that the most significant insect-borne bacteria diseases would be plague, tularemia, and rickets. Because of his own background in conducting research in the tropics, he also was intensely concerned with viral diseases such as yellow fever, dengue, and encephalitis. His perspective was that of an imperial man of science, which is clear in his discussion of the risks from plague from a "cloud" being dropped on a city:

> The intention would be to start an extremely fatal epidemic of pneumonic plague among human beings. Some of the droplets might lead to the infection of other animals, including rats, and flea-borne outbreaks of plague among rats might follow. Compared with other disasters, this would not provide an immediate and urgent problem in a European city. But if the cloud were liberated in a tropical city, consisting of badly built, ramshackle houses, with thatch roofs in which rats nest, and grain-stores, in which rats multiply in close contact with man, then a much more serious outbreak among the rats might follow. If rat plague were established in such a place, it might continue for an indefinite number of years and could lead to outbreaks of bubonic plague in man.

Buxton routinely offered such contrasts between the metropolitan world of Europe and the poorer conditions of the colonial world. He also attempted to look beyond the immediate object of a biological attack—killing humans—and to consider some of the collateral ecological consequences that might lead to recurrences of epidemic disease for the foreseeable future.[12]

Using language that anticipated the fears of Chinese and Korean soldiers during the Korean War, Buxton saw the greatest potential threats in areas of poverty, hunger, and, above all, close living quarters with poor sanitary conditions. He recalled that during World War II he had worried that Londoners huddling in shelters would become lousy, making them susceptible to biological attack. "A nation with considerable laboratory facilities," he wrote, "could practice something of the sort against such people as the Chinese, who are always lousy and heavily clothed in winter. Moreover, as the Chinese regard a certain amount of typhus as normal, small outbreaks here and there would perhaps not receive much attention at first."[13]

In tropical areas, Buxton saw catastrophe on the horizon. He was particularly concerned about the possible introduction of yellow fever to Asia. This disease, which often produces jaundiced skin (hence "yellow"), had helped earn Africa the name of "White Man's Grave" in the nineteenth century and had been a decisive factor in imperial conflict in the

Caribbean for centuries.[14] Due to its presence in West and Central Africa for millennia, yellow fever already had culled Africa's population of great numbers of non-immune people, and many Africans in the modern era had inherited the immunity of the survivors from past generations. By contrast, due to the relative lack of exposure over generations, yellow fever killed white Europeans in high numbers, and it also was lethal to people from India, China, and Japan. Buxton predicted an "immense epidemic" should yellow fever ever penetrate into Asia. If the Soviet Union wanted to cripple European empires, introducing yellow fever would be the way to do it.

Yellow fever had not made inroads into Asia, despite routine maritime contacts between East Africa and India over the centuries. But Buxton warned against complacency. "I feel that we must reject this foolish view that what has not happened will never occur; I would as soon argue that as my house has never been burnt down it never will burn." His particular concern was again ecological, taking into account not only the ubiquitous presence of mosquitoes (yellow fever's principal vector), but also of monkeys. The rhesus monkey *Macaca mulatta*, for example, ranged widely from India to southern China and throughout Southeast Asia—the treasures of colonial Europeans. Not only was it highly susceptible to yellow fever, but it also was a sacred animal in parts of India where it came into daily contact with humans. He left little room for ambiguity:

There seems little doubt that the deliberate introduction of yellow fever might be attempted. The right sort of mosquito is readily available in many parts of the world and many laboratories maintain stocks of it for experimental purposes. Laboratory strains of yellow fever, some of them virulent to monkeys are available in many places; the enemy may be supposed to possess the strain if he wants it. To bring it into use offensively, he would presumably infect monkeys and feed the mosquitoes (*Aedes aegypti*) upon them. These insects travel well in quite small cages, provided they are fed, which would present no difficulty, with an agent immunized to yellow fever. A considerable proportion of the mosquitoes would live about a month. They would require to be liberated in a village or town among human beings. It would not appear to be difficult for an oriental agent to enter some small port in Malaya, perhaps liberating some insects in the port and going on with others to other places.

The only defense against such an epidemic would be massive campaigns of vaccination and insecticide spraying.[15] It would be nearly impossible to tell whether an outbreak was deliberate.

Although they often disagreed about how to incorporate knowledge of natural vulnerabilities into war plans, officials from the military, intelligence, agriculture, and public health all clearly took the lessons of ecology seriously. According to the director of British scientific intelligence, chemist Bertie Blount, the Soviet Union would lose no opportunity to attack an enemy's economy in order to undermine the capitalist system. With pathogenic agents, this could be done without declaring war. Blount was a creative thinker on pathogenic matters—during World War II he had suggested using anthrax to kill Hitler.[16] In 1950, Blount warned of clandestine biological attacks, which "would appear as a catastrophic 'act of God' and as such be blamed on the government, which would suffer the twin discomforts of economic embarrassment and political unpopularity."[17] He also warned that the past naïve enthusiasm for biological weapons had led to a backlash within government, with most experts too quickly discounting their possibilities.

Blount knew a few details from history on how an insect or plant disease could bring an entire country to its knees. Now he was afraid the Soviets might introduce an exotic fungus into an area that concentrated on one particular crop. Man's simplifications made his land weak. As a matter of national security, Blount used a range of examples that pointed out the vulnerability of cultivated land. The most obvious was the 1846 Irish potato famine, which led to mass starvation and emigration out of Ireland. The cause was a simple fungus: *Phytophthera infestans*. And there were other ominous episodes. A fungus had imperiled the wine industry in Western Europe. A rust fungus had caused Ceylon to abandon its coffee plantations. The "sudden death" of clove trees had crippled Zanzibar. "Swollen shoot" in cocoa, along with the policy of cutting out infected trees, had harmed not only the economy of West Africa but was also a major cause of unrest there.[18]

"But there is one case of outstanding importance," Blount warned. He singled out rubber, in Britain's restive Southeast Asian "protectorate" in Malaya. Rubber had been a principal reason for Japan's invasion of Malaya during World War II. When Japan captured Singapore and the Dutch East Indies, it had secured some 90 percent of the world's supply of crude rubber. That serious strategic shortfall motivated American companies to perfect and mass produce synthetic rubber. But after the war, the European colonial powers still depended upon natural rubber. Worries about rubber in Malaya would lead Britain down a tangled path toward its own experiments with crop destruction. Its successes became a model for American activities in Vietnam.

Rubber had seen crippling blights before. The rubber trees in Southeast Asia were not native. They had been planted there in the nineteenth century, quickly becoming a major commodity for the British, French, and Dutch. Their origin was actually the Amazon region of South America. In the early twentieth century, the once-dominant Brazilian rubber industry was paralyzed by a "leaf blight" caused by the fungus *Melanopsammopsis ulei*. Brazil never recovered its dominance in the rubber trade.[19]

Blount feared the same future for Malayan rubber, which seemed vulnerable because the fungus would spread very quickly within the plantation systems. In Malaya, he worried, rubber was planted "in huge and continuous blocks which cover big tracts of the country." It would not take long for the leaf blight to destroy Britain's entire supply of rubber within a few seasons.

Imperial holdings in Southeast Asia seemed exceptionally vulnerable to ecological invasions, because human hands were poised to start them. With the French already waging war for control of its colony in Indochina, not far from Malaya, a clandestine communist attack seemed possible, even likely. And if the leaf blight came to Indochina, it would spread uncontrollably to Malaya. That would cost the British some US$80 million annually in exports, while necessitating major purchases of synthetic rubber from the Americans. Fearing for the rubber plantations, British intelligence officers carefully monitored the French Indochina war. Confirming their fears, the French informed them that the Viet Minh (the communist forces) had issued a directive to attack rubber plants with indigenous plant diseases. Although such diseases did not prove as catastrophic as the South American leaf blight, the idea appeared to be on the minds of the Viet Minh. It seemed only a matter of time before the Malayans attempted the same kind of sabotage.[20]

Not helping the situation, American synthetic rubber manufacturers were quick to point out this vulnerability. The president of the B. F. Goodrich Company, John L. Collyer, adamantly opposed the strategy of strengthening allies by helping them to raise the price of crude rubber—doing so would force companies like Goodrich to limit synthetic production while tying American markets to natural rubber production. He heaped scorn on the idea, calling it a "cartel road which leads to totalitarianism." Trying to protect his assets, Collyer lost no opportunity to play up the vulnerability of rubber plantations to disease. After the victory of the communists in China in 1949, Collyer pointed out that the rubber lands in Southeast Asia were at risk. "We know that rubber trees can easily be destroyed," he said.[21] In January 1950, English-speaking newspapers in Malaya carried a story in which Collyer suggested that the introduction of the South American leaf disease would annihilate the British rubber crop.[22] Upon reading such reports, one British biological warfare expert said he was concerned about the "sinister potentialities" of such pathogenic agents, which "may represent a powerful weapon for use in either cold or hot war."[23]

Britain's fear of a biological emergency in the tropics seemed more justified than ever in the early 1950s, as it began to lose its grip on its extremely profitable rubber and tin supplies in Southeast Asia. In the wake of communist victories in China, ethnic Chinese in Malaya tried to lead a war of liberation against the British Empire. That put the rubber supply at risk. The "Malayan Emergency," as the British called it, reached a new level of crisis in October 1951 when communist insurgents assassinated the British High Commissioner, Henry Gurney. The event led Prime Minister Winston Churchill to send the hard-nosed military commander Gerald Templer to resolve the crisis. The resultant campaign against ethnic Chinese communists has become the textbook case for modern counterinsurgency tactics.[24]

Military commanders in Malaya thought of the "bandits" themselves as a disease to be controlled. Prior to Templer's arrival, General Harold Briggs wrote that "the problem of clearing Communist banditry from Malaya was similar to that of eradicating malaria from a country. Flit guns and mosquito nets, in the form of military and police, though giving some very local security if continuously maintained, effected no permanent cure. Such a permanent cure entails the closing of all breeding areas."[25] These breeding areas, in part, were the villages comprised of ethnic Chinese, among whom the communists found the most sympathy. Those villages also supplied food to the insurgents—and Briggs, Templer, and other British commanders were bent on denying the communists this sustenance.

Unlike his predecessor, Templer managed to beat down the "bandits," as they were called, so decisively that later American experts would use British Malaya as a model for prosecuting the war in Vietnam. Templer spoke of winning "hearts and minds" long before it entered the American military lexicon, and his effort to relocate Chinese farmers into new, more easily defended villages away from the jungle inspired the United States' "strategic hamlets" strategy.[26] Templer's purpose was to undermine his enemy's support infrastructure. Unlike the Americans, who would attempt to couple nation-building with carpet bombing, the British under Templer attempted to apply minimal force to the local people. Templer commanded both the civilian and military sides of government, giving him unprecedented ability to undermine the enemy by giving Malayans a stake in the survival of a British-dominated regime. On the one hand, he promised citizenship and ultimate Malayan independence, undercutting the communist anti-imperial rhetoric. On the other hand, he starved out the enemy in an intensive food denial campaign. After relocating the villages and farms, controlling food supplies of the insurgents operating in the jungle proved much easier.

Moving villages was only part of Templer's strategy, however. Templer also was profoundly aware of the dangers and opportunities posed by diseases and crop destruction. His arrival in Malaya coincided with the first Chinese accusation that the Americans had begun bacteriological warfare in the Korean War. Beyond the diplomatic rhetoric in that debacle was a disturbing truth: the deliberate introduction of a disease would not be easy to differentiate from a natural, or accidental, one. Colonial Europeans took such threats seriously, because in their important possessions in tropical Africa and Asia, tropical diseases were a constant peril. Templer met not only with Buxton, but also with scientists of every stripe, from the esteemed Oxford men to the Porton chemical weapons specialists, to find ways to use scientific knowledge to protect rubber and to prosecute a food denial campaign.

As the "emergency" in Malaya intensified in 1951 and 1952, with the insurgents striking hard at the rubber plantations by killing foremen, rumors began to spread that the British were preparing to destroy their food crops. The Americans were intrigued, wanting to find out if destroying crops in a limited war might work. In 1952 the US Army Chemical Corps began asking questions about the use of crop killers in Malaya. American newspapers and radio had reported that the British Royal Air Force had been using sodium trichloracetate and hormones to destroy the crops that guerrilla forces depended on for sustenance. The Americans wanted to know if it was true and if they might send a technical observer. Repelled at the thought of American oversight, the British insisted that only the Malayan government should invite observers. The Ministry of Supply insisted internally that its efforts were aimed at jungle defoliation, not destruction of crops, but that "all methods to defeat banditry" were actively under discussion.[27]

Even within the British government, few knew the extent of Templer's mounting food denial campaign in Malaya. The truth was that the Malayan government, with the cooperation of the British firm Imperial Chemical Industries, were indeed experimenting with sodium trichloracetate as a defoliant—the chemical itself procured from American sources. They were doing so from the ground, not the air. The Malayan government also had asked the British Colonial Office for advice on crop destruction and had begun experimentation. Moreover, Malaya's Rubber Research Institution had been spraying rubber trees from civilian aircraft to test the effectiveness of growth inhibitors developed in World War II such as 2,4,D.[28]

The Malayan government soon issued a press statement confirming that it was working on both defoliants and crop killers to combat communist insurgents. Both options found their way to discussion on the floor of the British Parliament, and it became clear that Britain was trying out chemical warfare against "bandit crops" to starve out the enemy.[29]

Aside from the moral issue of focusing on starvation, there was a legal question: the Geneva Protocol of 1925 outlawed chemical warfare in very general terms. Crop destruction could have been classed as chemical warfare, and British officials worried that even the smallest-scale crop attacks could be interpreted as breaking an international treaty. Given the international furor over biological weapons accusations against the United States in Korea, it seemed an inauspicious time to start contaminating enemy crops with chemical weapons. The United Kingdom had opened itself up to communist accusations that it was waging chemical warfare in Malaya.[30]

The British government found an easy way out. The Geneva Protocol prohibited the use of chemical weapons against the enemy in a war. The solution, then, was to deny the existence of war. As one official explained, "In Malaya there is neither 'war' nor an 'enemy' in the accepted sense." Instead, there was civil unrest. The Malayan government was "entitled to do what it likes in the interests of national security, within its own frontiers against its own people." It was no different from using tear gas for riot control.[31]

Crop destruction was not the only means of using agricultural knowledge to fight a war. Plant physiologists such as Oxford professor Geoffrey Blackman conducted research on plant uptake. Even when chemicals did not prove fatal, plants might absorb (or "take up") enough of them to be absolutely poisonous for mammals. Blackman worked closely with scientists at Porton to perfect such techniques in the early 1950s. It was true that using conventional chemicals—such as 2,4,D, the same one used in Malaya—Porton scientists attempted to destroy or inhibit their home-grown crops of barley, sugar beets, and mustard. But they also wanted to know how much sodium fluoroacetate was needed to turn them into poison. Blackman and his colleague, Edwin Kenneth Woodford, managed the Agricultural Research Council's Unit of Experimental Agronomy at Oxford. Both men were specialists on plant uptake and became widely known in Britain for helping to revolutionize domestic agriculture with new, more selective herbicides that could control weeds without killing crops. Less well known is their activity in the crop destruction research at Porton.[32]

In December of 1952, Woodford found himself in Southeast Asia at the military headquarters of the Malayan government. He and a colleague quickly confirmed that an effective spraying campaign deep in the jungle would require helicopters, not airplanes. These helicopters could dip below the tree level and slowly saturate the small clearings used for crop cultivation. Woodford told the military commanders there that the downward pressure generated by the helicopter's giant rotors would help drive the chemicals into the crops. He recommended a chemical manufactured by Du Pont in the United States called CMU. In a matter of weeks, Woodford claimed, two pounds of CMU per acre would not only destroy seedlings but would also render the soil infertile for at least a year.[33] CMU was an organic compound that had extremely high toxicity to plants when absorbed from soil by roots. Its main requirement was the presence of moist soil, making it perfectly suited to the rainy hills of Malaya. Already it was being used in Canada to sterilize the soil underneath railways.[34] Now it was going to be used in Malaya to target tapioca, sweet potatoes, groundnuts, vegetables, hill padi, and maize.

It is often thought that most of the scientific research at Porton was oriented toward defoliation, not crop destruction. After all, the main reason for diminishing roadside vegetation was to prevent possible ambushes. But defoliants would not remove the heavy wooded underbrush. Hand cutting and removal was far more effective, and the Malayan people could be used as cheap or free manual labor. So scientists at Porton directed their energies primarily toward destroying the crops upon which the insurgents depended for survival.[35]

The logistical problems in the Malayan campaign proved what military strategists suspected. Chemicals might be used in a country as small as Malaya (or as the Americans later decided, Vietnam), but spraying the

Soviet Union would be impossible. In a global conflict, biological means—insects and pathogens—made far more sense. Chemicals appeared ideally suited to small conflicts, as a supplement to other activities like relocating villages and defending them with conventional forces. In a 1955 secret memo assessing a report on the use of chemicals in crop destruction, British Wing Commander F. H. P. Austin put it succinctly: it "makes interesting reading but its application to the type of future war now envisaged is dubious. It is not a weapon which can produce immediate results and therefore becomes of little significance in total war. It might have an application in a limited war."[36]

As in the case of biological weapons, crop warfare had appeared as a legitimate way to exploit basic human vulnerability on a massive scale. The evidence of that vulnerability was everywhere. At the end of World War II, millions of Europeans faced starvation. The United Nations Relief and Rehabilitation Administration (UNRRA) offered food aid to areas previously occupied by Axis powers. Just as the World Health Organization was created to combat disease, the Food and Agriculture Organization (FAO) came into being to ensure that the people of the world had enough to eat. The United States contributed billions of dollars in aid to Europe, through UNRRA and later through the Marshall Plan, partly to prevent starvation but also to prevent the region from plunging into political chaos and military weakness in the face of the Soviet Union. Just as the movement of people during the war and its aftermath had contributed to the spread of disease, so too did disruptions in food trade and consumption lead to the circulation of pathogens and insects along unexpected pathways. Food was vulnerable, and farmers and merchants resorted to heavy use of chemical insecticides.

The immediate postwar years provided numerous case studies of regional food insecurity. Despite an end to the war, poverty-stricken countries still had inadequate access to chemical defenses and often had under-funded food inspection offices. The Italian government, for example, complained that much of the population consumed bread made from spoiled wheat. It had proven impossible to control insects, so the solution was simply to consume the wheat as soon as possible to maximize freshness. Doing so kept the Italians constantly on the brink of starvation. The accepted methods of control for insects and rats included spraying DDT, strychnine, cyanide, and various chemical compounds. At one FAO meeting in 1948, it became clear that sprayers, dusters, and other equipment often were in short supply throughout Europe; Austria, Czechoslovakia, Denmark, Finland, and France all admitted shortages.[37]

Insects and plant pathogens had slipped out of control during the war, and farmers and government agencies relied more than ever upon their most effective instrument—chemical pesticides. This was especially so because they knew precious little about the range of insects they were up against. Pesticides like DDT killed them all.

The war had disrupted the usual global routes of trade, forcing combatants to acquire commodities wherever they could. Doing so revealed a vast disparity in the quality of food from one country to the next. Partly this was due to a difference in control measures, but also it was due to climate and commodity differences—and of course biological differences among predatory organisms. According to the FAO, losses in shipments exported from Honduras, Ecuador, or Haiti, for example, might be as high as 50 percent.[38] Although the British were lucky to have access to the Commonwealth nations during the war, they were always pleased to see shipments coming from Canada but rather dreaded what might await in shipments from Central America, Africa, or India.

Because of the reshuffling of trade routes, insect species often showed up in the most unexpected places. Even relatively "clean" shipments still carried organisms—sometimes ones that had been carried aboard ships with a completely different commodity, leading to bizarre food-insect-environment combinations upon arrival. A government official once gave a telling example about copra, the dried "meat" of a coconut:

> One vessel carried copra from the Philippine Islands to Vancouver. After discharge of the copra, the ship loaded wheat, which was found on arrival in the United Kingdom to be infested by a number of species associated with copra, and not usually found in Canadian wheat. Another instance was of a ship which carried Argentine barley to Portugal. The ship then went to Australia, where it loaded cased goods which were found to have a heavy superficial infestation of grain insects upon arrival in the United Kingdom. These insects had been derived from residues of the barley cargo.[39]

Similarly, the French had been surprised to find a shipload of peas from Morocco infested with weevils, an unexpected combination. The reason was that the ship had previously been used for grain. Britain estimated that an average of 190 insect and mite species were imported each year during the war. Most died off because they could not survive the British climate, but many persisted as new postwar pests.

With their lands, people, and infrastructure devastated, most European countries relied heavily on imports in the postwar years. In doing so, they had to contend with a host of unwanted organisms. Finland imported 50 percent to 60 percent of its cereals from abroad, leaving it open to "foreign invaders" such as the Mediterranean mill moth (*Ephestia kuhniella*) that plagued mills, flour stores, groceries, and bakeries. "In imported food and forage products," the Finns lamented, "have been found almost all the species that occur all over the world."[40] The British also complained about the mill moths, whose numbers increased tremendously. But mill moths had existed in Britain prior to the war. What was shocking was that between 1942 and 1947, an estimated 150 species of beetles previously unknown in the British Isles had been imported. H. E. Hinton, an entomologist from the British Museum, pointed about that about 10 percent of these were species new to science.[41]

Given the immense disruptions caused by crop failures, infestations, and shortages, research on crop destruction assumed a new importance. When the war ended, and the US-Soviet confrontation escalated, serious questions loomed about whether to bother investigating crop destruction with synthetic chemicals. It was expensive, requiring many tons of material and lots of aircraft. It only seemed feasible when an enemy could be blockaded effectively, so that crop destruction could hasten the process of starving him out. Was this likely with an enemy as vast as the Soviet Union?[42] Meeting together, the consensus opinion of the US Air Force, UK Royal Air Force, and the Royal Canadian Air Force was fairly adamant: chemical crop destruction offered no feasible means of hindering staple crop production of any major continental power. On the other hand, the British were not a continental power and thus might be vulnerable to it.[43]

The insect invasions during the war pointed to a better strategy. If scientists could develop weapons that destroyed crops indirectly—through the food chain, with pests, or with plant-specific diseases—the logistical problem might be overcome. Even small amounts might spread naturally over time, harnessing the power of nature itself. All one had to do was to introduce something harmful, such as a plant pathogen, and let nature do the work. One British analyst put it thus: "Accuracy of aim is of no great importance when shooting at millions of acres of wheat."[44]

Research on all kinds of crop killers progressed on both sides of the Atlantic, despite uncertainty about their real value in wartime operations. By 1949, the American work had received enthusiastic endorsement from top scientists at Camp Detrick, particularly the Englishman Arthur Geoffrey

Norman. At Porton, the UK center for chemical and biological weapons research, scientists agreed with Norman that the potential for crop killers deserved more support. But military leaders were deeply skeptical. In the United Kingdom, the Air Ministry was surprised that Porton should associate itself with unrealistic goals that diverted money from research on much more suitable and large-scale weapons. It was true that during World War II, they had laid down plans to poison rice fields in Japan, but this was a special case: Japan was an island. Air Vice-Marshall G. A. H. Pidcock was particularly adamant about wasting resources on what seemed like a fool's errand. He observed that using chemicals to destroy the crops of an enemy that controlled the greater part of two continents "would involve an airlift utterly beyond our resources." Once again, the British insisted that the only effective crop killers would be those that introduced pests or spread disease. Research on such pathogenic agents, however, was still in its infancy.[45]

Chemicals had limitations on defense as well. Farmers in Europe already had proven how dependent they were on DDT. Those lacking facilities, fuel, and equipment had let the potato bug run rampant. And DDT was critical to halting malaria in Italy and Greece. Although DDT was effective, Europeans depended on the goodwill of American chemical suppliers. Western Europe was both economically and technologically beholden to the United States. This alone meant that a country relying on DDT could not call itself truly independent. But as ecologists soon would point out, there was evidence that DDT was doing more harm to national security than good.

How vulnerable were countries, even those with ready access to DDT, to invasions by plant pathogens and insects? This became the subject of one of the seminal works of modern ecology, Charles Elton's 1958 *Ecology of Invasions*. Although the environmental critique of the indiscriminate use of chemical weed killers is most closely associated with American writer Rachel Carson's 1962 book *Silent Spring*, Carson quite freely acknowledged an intellectual debt to Elton. The English ecologist had made fluctuations in the abundance of species his life's work and had made Oxford's Bureau of Animal Population a mecca for animal ecologists worldwide. Like Carson's later book, Elton's 1958 *Ecology of Invasions* contained a critique of chemical pesticides such as DDT and plant hormones such as 2,4-D, the modern world's principal tools for protecting plants and ensuring the food supply.[46]

Elton pointed out that overreliance on chemicals had not made food supplies more secure. Quite the contrary, they had cleared the way for invaders. Although he criticized pesticides, he did not favor the complete abandonment of DDT. "No realist," he argued, "would for a moment suppose that either counterpests or chemical warfare can be abandoned," though he hoped they could be employed intelligently rather than indiscriminately, to suit ecological relationships.[47] But no amount of spraying could provide true and lasting security. In the short term, massive spraying campaigns could have a stunning effect—Elton called DDT an "astonishing rain of death upon so much of the world's surface."[48] But from an ecological point of view, it was "not very subtle."[49] Permanent control would require strengthening biodiversity, or what Elton called the conservation of variety. With an abundance of different species, nature would conform to a system of checks and balances, preventing any one organism from spreading too readily as an invader. The most vulnerable areas were the ones whose food chains had been most simplified artificially by man—through agriculture, development, or pesticides. The best defense against attack was a huge variety of potential counterbalancing organisms. Complexity appeared to be the key.

Understanding this vulnerability soon became an anxiety of writers and commentators from various quarters, which fed into a nascent environmental movement. However, governments also concerned themselves with the issue, not in order to curb development, save wildlife, or prevent cancer, but rather to understand how to protect national or imperial interests, and to fight and survive wars. Elton was part of a tradition of ecologists who served the British Empire's interests overseas, understanding problems of plant and animal acclimatization and protecting lucrative commodities gleaned from nature.[50] Elton relished the language of human conflict, describing himself as a "war correspondent" on the front lines, sending dispatches about "the quiet infiltration of commando forces, the surprise attacks, the successive waves of later reinforcements after the first spearhead fails to get a foothold, attack and counterattack, and the eventual expansion and occupation of territory from which they are unlikely to be ousted again."[51]

Just as the UN Food and Agriculture Organization had convened experts to discuss the stunningly widespread migrations of organisms during and after World War II, ecologists stood in awe of the rapid transfers of species from field to hedge, city to countryside, one continent to another. It was, as Elton so aptly put it, one of the great historical convulsions in the world's flora and fauna. It suggested the possibility of rapid change and the extraordinary vulnerability of human habitations to disease and crop destruction.

Because of the interdependence of food chains around the world through global trade, every geographic area was open to invasion from any of the world's species, with only a few degrees of separation. Indeed Elton was fond of quoting the American mathematician Alfred J. Lotka, who spoke of the global food web as a physical system: "The entire body of all these species of organisms, together with certain inorganic structures, constitute one great world-wide transformer. It is well to accustom the mind to think of this as one vast unit, one great empire."[52]

Both Elton and, a few years later, Rachel Carson cited some "experiments in Maryland" that showed how much DDT, in the process of killing insects, depressed crop yields by inhibiting seedling growth in beans, wheat, and barley. Although these referred to work by the US Department of Agriculture in Beltsville, another group of researchers just 50 miles down the road were looking at much the same question. Camp Detrick, which would change its name to Fort Detrick in 1956 to reflect its permanent status and increasing size, employed numerous scientists to work not just on spreading diseases in man but in understanding crop vulnerabilities for both offensive and defensive purposes.

Scientists at Fort Detrick had the benefit of an extraordinary amount of funding to explore a wide range of possibilities, enabling them to embark on large-scale field tests. For example, American scientists tested out Patrick Buxton's nightmare scenario about yellow fever. During an outbreak in Trinidad in 1954, they obtained infected blood from one individual and then inoculated Rhesus monkeys with it, giving scientists an experimental reservoir of yellow fever virus. In what was known as Operation Big Buzz, scientists tested out the vector: they packed hundreds of thousands of uninfected *Aedes aegypti* mosquitoes into bomb canisters and dropped them on the backcountry of the state of Georgia. The experiment was one of several entomological ones. The previous year, Operation Big Itch tested the dissemination of fleas over Dugway Proving Ground, Utah. Another yellow fever test, Operation Drop Kick (1956), followed Big Itch and Big Buzz, dumping *Aedes aegypti* mosquitoes on a bombing range in Florida, and upon a residential neighborhood in Savannah, Georgia. Later that year, Operation May Day released more of the same species of mosquito in Savannah.[53]

Camp Detrick had embarked upon these projects in 1953, having determined that insects would help to bypass the protective measures typically employed against chemical warfare, such as masks. The insects would continue to pose a threat as long as they lived, and human death rates from yellow fever were extremely high: about a third of all cases were fatal. One American report repeated Buxton's warning that it had never broken out in Asia. While Buxton had seen the disease as a threat to the British empire, the Americans saw it offensively: "Yellow fever has never occurred in some areas, including Asia, and therefore it is quite probable that the population of the U.S.S.R. would be quite susceptible to the disease." Although there was a yellow fever vaccine, American scientists doubted that the USSR could mount an immunization fast enough to counter a widespread epidemic.[54]

Scientists at these laboratories knew that they were harnessing humanity's ancient enemies, not truly developing new weapons. As one researcher at Fort Detrick, LeRoy Fothergill, told a group of civilian medical doctors in 1956:

> One must be unremitting in emphasizing that there is *no* secrecy concerning the agents which might be included in an overall BW [biological warfare] arsenal. Only certain agents will meet the general and specific BW requirements. Both we and any potential enemy know them. This is not like inventing or rather synthesizing a new chemical poison. One frequently hears it said, "If we only knew what agents our potential enemies were working on we would know what to defend ourselves against." This platitudinous statement is parroted ad nauseam. This is the kind of statement that is made by an ostrich before burying his head in the sand. A more appropriate conjecture would be to ask ourselves, "What are we doing about it? Are we doing enough?"[55]

For Fothergill and his like-minded colleagues, the problem was not the pathogen itself, but the vulnerability of the population. How vulnerable was America? How vulnerable was Russia?

Such vulnerability could only be understood ecologically. Arming nature to spread diseases in humans or to destroy crops depended on a deep knowledge of crucial biological links. For example, it might be possible for an enemy to develop an effective aerosol containing the causative agent of epidemic typhus (*Rickettsia prowazekii*), and to saturate a city with it. Although many people would die from that initial exposure, Fothergill observed, no epidemic would ensue without the ubiquitous presence of lice. Lousiness was a prerequisite for epidemic typhus. Understanding such pathways was the key to preparing for a war against the Soviet Union.

Scientists working on biological warfare, particularly on crop destruction, had a profound respect for strengthening crops through biodiversity. Conversely, they understood that man's simplifications of his surroundings with agriculture simply invited invasions by insects, fungi, and pathogens. Fothergill took comfort in the knowledge that the United States was a large, biologically diverse nation. Although its agricultural areas were vulnerable, the country did not depend on any particular crop for survival. "Our cropping is very diversified and biological agents are, of course, specific for particular crops," he argued. "Those countries that are generally dependent, for agronomic, climatic, or traditional reasons, on a single crop are the most vulnerable."[56] Fort Detrick preached biological diversity whenever it could.

It fell to scientists at Fort Detrick to match potential invaders with their environments around the world. One three-year study, for example, revealed the Ukraine to be an ideal target for an attack by cereal rust spores. Such spores, carried by the wind, led to fungal disease in wheat, barley, and oats. It was a problem the Americans knew only too well: rust epidemics had swept through the American breadbasket in 1953 and 1954, reducing production by over 30 percent in the Dakotas. If released in the Ukraine, cereal rusts could have a crippling effect on the ability of the Soviets to feed themselves.[57] In a 1957 secret study conducted for the US Joint Chiefs of Staff, American intelligence analysts calculated that cereal rust spores would likely be the preferred form of attack by the Soviet Union against American farmland. In addition, because of American reliance upon livestock, the Soviets were likely to hit the United States hard with rinderpest and foot and mouth disease.[58]

Such vulnerabilities often were quantifiable and rather specific in their implications. Attempting to assess the likely benefits of anti-crop and anti-livestock biological weapons, American intelligence agencies calculated:

In order to have a crippling effect on the economy of the USSR, the food and animal crop resources of the USSR would have to be damaged within a single growing season to the extent necessary to reduce the present average daily caloric intake from 2,800 calories to 1,400 calories, i.e., the starvation level. Reduction of food resources to this level, if maintained for twelve months, would produce 20 percent fatalities, and would decrease the manual labor performance by 95 percent and clerical and light labor performance by 80 percent.[59]

Any reduction in average caloric intake, these analysts predicted, would have an adverse effect on the Soviet economy. The same was true of China, which was even more vulnerable due to its extraordinary reliance on rice and its comparatively low average caloric intake, already hovering just above starvation levels. Other communist areas had already felt this sting: North Vietnam once had gotten its rice from the south, but now had to import it from China and Burma. North Korea was entirely dependent on imports. The problem of food production was less severe in Eastern Europe, but even there the countries had to rely on imports.[60]

In a 1959 article in *Harper's*, retired US Army Brigadier General J. H. Rothschild laid out this vulnerability quite openly:

> Biological agents can attack a nation's food supply and greatly decrease its ability to make war. This is particularly true of a country which depends to a large extent on a single crop, as the Soviet Union does on wheat. The United States is much less vulnerable than Russia in this respect—we do not crucially depend on any one crop and, in general, our crops are more resistant to the various diseases.[61]

Rothschild's goal was to persuade his readers that abhorrence of such weapons defied all logic since they were far more humane than conventional or nuclear weapons. After all, a nation could surrender at the point of starvation and food might then be shipped in. From Rothschild's point of view, Americans understood this far better than the Soviets did and would have the advantage in a war with biological weapons.

Candid statements from Fort Detrick about biological diversity drew distinct connections between national security, ecology, and agriculture. Although one could argue that the Soviet Union and China were more reliant on just a few crops, the United States and its allies had to consider their national weaknesses as well. This kind of self-assessment turned out to be rather shocking, particularly in attempts to imagine biological survival after a nuclear attack.

The first tests of hydrogen bombs in the early 1950s complicated the scientific picture of surviving a third world war. While scientists had grown accustomed to imagining ways of manipulating nature to attack the enemy with insects and pathogens, few yet understood the long-term consequences of harnessing the forces of nature on a large scale. Naturally, nuclear war seemed the most likely candidate as a catastrophic event that could transform the natural world in myriad ways. Some ways were expected: fires, radiation sickness, physical destruction. But what about the effects on farm animals, on fish, on the ability of soil to grow crops, or even upon the genetic makeup of all living things?

No one doubted that a nuclear war would devastate North America, Europe, and much of Asia. Recovery after the war would require practical knowledge of what to expect from nuclear fallout and of the most reliable sources of food. Governments in North America and Europe developed emergency plans and even began to encourage average people to keep stocks of food on hand and to build fallout shelters in their own homes. But beyond this period of immediate survival—the first few days after the first nuclear explosions—few had any conception of what to expect. Only one thing seemed clear: the landscape and the people would be changed radically.

In North America, the vast landscape would be grossly contaminated, to be sure, but scientists believed it still would produce food for most Americans. The vast breadbasket in the heartland would continue to supply staple foods such as wheat and corn in the long term. By contrast, in Europe the commodity problem—getting the right food, equipment, and other supplies to the right countries in the most efficient way—was beginning to look nightmarish. Within NATO, the simplest—and most troubling—situation appeared to be in Britain. Its two main islands would be cut off from the rest of the world, in the short term certainly and perhaps even longer as other countries dealt with internal difficulties. In all likelihood, most of the British Empire would be inaccessible to the home country. Imports might be hard to come by, even from the best of friends. Clearly a nuclear conflict would differ fundamentally from the last war. Thermonuclear weapons left a basic, still unanswered question: even if some were to survive the warheads themselves, would they then starve to death?

In Britain, the revelation that military planners had merely scratched the surface of the long-term problem of survival came in 1957 during a war game. This first serious attempt to play out a war scenario that addressed food was the so-called Ishmael study. Held at the Civil Defense Staff College in January 1957, its primary object was to understand how to protect those left homeless after a nuclear war. What made Ishmael unique was its attention to human survival rather than battlefield tactics. It immediately shattered all illusions of preparedness. Planners were not equipped to deal with the brisk pace and immediate wide-ranging problems of a war involving hydrogen bombs, which could be a thousand times larger than the atomic bombs dropped on Hiroshima and Nagasaki. People would be afraid of the dirty and poisonous fallout, but even more fearful of the more obvious threat of blazing fires. Fires would rage up to 10 miles from ground zero of a 10-megaton blast. The Ishmael plans were short on specific measures to be taken after the war began. There seemed little to be done except fight fires and keep people inside. Beyond that, the study called for individual self-sufficiency and neighborly conduct. It also suggested that the British government remind people that, in the event of nuclear war, "they should wear stout shoes."[62]

Aside from the problems of blast, fire, fallout, and finding a good pair of shoes, the short-term prospects for survivors would depend on ready access to some form of sustenance. Preparations would have to include a far more sophisticated understanding of the peacetime interdependency of humans, crops, livestock, and the material infrastructure that kept it all thriving. Post-nuclear survival required thinking about the nation as a system, with an eye toward preserving the elements fundamental to humanity. Such planning would have to dig deeper than fallout shelters and fire brigades.

Oddly enough, the first positive opportunity to make an educated guess about a nuclear war occurred during a major scare at a British nuclear facility in 1957. An unexpected fire at Windscale released considerable levels of radioactivity into the air. British scientists looked at it as a chance to measure the effects of radioactive fallout on local products such as milk. They also hoped to gauge the effects upon livestock. The Windscale fire provided the opportunity to imagine nuclear scenarios at home. Where did wind take the radioactivity? What animals were most poisoned?

In the year or so after the fire, a rumor spread that conception rates in cows had dropped as a result of exposure to radiation, or that cows took longer to calf their young. After a comparison with unaffected areas, scientists at Britain's Milk Marketing Board determined that this was not the case.[63] But the issue reopened disturbing questions about post-nuclear survival. Nuclear war would kill a huge number of cows. The surviving bulls might not have worthwhile sperm. The herds studied had been produced by artificial insemination, which was quite common in the United Kingdom. It was so common that the number of bulls was quite low, and Britain relied on artificial insemination centers throughout the country.

Would it be possible to use artificial insemination to breed stocks of cattle after the initial wave of destruction? Radiation undoubtedly would have introduced mutations in the semen of animals out in the open. Semen in surviving bulls would be tainted to an extraordinary degree, but if relatively "clean" stocks could be stored far from the bomb areas, they could be used to reconstruct the population.

The question itself revealed an uncomfortable degree of ignorance in scientific and defense policy circles. Despite it being a "vast and important question," one scientist doubted that anyone had any information about the effects of radiation on stored semen. Surely there was a dosage that could be deemed tolerable, "without injury being caused either to the semen or the progeny."[64]

Bull semen, perhaps understandably, made for an uncomfortable topic of discussion. Aside from forcing war planners to talk to each other about semen, it threw into sharp relief the reality of genetic effects upon humans. When Stanley Kubrick's 1964 comedic film *Dr. Strangelove* had an American officer panicking about the need to protect "our precious bodily fluids," it was not far off the mark. Defense planners were not worried that communists were trying to steal Western men's "essence," but they were deeply worried that a nuclear war would subject semen to extremely harmful doses of radiation. And geneticists made it abundantly clear that sexual organs' exposure to any amount of radiation would produce mutations in future generations. Radiation, then, would be dangerous not just for humans but also for the livestock on which humans depended.

As was the case with agricultural problems, with their dependence on fertilizer and fuel supplies from industrial centers, this way of looking at the livestock problem presented intractable logistical problems. Who could guarantee the integrity of any semen bank during a nuclear war? Even if such banks could be isolated successfully, they required sustained low temperatures of about $-70°C$, made possible by a steady supply of solid carbon dioxide—also known as cardice, or "dry ice." Even missing one day's supply of cardice would render the semen useless. Alternatively, some other form of refrigeration would be needed, which would involve a facility generating electricity.

Numerous scenarios were presented. Should the government keep a certain number of bulls underground at all times? Should semen be stored in the Arctic?[65] After canvassing the most knowledgeable scientists, one official came to the pithy conclusion: "the short answer is that they do not know."[66] With scientists slow to offer helpful solutions, defense planners saw hope in some transformations occurring in the artificial insemination industry. By 1962 the future of semen security appeared to lie with the adoption of liquid nitrogen as a coolant. It kept the semen frozen at about −200°C, which provided a better margin of error than solid carbon dioxide (dry ice) at −79°C. British war planners encouraged their industry colleagues to make the change as quickly as possible, so that by early 1965 "as much as possible of our wartime planning should be in an advanced state of readiness."[67]

The years-long effort to find a way to save bull semen was symptomatic of how vulnerable scientists and war planners felt with the advent of hydrogen bombs. All the NATO allies considered stockpiling seeds and sheltering livestock on a large scale, so that man could redeploy his ecosystem after the Apocalypse. In 1959, emergency planners in Britain began thinking about ways to protect future crops by building radiation-shielded facilities. Because potato seeds did not last very long in storage, other crops such as swede and turnips had to be considered. But swedes (also known as rutabagas) were hardly popular. Ever since the First World War they were known as famine food. Would the future inhabitants of the British Isles have to live on fish and rutabagas?

There was a particularly troubling question implicit in the worries about survival commodities. Was it possible for any nation to be self-sufficient? The extent to which home production of basic life supporting commodities could replace imports remained a wide-open question. Potatoes were doomed. Their propagation would require an impossible amount of storage for seed tubers, kept under ideal temperature and humidity conditions.[68] Instead Britain regarded the following seeds as critical: brassicas, legumes, carrots, turnips, and swedes. Of the brassicas, they wanted to focus on cabbage and Brussels sprouts, because Britain already was self-sufficient in their cultivation. Of those, cabbages had two to three times the yield of Brussels sprouts and were easier to handle and distribute. That meant a post-nuclear diet of cabbages, peas, carrots, turnips, and swedes, with leeks tossed in for flavor.[69]

Biodiversity became a strong justification for *not* stockpiling at all. After failing to come up with a workable plan to save large amounts of seeds or tubers, officials came around to the idea that the best defense was in conserving as much variety as possible. The stocks held by merchants at any given time in Britain would make a better stockpile than anything the government might save. If nuclear war broke out, it would be best to rely on the bounty provided by the dynamism of trade. The seeds would be plentiful, varied, and dispersed. The only seeds considered for special storage—because of long-term genetic effects—were cereals (for staple human consumption) and grass (for livestock).[70]

The Americans had come to a similar conclusion. Less constrained by finances than the British, they were eager to preserve as much variety as they could. They had set aside funding for the long-term storage of genetically valuable seeds and maintained an operations center to identify and store stocks of key plants in Fort Collins, Colorado, at the US National Seed Storage Laboratory. But the seeds there were used for breeding purposes, and only small numbers of them were kept—at times just a few pounds for each variety. The Americans had abandoned hope that they could protect or stockpile seeds on any significant scale in wartime.[71] Instead, they thought even longer term and just preserved samples of a much greater variety.

These efforts to protect the vitality of Britain and the United States after a nuclear war highlighted just how fragile a modern nation could be. Even leaving aside the widespread destruction of a nuclear war, agriculture would be paralyzed simply because it relied so heavily on the healthy functioning of a much larger system. As one official put it: "Today agriculture is highly mechanized, and its present level of output is achieved at the cost of dependence upon public utilities and a continuing flow of products such as fuel oil, tractors, farm machinery, feedingstuffs, spare parts, tyres, artificial fertilisers, antibiotics, herbicides, insecticides and fungicides, all of which come from factories mainly situated in urban areas."[72] The breakdown of any of these would imperil the lives of millions. Because of the possibility of nuclear war, farmers would be better off with more diversified crops. Man's simplifications of the landscape had made him extraordinarily vulnerable. National and allied vulnerabilities, troubling though they were, barely scratched the surface of what scientists tried to understand about the environment in the 1950s. With the arms race came an increasing military interest in environmental sciences on a global scale.

PART TWO

Forces of Nature

4

Earth under Surveillance

Since the war, a new phrase has been added to our vocab-
ulary—the polar concept. This concept is based upon the
following facts: all continents in the Northern Hemisphere
meet at the ice-covered beaches of the Arctic Ocean; nearly
all of the most important industrial and military concen-
trations are situated well north of 35° North latitude; and
the shortest routes—the great circle courses—between the
industrial and military centers of the US and USSR cross
the polar regions, some of them quite close to the North Pole.

—U. S. Central Intelligence Agency, "Recent
Developments in the Soviet Arctic" (1954)

Human beings are now carrying out a large scale geophys-
ical experiment of a kind that could not have happened in
the past nor be reproduced in the future.

—ROGER REVELLE and HANS SUESS, 1957

IT HAS BECOME SO commonplace to point out the hubris of those who
meddle with nature that it is difficult to approach the subject without
stepping on some kind of trope or cliché. There are myriad examples of
attempts to modify nature on a giant scale—from America's Tennessee
Valley Authority, to the Soviet diversion of major rivers to make deserts
fertile, to the dream of using nuclear explosions to carve out harbors in
Alaska. A philosophical environmentalist today might shake his head at
these projects that irrevocably would replace natural regimes with those designed by humans, and perhaps quote the advice of the American prophet
of environmental ethics, Aldo Leopold, who said that the first rule of tin-
kerers is to save all the parts.[1] Yet there was considerable appreciation for
this perspective among scientists imagining a third world war. One conclusion of defense planners was actually quite similar to Leopold's—abandon

faith in particular commodities and try to bring into a post-nuclear world as many of the "parts" provided by nature. Military planners did in fact consider ecological and environmental questions. To understand how the sense of environmental vulnerability became global, it is more helpful to explore the question of why scientists started keeping track of large-scale environmental change.

Much of the scientific knowledge about the physical environment—the earth, the atmosphere, the oceans—came about due to a pressing military need to expand American and allied knowledge of the forces of nature on a global scale. That knowledge began with *monitoring*. The word has a military ring to it, and for good reason. Global environmental monitoring began as an explicitly Cold War activity. This chapter explains in detail how several kinds of environmental monitoring grew to importance in the 1950s as the United States and its allies made plans for war and kept watch over the Soviet Union. It also reveals the early disagreements about whether man-made changes to the environment, detected quite easily by such monitoring, could be justified as part of the struggle against the Soviet Union.

In the late 1940s, few regarded the coming war with the Soviet Union as an impending nuclear holocaust. This is an anachronistic image that fits a later period, after the advent of hydrogen bombs, massive stockpiles, and intercontinental ballistic missiles. In the half-decade after World War II, there simply were not very many atomic bombs in existence. Some leading strategists saw the atomic bomb as a wasting asset—one that might become meaningless after the Soviets achieved weapons parity—and argued for declaring war against the Soviet Union to capitalize on the temporary advantage.[2] A few scientists, including the eminent mathematician and game theorist John von Neumann, were pointing out that radiological weapons—based on contamination—might actually prove more decisive than bombs. In the 1950s, this view changed because of the advent of hydrogen bombs, the expectation of extraordinarily wide physical destruction, and worldwide contamination. Yet even in those early years, it seemed extremely important to assess the residual effects of atomic explosions—namely, the environmental contamination that might ensue after a series of blasts, whether on Russian or American soil.

The United States had one overriding reason to put the entire earth under environmental surveillance in the late 1940s. American espionage activities in the Soviet Union were failing miserably. Although Soviet agents seemed to have had little trouble penetrating the Manhattan Project during World War II, there is little evidence to suggest that the Americans were equally adept at spying. Soviet counterintelligence operations sniffed out American agents and promptly shot them. That meant there were few "eyes" on the ground to tell the Americans when and where Stalin might test his first atomic bomb. Fear of a secret explosion, and thus of a secret arsenal, drove the Joint Chiefs of Staff to insist upon the development of a worldwide radiological monitoring network in the late 1940s. In time this would become the largest data collection network in history.

Because such monitoring required taking samples from the atmosphere, establishing this radiological network became the perfect job for the brand new US Air Force. When President Truman signed the National Security Act of 1947, the Air Force had been born—along with other staples of the American defense establishment, such as the Joint Chiefs of Staff, the National Security Council, and the Central Intelligence Agency. Unlike the other armed services, the Air Force adopted a scientific worldview from its very start. General Henry "Hap" Arnold, who commanded the air force when it was part of the Army, was intent on using scientists as fully as possible. He was instrumental in founding the nation's first "think tank" in 1948—the RAND Corporation. As an advisory body on policy and strategy, RAND helped the nascent Air Force find its way, by bringing its mission and goals in line with the latest and projected developments in science and technology.[3]

The radiological monitoring network was one of the Air Force's first genuine contributions to national security. The Air Force Office of Atomic Energy (AFOAT-1) kept B-29 bombers in the air routinely, carrying "bug catchers"—air sampling contraptions—across the sky between Alaska and the Soviet Union. This project was a great motivator to other armed services, particularly the Navy, which already was struggling to convince the secretary of defense that it was not obsolete. Under the influence of oceanographer Roger Revelle, the Naval Research Laboratory sponsored Project Rainbarrel, a monitoring operation that analyzed rainwater. In September of 1949, the Air Force detected a suspicious cloud of radioactivity. Tipped off by the Americans, British planes sampled it when it passed over Scotland. Then the Navy's group reported uncharacteristic levels of radioactivity in Alaskan rain. Together they accomplished what none of their spies had been able to do: to peer inside the Soviet Union and discover that Joseph Stalin had an atomic bomb. The Americans called the blast Joe-1.[4]

Detecting Joe-1 was just a taste of what environmental monitoring could accomplish for gathering intelligence and helping the armed services prepare for war. After this success, atmospheric and ocean monitoring expanded considerably. The Air Force, Navy, and Atomic Energy Commission wanted to learn a great deal more about the composition of the atmosphere, the sea, and the fission products from different kinds of blasts. Measurements of air and rainwater became a routine matter, as the US military attempted to keep tabs on Soviet tests and, 15 years after Joe-1, the first Chinese test. The Atomic Energy Detection System (AEDS) became a central part of the daily operations in the American armed services.

What these sampling efforts could not do, however, was detect the location of nuclear tests in the vast Soviet Union. To do that, the US government needed still another monitoring operation to take different kinds of data. By 1951 geophysicists such as the University of Minnesota's Athelstan Spilhaus were helping the Air Force find the epicenter of any given nuclear explosion, using acoustic data based on variations in atmospheric pressure. This required considerable knowledge of normal meteorological conditions, to be certain that any fluctuations were due to the shock waves of a nuclear blast. Geophysicists also helped to triangulate seismic data— the transmission of pressure waves through the earth—though this was complicated by the need to differentiate nuclear blasts from earthquakes and ocean surf. Like detecting radioactivity in rainfall and the atmosphere, all of these methods required a worldwide network of monitoring stations. Some would be operated with the consent of allies, while others—for example, atmospheric detectors of rare gases such as Krypton-85—could be operated out of American embassies, with or without permission from host governments.[5]

What all these projects required was abundant data. And it had to come from all over the world. Reliable geophysical information was the single most important piece missing from the arsenals of all of the armed services, whether American or Soviet. Even more than nuclear physics, the earth sciences soon became the quintessential exemplars of "Cold War Science." This was based not only on detecting atomic bombs but also on understanding their effects and finding reliable ways of getting them to their targets with bombers and—so the future plans went—with submarines and rockets. Ignorance of the earth's true shape and of its dynamic systems—the interaction of the atmosphere, the oceans, and crust— would render nations impotent.[6]

The American armed services were well on their way to becoming the largest, most thoroughly scientific-minded organizations on the planet. This was not merely a matter of funding more science than anyone else (which they did), but also of anticipating scientific and technological developments and including them in their respective missions. The Navy learned this lesson from the Air Force in 1949. The secretary of defense had cancelled the construction of the Navy's gargantuan supercarrier USS *United States*, on the grounds that resources were better spent elsewhere— such as on the Air Force's fleet of strategic bombers. Reeling from this embarrassment, the Navy failed to reverse the decision by openly contesting it. That brief "revolt of the admirals" resulted mainly in a few very good naval officers getting fired. With the advice of scientists, the Navy's more successful answer was to start developing submarine-launched missiles. Scientists helped the Navy to stay relevant to America's geopolitical posture against the Soviet Union.[7]

Understanding the natural environment meant more than detecting radioactivity. It also meant understanding the operational environment for ships and planes. No one spent more time, energy, and money attempting to advance science about the oceans, atmosphere, and lithosphere than the US armed services. They literally put the entire earth under surveillance in the 1950s. Most of the data we now possess about the environment and about environmental change can be traced back to their efforts to understand the earth's dynamics.

One great irony of science in the Cold War was how easily this critical geophysical information lent itself to the rhetoric of peaceful international cooperation. When President Eisenhower announced that dozens of nations were going to work in concert to collect these critical data, in what became the International Geophysical Year (IGY) of 1957–58, he mentioned that the project might help ease the tensions of the Cold War. After all, scientists spoke the common language of mankind. Now they could work together. The argument seemed logical: science itself was not nationalistic, knowledge knew no borders, and ideas were universal.[8]

The president did not mention that the United States was trying to understand atmospheric conditions and the state of the oceans in key strategic areas. In pursuit of this aim, the federal government's budget allocations for science skyrocketed to unprecedented levels during the IGY. The Soviets surprised everyone by agreeing to take part. They had a card to play, however—they used the IGY as a peaceful scientific venue through which to launch the first artificial satellite (Sputnik). Thanks to that Soviet challenge to American technological supremacy, the National Science Foundation's budget would never return to its pre-IGY levels. That was just on the civilian side. It did not account for what the armed services spent doing the preparatory work moving men, equipment, and entire construction sites from one part of the globe to another, setting up bases in remote areas—including one at the most remote of all, the South Pole.[9]

The whole point of the IGY was to attempt what no one had ever tried: a truly synoptic study of the earth. The idea was to take the same kinds of measurements throughout the year in many different locations. By the end of the 18-month "year," it was hoped, there would be enough raw data to help scientists comprehend what the earth looked like in a relatively short period of time. It would be like taking a snapshot photo. That photo could be used in subsequent years, decades, or even centuries. Even if no genuinely original scientific work ever got done during the IGY, it would not matter. The scientific data would be priceless.

In reality the IGY was the perfect answer to several different problems. Both the US Air Force and the US Navy desperately needed to cooperate with other nations to keep a steady stream of data coming in from the far-flung reaches of the world. Granted, it was shared (and thus suspect) information, but it was better than nothing. The IGY also promised geophysicists an opportunity they had only dreamed of—not only lots of money but also naval vessels willing to cart them where they needed to go. They could finally gain a better understanding of the properties of the atmosphere, oceans, and the continent of Antarctica—embracing many scientific fields from glaciology to marine biology. The late 1950s were boom times for science in the United States.[10]

The men who dreamed up the IGY were keenly aware of these needs. The idea was hatched at a dinner party in 1950 at James Van Allen's house. Van Allen was an atmospheric scientist from Iowa, then working in Maryland at the Applied Physics Laboratory of Johns Hopkins University. He was keenly interested in rockets and dreamed of using them to explore the upper atmosphere. Van Allen was no stranger to military work, and during the IGY he would be instrumental in designing one of the most scientifically interesting atmospheric nuclear blasts to date—an explosion in the earth's radiation belts. One of the others in attendance, Lloyd Berkner, at the time was in the midst of authoring the "Berkner Report," a kind of government manifesto about linking science with foreign relations—setting up science attaché offices abroad to make best use of scientific ideas and to forge cooperative data-sharing agreements. The IGY turned out to be an opportunity to do this on a scale that defied the imagination: not only did more than 60 nations record relevant data diligently over a period of 18 months, but they also quite willingly forked over the data, no questions asked.

The strategic areas most in need of data were the poles. The IGY had been modeled after the International Polar Years of 1882–83 and 1922–23, and the focus on the polar regions always was the most decisive justification for the armed services to support it. Most of the public attention went to Antarctica, including the territorial disputes there. But both the United States and the Soviet Union kept their eyes on the prize: the Arctic, easily the most strategically important area on earth. This was especially so because neither country knew very much about it. The US Navy knew that ice and poor weather would impede their operations in the waters leading to Soviet ports, and it needed data. Perhaps more crucially, the northern latitudes would be the path of approach for incoming bombers, armed with nuclear bombs. The Americans and Canadians were well on their way to implementing the "DEW line," a defense early warning network of radar stations at the northern reaches of Alaska and Canada. But there was so much more that scientists and military officers did not know about the conditions that they would need to operate in.[11]

The Americans needed polar data and were willing to cooperate with allies to get it. The Soviets already had shut the curtain on polar information. In 1947, the Soviet government had decreed that all Arctic information would be put on the list of state secrets. Polar scientific observations were placed under lock and key. But there was evidence of considerable research activity in that region, as the Soviets collected information on every conceivable subject. Partly these data were supposed to improve weather forecasts in the Soviet Union, but more important, they would aid the Soviet Air Force on long-range trans-polar missions to the Western Hemisphere. Further, measurements of terrestrial magnetism over the North Pole would prove invaluable in future guided missile technology. The Soviets, the CIA believed in 1954, were attempting to master the northern route.[12]

American intelligence analysts knew that the Soviets guarded geophysical data very closely, and they worked hard to use the IGY to gain access to it. Often Soviet scientists would publish articles in Soviet journals without citing any data except those publicly available in the West. Yet all the evidence suggested a great deal of research activity, but with almost all results typically staying inside the Soviet Union. "Only recently have some cracks in this iron curtain of secrecy begun to develop," one CIA report pointed out, mainly due to cooperative ventures like the IGY.[13]

The IGY raised the geopolitical stakes of geophysics, as the superpowers raced to collect data and to develop comprehensive and militarily significant portraits of the whole earth. Scientists were thinking big, as were military planners. They tried to make sense of the deluge of scientific research on subjects affecting large swathes of territory. By 1956, as all the IGY participants were finishing their final preparations, the armed services found themselves drowning in information: the crack in the iron curtain had become a flood. Because of the IGY, the Soviet government greatly expanded the number of scientific journals available to Westerners, including an enormous amount of information indirectly relevant to atomic energy, guided missiles, electronics, biological weapons, and chemical weapons. Both the Air Force and the CIA compiled regular summaries, with the CIA issuing digests of new Soviet bloc scientific information twice a month. In addition to that, the CIA made an intense effort to keep tabs on all International Geophysical Year activities, regardless of their source. With over 60 participant nations, this was no easy task, but the agency had the manpower and the funding to accomplish it. Not wanting to draw attention to CIA interest, these reports were published under the cover of the US Department of Commerce. Intelligence analysts did their best to keep up with the windfall of information coming out of the Soviet bloc.[14]

Scientists and their military partners never kept atmospheric sciences or the polar regions far from sight. These would be the keys to fighting a war with nuclear-armed missiles or bombers, or even fighting a conventional war against an enemy located on the other side of the North Pole. American and Western European scientists collaborated on what seemed like a project for weather prediction: the IGY's Polar Front Survey. In reality it added year-round ocean and atmosphere observations of the most crucial future battleground, in an effort to understand how the warm and cool air masses shaped weather and climate. The area had been studied before, but new observations helped fill in winter data that previously had been thin. The IGY studies also permitted the direct measurement of subsurface currents, reinforcing key ideas about ocean circulation.[15] Scientists were happy with this military monitoring, and they tagged along to explore their own ideas too. For example, one drifting observatory, put into the Arctic Ocean during the IGY by the US Air Force, became the platform for the first photographs of the Arctic's ocean floor, its living organisms, and its sediment clouds.[16]

The new wave of research on global data collection was in keeping with American national interests, and scientists benefited too. During the IGY, the US Navy built the installations in Antarctica that would serve scientists' interests for decades to come. At the tops of mountains like Hawaii's Mauna Loa, the armed services built roads and buildings to keep track of satellites. These same locations became centers of scientific observation. Meteorologist Harry Wexler and Roger Revelle, the director of Scripps Institution of Oceanography, were instrumental in using the Mauna Loa location to begin measurements of carbon dioxide in the atmosphere (a station in Antarctica also was used for this purpose). The subject was close to Revelle's own research interest in ocean circulation—an interest itself linked to the Atomic Energy Commission's desire to understand how radioactivity was dispersed in the sea. He and other collaborators had concluded that carbon dioxide molecules did not spend more than 10 years in the atmosphere before dissolving into the ocean. That meant that the carbon dioxide produced by the burning of fossil fuels was taken in by the ocean. During the kickoff year of the IGY, 1957, Revelle and Hans Suess published an article saying as much, but concluded with a paragraph warning that the oceans could not continue to absorb all the carbon dioxide indefinitely.[17] So it seemed reasonable to begin taking measurements of carbon dioxide levels in the atmosphere during the IGY. It was better late than never—no one had ever measured the "normal" levels of carbon dioxide, but the IGY seemed like a good time to start.[18]

There were several "starts" in global monitoring in the IGY, but the carbon dioxide measurements have become famous. Revelle and Wexler saw a new opportunity to collect more data with more precise instrumentation using expensive spectrophotometers. Revelle's previous calculations had relied on a small dataset, and he argued for intensive, sustained efforts to collect new data over a long period. The man selected to take these measurements in Hawaii, Charles David Keeling, later lent his name to the famous "Keeling curve" showing the accumulation of carbon dioxide in the atmosphere. By 1960, Keeling's work with the IGY's Atmospheric Carbon Dioxide program had produced the most accurate time series of data yet, designed to discern any increase of CO_2 in the atmosphere. And he did detect a rise. This in itself would spark scientific demand for more global, more synoptic, more continuous data collection to determine the extent of CO_2 increase and the possibility of global climate change. The Navy and other military sponsors were often happy to oblige.[19]

Perhaps more important than these global projects and synoptic monitoring, scientists in the 1950s began to look at the earth differently than in the past. In particular, they became increasingly interested in large-scale change due to human actions. Revelle and Suess wrote in 1957 that humans were carrying out a major experiment on the earth. They were talking about carbon dioxide, but Revelle learned this first with radioactivity. Preparing for the IGY, scientists began to recognize an opportunity to monitor the environment more effectively for radioactive debris from nuclear tests. In the process, they came to a startling revelation that the "normal" earth was retreating into an irretrievable historical past. With each nuclear test, the environment became a different place. How different? That was a matter of conjecture, because no one had taken the time to make an intensive global observation prior to the tests. That effort was only possible during the global snapshot of 1957–58.[20]

In fact the International Geophysical Year came at a perfect time for this mode of thinking, because scientists and military planners had begun to ask tough questions about the global consequences of such vast enterprises as hydrogen bombs. The explosions of hydrogen bombs could be much, much larger than atomic bombs. A single hydrogen bomb, based on fusing light atomic nuclei together rather than pulling heavy ones apart, could produce the energy of a thousand of the bombs that destroyed Hiroshima. Both the United States and Soviet Union tested hydrogen bombs in the 1950s, and with the Soviet launch of Sputnik in 1957 the world got a hint of a future with nuclear warheads delivered by rockets. Although work on biological and chemical weapons went forward, few continued to believe that these weapons would be the main threat in a third world war. Crop destruction, epidemic diseases, even contamination with radiological bombs—all these would be sideshows. In a total war, the main event would be the weapon with many names—the "Super," the "thermonuclear bomb," the "fusion bomb," the "megaton bomb," the "H-bomb." Should conflict commence between the United States and the Soviet Union, it might engulf the entire earth in a fiery, immensely destructive holocaust. World War III promised an unprecedented level of devastation, convincing some survival planners to abandon civil defense entirely and focus purely on laying the groundwork for the postwar survival of the human race.

Aside from ratcheting up anxieties about the Cold War, peacetime tests of hydrogen bombs changed the way scientists around the world thought about the earth itself. It began when radioactive ash from a 1954 American nuclear test fell out of the sky and blanketed a Japanese fishing vessel, the *Fukuryu Maru* (*Lucky Dragon*). The crew was hospitalized, one man died, the fish market collapsed—and the chairman of the US Atomic Energy Commission, Lewis Strauss, unwisely blamed the Japanese for having been at the wrong place at the wrong time. The international incident introduced a new word to people around the world: fallout. It turned out that fallout did not simply imperil local fishermen. In addition, the blast from an H-bomb would send debris high into the stratosphere, where it might circulate for years before falling out of the sky and could subject everyone on the planet to exposure.

The fallout controversy was a major turning point in global environmental awareness. It engaged the attention not only of scientists and concerned laymen but also of governments sending representatives to the United Nations. It raised questions of culpability and responsibility. It suggested that the Soviet Union, the United States, and, in fact, all nuclear powers had the ability to take actions with far-reaching, unpredictable, and deadly consequences even in peacetime. They were already subjecting the world to radiation but arguing that it was relatively harmless. Accepting this required an enormous level of trust, and that was never fully achieved.[21]

What is most remarkable about the controversy was how it altered the questions scientists asked about the earth's vulnerability to human-induced change. The "fallout" controversy ensured that scientists would never look at the earth in the same way again. Suddenly and on a global scale, scientists wanted to measure everything, to see how it was changing.

Earth scientists around the world in the 1950s found themselves unable to define contamination because they had no idea what the normal levels of radioactivity were. By the time they thought to measure them, bomb tests had already changed them. That left an open question: what were the normal levels for the oceans, for the soil, for atmosphere? That the Americans could conduct a major series of thermonuclear tests in the Pacific without knowing this might seem strange. But it was consistent with how most scientists thought about radiation. Radiological safety at the nuclear tests meant ensuring that humans were far away or shielded so that their exposure stayed low. It ignored questions about the long-term changes bombs made to the natural environment.

Such questions did not come from the United States—at least, not at first. The AEC was busy trying to control the diplomatic damage from the *Lucky Dragon* incident. After these Pacific tests, was the ocean contaminated? From the AEC's perspective, it could not be. The expected radiation exposure humans might receive from the ocean while steaming through it was below accepted thresholds. The Americans did not measure the radioactivity in the ocean before the tests. And at first, they did not measure afterward. Why would they? They did not think in such terms.

Japanese scientists did, aboard another ship voyaging near the Pacific testing grounds. Japan's reaction to the *Lucky Dragon* incident had received unsympathetic coverage in major American newspapers—the *New York Times* belittled outraged Japanese as professional anti-Americans. "Even in excitable Tokyo," one article sneered, "it is long since so much rumor, sensationalism and drummed-up indignation have been perceived."[22] Unsurprisingly, the Japanese felt differently. In short order a scientific vessel, the *Sinkatsu Maru*, voyaged to the blast area to sample the water. The results were published eventually by an ocean chemist named Yasuo Miyake. Realizing that Miyake and his colleagues were bona fide scientists, American oceanographers hastily put together a follow-up expedition. However, it was plagued by measurement problems. Miyake's study became the principal post–*Lucky Dragon* scientific work about the effects of radioactivity on the oceans.

Atomic energy establishments were wholly unprepared for Miyake's work, for the simple reason that it raised a new standard of inquiry: in the future, scientists would have to describe the extent to which nuclear tests changed the ocean from its normal levels. As innocuous as this statement may seem, it was a radical departure from the typical studies of radiation. Previous studies had been confined to effects on man. Suddenly they had to frame their analyses within the context of the ocean, not of the risk of exposure to humans. They would keep track of environmental change.

Not to be outdone by the Japanese, American oceanographers began to measure radioactivity routinely on their expeditions. Although the "normal" ocean was now beyond their reach, impossible to assess, they saw these measurements as an important part of understanding the effects of nuclear tests. Why? Did they believe that these levels would approach the safety thresholds? No. Rather they wanted to understand the role of this radioactivity in the ocean itself, to put it the context of ocean circulation, chemical composition, and sea life. But as they did so, contamination took on a new meaning that recognized the extent to which nuclear tests were changing the ocean from its "normal" state.

Political pressure to halt atmospheric testing led to even more surveys of radioactivity around the world. The United Nations encouraged them, and by the early 1960s the UN Food and Agriculture Organization's global soil survey was in full swing. Initially atomic energy establishments saw such surveys as a way to grind axes about the need to stop nuclear tests. But perhaps cynically, they also saw that such surveys could be interpreted as monitoring the environment—a phrase that suggested vigilance and precaution. In this case, monitoring meant data collection.

The fallout controversy led to heated debate about catastrophic biological effects on future generations. Scientists such as American chemist Linus Pauling claimed that the links between fallout exposure and cancer were disturbing enough to justify an end to the tests. Many scientists in the United States and elsewhere agreed. In Japan, geneticists did not hesitate to point out the consequences. The Genetics Society of Japan issued a statement in April 1957 warning that radiation induced genetic change, regardless of the amount, and the great majority of these changes are harmful. The increase in mutant genes in the population "will lead to a gradual increase of individuals handicapped in physical strength or in mental capacity, increases the sacrifices of individuals and the burdens of the society, and leads to eventual disaster for mankind." They urged that a solution to the problem be found as soon as possible.[23] The fallout controversy suggested global catastrophe even in a time of peace.

Rather than answer this criticism, the AEC looked for ways to label the Japanese work as biased. One of the Japanese geneticists, Yasushi Nishiwaki, had written that methodological problems in measuring radiation exposure had led the Americans to underestimate the harm. The AEC claimed that Nishiwaki's views were prejudicial because he disliked American nuclear testing and was married to an American woman with communist leanings.[24]

How could the AEC so brazenly ignore genetic effects? For one, most people understood radiation sickness to be a condition that either was immediate or a long-term disease that might cause premature death. Genetic effects fit neither category. Causing problems in one's future grandchildren, or great-great grandchildren, did not rankle people as much.

Genetic effects also were impossible to demonstrate. The AEC could point to children of victims of Hiroshima and Nagasaki and truthfully point out that they showed no signs of harm, although this ignored the fact that genetic mutations were unlikely to manifest in the first generation. Genetic effects were thus "unproven." The irony was that, compared to the risks of getting cancer and dying, these genetic effects were not controversial among geneticists. American geneticists agreed with the Japanese that radiation exposure to sexual organs caused genetic mutations. Moreover, mutations would occur at any level of exposure. Naturally occurring radiation, such as cosmic rays and radioactivity in the rocks, already caused mutations. Further exposure simply added to them.

To admit publicly that each nuclear test put new harmful mutations into the gene pool seemed daunting indeed. To prevent such mutations from happening would have meant not only a cessation of nuclear tests but possibly a halt to commercial nuclear power, weapons production, and the use of radioisotopes in agriculture, medicine, and research. Even geneticists were uncomfortable emphasizing this. Advising the National Academy of Sciences in 1955, geneticists argued among themselves about what kind of practical advice they might give, if all radiation produced mutations. In the end they decided that "as little as possible" was not practical enough. Remarkably, they chose an actual dose level to be published in their official 1956 report. It was an arbitrary level based on what seemed reasonable to them. Members of the British Medical Research Council, which issued its own report, were shocked that the Americans had the audacity to name a number at all. But the Americans reasoned that if they did not do it, someone else would.[25]

Although some scientists attempted to deny that the mutations were harmful—after all, mutations were the mechanism of evolution, so they might benefit the species—most turned toward justification rather than denial. In the United States, prominent geneticists misled the public by identifying, arbitrarily, a radiation dose recommendation for the population. They did so despite knowing that it would mislead, and despite their consensus that there was no scientific basis for setting any dose.[26] All levels of radiation produced mutations. The scientific consensus about the worldwide damage from nuclear testing that seemed to emerge in 1956 was in fact deeply subjective, based on what seemed reasonable to Americans given their desire to have nuclear weapons. In a letter to Lewis Strauss, mathematician and AEC member John von Neumann acknowledged this problem, pointing out the dangers of having the United Nations conduct its own assessment throughout the UN Scientific Committee on the Effects of Atomic Radiation. He complained that the UN undoubtedly would take a dim view of damage to human life, despite the fact that no human endeavor has ever succeeded without costs. "Every worthwhile activity has a price, both in terms of certain damage and of potential damage—of risks—and the only relevant question is, whether the price is worth paying."[27] So, was the price worth paying? Von Neumann believed that, for the United States, it was. Other countries not as committed to standing up to the Soviet Union might have disagreed.

The AEC commissioners made a strong case for human sacrifice, but called it risk. They dismissed Japanese suggestions of "disaster for mankind," choosing instead to encourage a public discourse about "risk," centered upon the dilemmas inherent in a risk-based society. After all, many people died in automobile crashes every year—far more than were harmed by nuclear testing. Moving from California to Colorado would expose a person to additional radiation from cosmic rays, they said. A traveler added to her body's radiation burden every time she went up in an airplane. Yet these were risks people were willing to take. Nuclear testing, which added a small amount of radiation compared to natural sources, was just another of these risks. Framing the debate in this way certainly helped the cause. Famous scientists such as Edward Teller (the "father" of the H-bomb), Willard Libby (the discoverer of carbon dating), and many others added to the reassurances of the AEC and President Eisenhower that the dangers from nuclear testing in the atmosphere were far overdrawn. Everyone, they maintained, took risks. Still, the intellectualized conversation about "risk" masked a transformation in public policy that allowed continued harm to people all over the world, permitting the sacrifice of hundreds of thousands of lives, most of them in future generations. Hawkish scientists such as Teller and Libby looked at nuclear fallout as an acceptable price to pay in the conflict with the Soviet Union. Even in peace, they saw the sacrifice as necessary. Great human cost now could prevent greater disaster later. The difference between risk and sacrifice was subtle, but undeniable: individuals took risks; nations made sacrifices.

While politicians and scientists debated how to address (or not to address) these changes to the atmosphere, the fallout controversy also forced war planners to reevaluate their survival plans and rethink the earth's vulnerability. One example of this was in fishing, which was a crucial part of European—especially British—survival plans. Everyone knew that radiation from fallout would limit supplies of relatively safe meat, dairy products, and vegetables. Fish, on the other hand, could be caught in deep water, away from the attacks and cleansed by the ocean.[28] Britain's nuclear war scenario relied on this explicitly. The Admiralty would tell fishing vessels to abandon England and head west, stopping to salt the fish in Iceland, Greenland, and Canada. Then, with salted (and thus easily preserved) fish, they could return to England and feed the people in a month's time.[29]

This plan had to be changed after the first American hydrogen bomb tests in the Pacific Ocean. When news of the *Lucky Dragon* broke, the fish market in Japan collapsed. Was this a reasonable response, and were exposed fish really dangerous to eat? At that time, the ocean was widely perceived as a great neutralizer, with virtually unlimited ability to absorb noxious substances. British fisheries scientist Michael Graham put it unequivocally to a colleague at the Ministry of Agriculture and Fisheries, "an explosion produces virtually no danger from contaminated fish." The surest way of ridding oneself of the danger from fallout was to use the ocean to clean it off. Washing down the ship with sea water would be "a complete antidote if done soon enough; otherwise death or at least chronic ill-health in a distressing form is very probable."[30]

Despite Graham's unambiguous statement, assessing the effects of nuclear war on fish was fraught with difficulty. Making broad generalizations about "fish" struck fisheries scientists as comical. Each species had different migration patterns and life habits—fishing for shallow-water herring was a different operation altogether from deep-water trawling of the "white fish," such as cod, haddock, and plaice. What kind of fish would survivors try to catch? The more they looked at the problem, the more uncertain it became.[31] Finding safe fish meant taking into account a complex array of environmental information. It required calculating rates of fish consumption, measuring fallout deposition with greater precision, understanding the effects of wind, and taking into account variations in ocean circulation. In the event of wide-scale nuclear conflict, there would be no nearby "clean" water with which the contaminated water could mix. That meant a long wait until mixing with deep water occurred.[32]

In one 1962 study, British scientists projected that if hydrogen bombs were dropped upon Glasgow (10 megatons) and Edinburgh (3 megatons), fish in the entire region between Scotland and Scandinavia would be unfit for consumption for at least a year. Because prevailing winds would blow most of the fallout to the east, fish on the west coast might be all right to eat in about month or so, but only as an emergency measure. On the east coast, the fish would remain poisonous even after the water itself ceased to be a hazard. Thus, in the event of war, all fishing vessels should be deployed to the west, and "fish as a long-term source of food should be sought from cleaner waters" such as the northwest coast of Scotland, the Faroes Islands, Iceland, and—only if no bombs were dropped on Ireland— the Irish Sea.[33] And this was the result of just two bombs.

Meanwhile the Americans continued to put stock in the ocean as the world's savior. In a National Academy of Sciences booklet "Damage to Livestock from Radioactive Fallout in Event of Nuclear War," American scientists asserted that fish would be *relatively* safe to eat after a nuclear war. Compared to cows, pigs, and chickens, fish would be exposed rather less. The booklet identified radioiodine (I–131) as the principal concern because of its tendency to concentrate in the thyroid of fish. After a bomb test at Eniwetok atoll, some 700 fish samples collected over 19 months showed that only about 1 percent of all beta activity was concentrated in muscle (the edible parts). Because there would be plenty of uncontaminated water nearby to help dilute radioactivity, the Academy pointed to the muscle of fish, crustaceans, and mollusks as a "highly recommended, relatively safe food source in a disaster situation."[34]

What emerged from these predictions was how little knowledge anyone possessed. One British scientist complained that the American view was based on "the briefest of supporting evidence" and seemed to assume a great deal of dilution by the ocean.[35] Another dismissed the American work, noting that "the whole marine side is dismissed in under one page!"[36] The Americans had taken the data at Eniwetok, out in the vast Pacific Ocean, and applied it to all seas, ignoring the fact that in some areas there was relatively little or slow mixing of water.

That shortfall of data was disappearing. The information collected during the IGY, along with scientists' interest in tracking change, gave war planners the tools to reevaluate prospects for post-nuclear survival. In this case, the result of the dispute about fish was a new British study, far more detailed, that attempted the first comprehensive portrait of a more realistic nuclear war. The previous American work had only dealt with the Pacific, and the previous British one had only dealt with the consequences of two bombs. Now the British scientists tried to imagine a large-scale nuclear war and its effects on fisheries in the entire North Atlantic. Completed in late 1964, a report of the study drew from a wide range of American and British sources on oceanography, fisheries, radiobiology, radioactive waste disposal, fallout, and nuclear explosions.

Unlike the American confidence that the sea would simply wash away most of the harm, this new study gave the opposite impression. The Pacific—the source of almost all previous data, because of nuclear tests there—differed in important ways from the Atlantic. The Pacific, for example, had more phytoplankton, where radioactivity would concentrate, whereas the Atlantic had more suspended matter to trap debris. This made the American views seem irrelevant, because most of the combatants would depend on fish from the north Atlantic, not the South Pacific. Another problem with earlier predictions was that fish comprised only about 1 percent of the average person's diet, in peacetime. Would people rely that much more on fish after a nuclear war? Further, there were only three major fish processing areas in Britain—the kind of concentration that was extraordinarily vulnerable to attack. Also, only fish caught in water deeper than 50 fathoms were considered safe. Unfortunately about

90 percent of Britain's fish currently were drawn from shallower waters. As for lakes and rivers, they would be off limits. Rain would wash contaminated soil into them.[37]

The US government was aware of these many problems and inconsistencies. Scientists in government knew far more about global contamination than they admitted publicly. Long before the fallout controversy, the armed services and the Atomic Energy Commission pursued secret research on what they perceived as "the problem of world-wide contamination."[38] After the Soviet Union detonated its first bomb in 1949, the United States had immediately taken action to estimate how many bombs would be needed to cause serious health problems within the United States. This was known as Project Gabriel, and its result seemed grim enough: if the Soviets were able to drop 3,000 Hiroshima-sized bombs on the United States, the landscape would be seriously contaminated by radioisotopes, particularly the bone-seeking isotope strontium-90. As if this were not frightening enough, soon the development of the hydrogen bomb (the Americans tested the first one in November of 1952) raised the ante. If each one of these could be the size of a thousand Hiroshimas, did that mean that only a handful of hydrogen bombs could seriously contaminate the United States?[39]

Working with scientists at the RAND Corporation, the Atomic Energy Commission tried to answer this question, but took it one step further: to what extent did the explosion of hydrogen bombs contribute to worldwide radiological contamination? Beginning in 1953, RAND invited scientists to its office in Santa Monica, California, to produce the first briefs on what became known as Project Sunshine. The project was the brainchild of University of Chicago radiochemist Willard F. Libby. His survey of the bones of a few dozen premature or stillborn babies in Chicago formed the basis of the Sunshine work, which attempted to track the fate of radioisotopes by sampling human and animal bones. Although initially concerned about the effects of war, the AEC attempted to nail down what was really happening to the earth and its inhabitants during peacetime nuclear tests.[40]

Project Sunshine started out as a secret, but it required a global network of participants well beyond the confines of RAND, the AEC, or any American agency. Strontium-90 followed the same metabolic pathways as calcium, which meant that its presence could be measured most readily in bones. The AEC developed a network of willing participants in hospitals throughout the globe, all of whom collected bone samples of recently deceased humans of every sex, age, and ethnic group—and dispatched them to American labs. The best measurements of strontium-90 came from babies. Collecting all these bones, as historian Barton Hacker has noted, required a "well-contrived cover story." Establishing that story was a simple matter: they would talk scientists into doing some "basic research" on the natural radium burden of human bones around the world. The fact that most of them were babies would not raise an eyebrow, as the Americans simply could say that these were the most readily available corpses.[41]

In addition to human samples, the AEC needed plant and soil samples, which it gained through an equally contrived network of researchers. Initially the project described the natural environment in fairly precise terms, even introducing the concept of "Sunshine units" to describe the radioactive content in each individual's bones. This unit was based on permissible levels to workers recommended by the National Bureau of Standards. But soon the project got bigger and more diffuse, with active participants all over the world. Eventually it became too big to keep secret, and it became public knowledge in 1957. Unveiling Project Sunshine was perfectly timed to benefit from the data sharing of the International Geophysical Year.

All of this suggests that the AEC did not merely act in response to the fallout controversy but in fact had been studying it from the outset as a global problem. That said, some of the earliest conclusions of Project Sunshine convinced die-hard weapons test advocates that the dangers from peacetime testing were overstated. Willard Libby became the leading scientific voice among the AEC commissioners, and he routinely dismissed the harm from fallout. The first conference at RAND, in 1953, had identified an astronomical figure—2.5×10^4 megatons—required to bring the world's population up to the existing maximum permissible concentrations. Although those maximum levels would change in subsequent years (and geneticists would invent theirs), the attitude of Libby and his like-minded commissioners would not. They believed that even giant fireballs like hydrogen bombs could not compete with the forces of nature, and they contributed only minuscule amounts of radioactive strontium to the atmosphere. Any changes to the atmosphere could be justified as necessary in the struggle against communism.

As data poured in, Libby did not change his view. But other scientists were more skeptical. Commenting on Sunshine, AEC scientist Hal Hollister pointed out in 1958 that such confidence assumed a lot. Libby and others postulated that there were "infinite sinks," where strontium-90 might be tied up long enough for it to decay without harm to man. Most people put the oceans in that category, and scientists such as Libby put the

world's soil at least partly in it. But the truth, Hollister pointed out, was
that no one knew. It was a matter of where to put one's confidence. Even
global radiological monitoring barely scratched the surface of the earth.
Scientists had to extrapolate from a tiny number of measurements. The
real fate of strontium-90 in the atmosphere and oceans—in terms of actual location and quantity—was unknown. "In fact, of course," Hollister
wrote, "we are no closer to measuring the environment for strontium-90
than we are for sand or needles."[42]

What Sunshine did provide was a large dataset about the worldwide
distribution of strontium-90 and, to some extent, cesium-137. But as scientists began to notice, the Sunshine studies had a wider potential. The project had begun as a study of the most likely risk to man but had evolved
into something much bigger in scope. It had gone from a study of fallout's
effects on humans to being a program of worldwide monitoring, sampling, and radiochemical analysis. Rather than assessing hazards to man,
Sunshine scientists were tracking the distribution of radioisotopes all over
the world and collecting data for the study of the earth's mechanisms.[43]

Because of the fallout controversy and the global Sunshine studies, a
huge range of people had become involved in radioactivity, not only to assess health effects but also to monitor how testing altered the environment. English-born Arthur Geoffrey Norman, who just a few years before
had advised Fort Detrick and Porton on methods of crop destruction, now
used his expertise to imagine the vulnerability of all American crops to the
perils of radioactive fallout. He headed the National Academy of Sciences'
group devoted to radiation effects on agriculture. Like so many others, he
lamented that it was impossible to speak logically about the "normal" state
of the world. Any policies about food were "clouded with uncertainties"
because natural states had disappeared because of the fission and fusion
explosions since 1945:

> The testing of atomic and nuclear weapons is placing in soil, water,
> and air, the world over, radioisotopes not formerly present, though at
> extremely low levels. The "natural content" of foods now consumed
> by animals and man is not the same as in the preatomic age. Though
> extremely small, the increment is measurable and inescapable.[44]

Even without a catastrophic event such as a nuclear war, agricultural products
around the world would see more and more radioactivity concentrated in
them. Humans were changing the world around them in measurable ways.

Norman and others pointed out the "great deficiency" in the amount of data available and called for more. The Atomic Energy Commission sponsored ecological research around its facilities, not nationwide. Norman wanted a broader survey of major agricultural areas, to find out what the current levels of radioactivity were in their crops and livestock. What was sorely lacking was any understanding of what "natural background" radiation even meant. What was normal for forests? What were the major differences between rangeland, rotation grassland, and plowland? To what extent did irrigation make a difference? Even if it was impossible to establish the normal, preatomic levels, scientists needed to start somewhere. They needed to start taking data, keeping a record, tracking changes over much larger areas, not just at AEC sites.

Because some organisms absorbed considerable amounts of radioactivity, often concentrating radioisotopes in their bones, radioactivity touched nearly every conceivable scientific discipline, not just physics. Meteorologists, oceanographers, and geologists all jumped into radioactivity research. The entire field of radioecology was devoted to tracing the paths and concentrations of radioactivity within ecosystems. Because all of the earth sciences blended physical, chemical, and biological processes, they could claim a significant stake in understanding the fate of radioactivity. And they could easily ask for money. Suddenly there were many more stakeholders in atomic affairs than ever before, many of them arguing for more and more data, playing up the perils of ignorance.

The same dynamic gripped the United Nations' specialized organizations. On the one hand was the coming International Atomic Energy Agency (IAEA; to be established in 1957), populated by pro-nuclear people who had worked as scientists, administrators, and regulators in their home countries. But at least two other agencies, the World Health Organization (WHO) and the Food and Agriculture Organization, resented the impending dominance of the IAEA. After all, who knew more about radiation's effects on health and food than WHO and FAO did? This little bit of competition spurred more intensive work by FAO in particular. As if echoing Geoffrey Norman's call for more research on a wide scale, FAO botanist Ronald Silow pointed out in 1956 that FAO needed to know how radioisotopes entered the food supplies of all mankind.[45]

The implication of FAO's outlook was staggering. The US Atomic Energy Commission already sponsored ecologists to study contamination of its nuclear sites. Geoffrey Norman's panel had suggested broadening this to include key agricultural zones throughout the United States. Now FAO wanted to track the fate of radioactivity in all of man's food supplies. And by "man," Silow meant humans all over the world.

These studies led to ambitious efforts to identify particularly vulnerable parts of the world. FAO began by asking about the distribution of soils deficient in calcium. One particular radioisotope, strontium, followed metabolic paths typically followed by calcium. The less natural calcium there was, the more likely it was that strontium would build up. To FAO this implied that plants grown in calcium-rich soils would be safer than those grown in calcium-deficient soils, because they would contain less of this dangerous radioisotope. Thus a major global project presented itself: why not conduct a global survey of calcium-deficient soils, to identify the most vulnerable parts of the earth?[46]

Mapping this vulnerability proved complex, and scientists again realized how little they knew. Crops and diets varied from one region to the next, so it was impossible to identify the true consequences of calcium deficiency in soil. In most Western countries, the main source was milk products. But in the Philippines and Japan, people got their calcium from cereals and vegetables, as did those in many countries in Africa and Asia. Japan also relied heavily on fish and other marine foods, receiving calcium by that route. Even within individual countries the differences could be quite large.[47] In underdeveloped areas especially, calcium might come from unexpected sources. Many areas relied heavily on the cereals ragi or quinoa, for instance, which were quite rich in calcium. The people of southern India and Ceylon inadvertently made up for their calcium-poor diet by using a crude sea salt, whose impurities included large amounts of calcium. Also the maize grain used to make *tortillas* was treated with lime water (a source of calcium) before being ground into flour. In Mexico, much of people's calcium came from *tortillas*.[48]

For these and other reasons, there never had been a strong scientific basis for surveying the calcium content in the world's soils. FAO's position was that it was at least a start, leading to more intensive global and regional studies of food security and environmental vulnerability.[49] Just having the data, FAO scientists argued, was reason enough to do it.

Other UN agencies were no less ambitious. Change was in the air, and the United Nations leaped into action to track it. Not content to leave nuclear matters to the IAEA, the UN Educational, Scientific, and Cultural Organization (UNESCO) carved out a niche by focusing on the relationship between radiation and cell growth. The World Meteorological Organization also got into the act with its own global agenda. Preempting the establishment of the IAEA, it announced in 1956 its goal of setting up a worldwide network of observation stations to record radiation levels. Strangely, by the time the IAEA was born in 1957, many of its responsibilities had been taken up by the existing agencies. This would create some bitter infighting within the United Nations over the years, but in the late 1950s it meant that several of the major UN agencies were monitoring global radiation levels in some way and expanding their data collection networks.[50]

By the early 1960s, it had become the scientific norm to take monitoring data, unrelated to any particular scientific question, simply to track changes to large areas of the earth. A new era had begun, with the earth under constant surveillance. As this monitoring was under way, with scientists collecting data on a continuing basis, others used these data to consider the possibility of manipulation.

5

Acts of God and Acts of Man

Effective knowledge is professionalized knowledge, supported by a restricted acquaintance with useful subjects subservient to it. This situation has its dangers. It produces minds in a groove.

—ALFRED NORTH WHITEHEAD, *Science and the Modern World* (1925)

We know how we can modify the ionosphere. We have already done it.

—EDWARD TELLER (1962)

THE EXPANSION OF knowledge about the earth in the 1950s fed an irresistible belief that humans could manipulate nature. Scientists and the military were not simply collecting data for the operational use of planes, ships, or even rockets. Saying so would ignore important goals—even dreams—of American and Soviet military planners throughout the Cold War, to use geophysical forces to alter the weather and climate in their favor. Scientists often were quite vocal in their confidence that manipulation of the environment was a human power not far beyond the horizon. For example, parallel to his top-secret work helping the Air Force to locate nuclear tests with seismic techniques, Athelstan Spilhaus became an outspoken believer in ultimate control of geophysical processes. "In all sciences," he wrote in the *Geographical Review* in 1954, "there should be a somewhat logical sequence of stages leading to control—observation, understanding, prediction, control." He argued that humans ultimately would be able to change climate for the better, by regularizing rainfall for farmers, maximizing numbers of fish in the ocean, and by turning even the most barren wastelands into fertile soil. Or perhaps by utilizing untapped resources, such as the freshwater locked up in polar ice. In order to achieve these ambitious goals, Spilhaus put forward a solution that the United States government already was promoting under the aegis of the military. "How should we organize to do all this?" he asked. "We should build up a global network of *observation* in sea and air. We should assist institutions where scientists in many different fields may devote their combined efforts to the problem of *understanding* the ocean and the atmosphere."[1]

There were two sides of global monitoring. One was military, designed to keep tabs on an enemy and to understand how to operate the latest weaponry on land, sea, and air. The other was peaceful—understanding the globe contributed to the betterment of mankind, improvement of conditions around the world, and control of the environment. The American scientists involved in the IGY tried to represent both sides at the same time. The observation tools being developed for military purposes—rockets, satellites, ocean buoys, artificial islands—"are engineering tools with no intrinsic immorality," as Spilhaus argued, "and may serve equally to promote peaceful living."[2] In practice, this meant that the lessons learned in one sphere deeply influenced thinking about the other. One lesson was that the earth's soil, atmosphere, and oceans might be susceptible to subtle and lasting change. The earth might be vulnerable.

With this knowledge came a corollary: human beings might already be capable in either war or peace of initiating such changes, intentionally or not. If scientists could tinker with large-scale forces, could they inadvertently bring about alterations, or even catastrophes, that they had not anticipated? The IGY would lead, among other things, to a fairly clear indication—the famous Keeling curve—that the carbon dioxide content of the atmosphere was on a steady rise. If taken as an indicator of the greenhouse effect, Keeling's data demonstrated that tiny, incremental additions to the atmosphere could amount to immensely significant changes in the dynamics of the earth. This finding was just one of many in a long-standing debate among scientists about whether humans had the ability to compete with the forces of nature, to match these forces, or possibly to manipulate them. The greenhouse idea pre-dated the IGY, but the continuous data collection did not.[3] At mid-century, carbon dioxide was an interesting question but not a very controversial one, certainly not when compared to the possibility that nuclear tests might be changing the climate, or that manipulations of the weather by overconfident scientists might have far-reaching consequences for the earth.

Because concerns about human-caused catastrophic change arose in the context of nuclear detonations, scientists and their military partners either downplayed the effects or justified their experiments in the name of national security. As long as the Soviet Union existed, they argued, there would be a need to take risks on a huge scale and test immense weapons in the atmosphere. In the 1950s and 1960s, the world debated the effects of fallout and the widespread impacts of hundreds of megatons of hydrogen bombs exploding in the atmosphere and in space. Some flops did occur, as when one 1962 American nuclear blast, named Starfish Prime, instantly blacked out some of the electricity in Hawaii. That had been unexpected. Scientists knew there would be some electromagnetic disturbance from the blast but had been surprised by its extraordinary range. Despite denials that hydrogen bomb tests had discernible widespread effects, laypersons, news reporters, and some scientists began to doubt it. Even those who did not deny serious long-term effects could claim that the Cold War struggle justified the chemical and physical alterations to the atmosphere. Scientists played with their experimental toys and manipulated the environment on a grand scale.

When it came to manipulating the environment on a large scale, military and civilian scientific work proceeded together. A prominent example of this was the American program of work from the late 1940s forward on weather control. Like the science of the IGY, weather control always maintained the veneer of being a positive social goal. Good weather meant better harvests and a better life. Shortly after the end of World War II, scientists at General Electric (GE) Laboratories began suggesting that they might already possess the tools to control the weather. One of them, Vincent Schaefer, demonstrated in 1946 that artificial nucleation might be the key to getting precipitation out of clouds. He acted on the premise that rainfall and snowfall were made possible by the presence of microscopic bodies in the air and that these acted as nuclei for snowflakes. Ice crystals formed around the tiny bodies, making them heavy enough to fall.[4]

Based on this work, GE scientist Irving Langmuir launched a major research program on weather control. He reasoned that by injecting hundreds of thousands of tiny bodies into the air, one could create these nuclei artificially and encourage precipitation. It would be like putting seeds into clouds. "Undoubtedly, some climatic or weather changes would ensue from vast area seeding," Langmuir predicted in 1947.[5] Over the next few years, Langmuir and his team at GE experimented with several different kinds of "seeds" and decided that silver iodide was the most effective under laboratory conditions.

These studies were conceptually simple but potentially revolutionary. All of the armed services recognized this immediately: General Electric created a cooperative research program, dubbed Project Cirrus, with the Army Signal Corps, the Office of Naval Research, and the Air Force. Together they tackled cold weather problems, such as airplane icing, which Langmuir believed could be eliminated by shooting dry ice into clouds.[6] Project Cirrus's experiments ranged far and wide, including desert rain in New Mexico, forest fire suppression in New England, cloud-seeding in Puerto Rico, and even an attempt to steer a hurricane.[7]

In the summer of 1950, Langmuir gained widespread publicity for the GE studies when the journal *Science* published his article on artificial rainmaking by cloud seeding. One of the advantages of cloud seeding, he wrote, was that it was capable of producing effects that did not occur naturally, such as creating rain in arid regions. He was dismissive of the failures of others, citing the supreme requirements of knowledge, skill, and experience. Noting that that US Weather Bureau's own experiments had yielded no rainfall of economic importance, he argued that this was simply due to the bureau's inattention to details such as seed type, place, time, and an understanding of the optimal clouds.[8]

In contrast with the Weather Bureau's failures, Langmuir claimed that scientists under Project Cirrus were having outstanding success. He said that by introducing silver iodide into clouds over the New Mexico desert, he and his colleagues had induced over a tenth of an inch of rain on average, over an area of some 33,000 square miles. He went on to suggest that this kind of "cloud seeding" had contributed to several days of unusually heavy rains over a huge area stretching from New Mexico to eastern Kansas. He went even further, urging an intensive study of hurricanes. Using silver iodide, he predicted with confidence, hurricanes could be modified and prevented from ever reaching land.[9]

Although it was no surprise that weather control might captivate the popular imagination, meteorologists were astonished at how readily people assumed that it was already within their power. Langmuir's unbridled enthusiasm, bordering on boosterism, caught on quickly. But he clearly stood outside the mainstream. In his *Science* article he cited only himself and the other two GE scientists who had published on the subject—in other words, the widely publicized article was based solely on Project Cirrus, with no corroborating data from outside. The president of the American Meteorological Society, Brigadier General Donald N. Yates, marveled at the reaction to press coverage of Project Cirrus's artificial nucleation studies in New Mexico. He reported that "Federal, State, and Municipal authorities have been besieged with requests to make rain, to stop rain, to put out fires, to destroy hurricanes, to eliminate icing, hail, and fog, and even to create major climatic changes."[10] People instantly believed it could happen. Such requests often fell far afield of actual knowledge or capabilities.

Scientists at the US Weather Bureau complained that Langmuir's conclusions were grossly premature. It was not unusual that New Mexico would see precisely the kind of rain pattern that Langmuir reported. One of the bureau's scientists, Ferguson Hall, produced a map of New Mexico showing the occurrence of rain and thunderstorms throughout the state, beyond the reach of the silver iodide. He insisted that Project Cirrus had generated "no conclusive proof" of making any difference at all, much less the sweeping claims made by Langmuir.[11]

Several scientists from New York University and the Massachusetts Institute of Technology concurred, reporting to the American Meteorological Society that the Project Cirrus studies were anything but conclusive. The truth, they wrote, was that despite Langmuir's and Schaefer's work, it was impossible to control or predict the atmosphere well enough to judge what might have happened in the absence of artificial nucleation. With no certain knowledge of what would have occurred normally, it was hard to tell whether it worked. After all, inducing artificial rainfall required there to be optimal conditions for rain. How much of the rain was due to cloud seeding, and how much of it would have occurred anyway? It was not possible to discern the difference, even for the areas immediately surrounding the test sites. As for the vast areas of rainfall cited by Langmuir, it "definitely has not been demonstrated."[12]

These naysayers halted neither Langmuir's studies nor the widespread belief that human actions could change the weather. Their military significance alone guaranteed these studies a long lease on life. Aside from rainmaking—itself a promising military tool—cloud seeding might be able to dissipate clouds, increasing visibility on the battlefield and making it easier for bombers to find their targets. Research groups in other countries, notably Canada, France, and the United Kingdom, paid close attention to the progress of Project Cirrus. It would have been hard to ignore Langmuir's confidence that relatively small amounts of silver iodide could alter weather systems many hundreds of miles away.

Although Project Cirrus was concerned with controlling the weather, it required no bold stretch of the imagination to suspect American experiments might have unintended consequences too. Some even thought that they might be causing strange weather patterns across North America.

After all, Langmuir had said so. Probably the most significant case of suspicion was related the disastrous Red River flood of April and May 1950, which led to the largest evacuation of humans in Canada's history. Unusually heavy snowfall during the winter had meant high water levels in the spring. The river rose to an unprecedented level. After multiple dike failures, about an eighth of the city of Winnipeg found itself under water. The river—normally about 150 meters across—turned into a lake, some 65 kilometers wide and 100 kilometers long. More than 100,000 people fled the city and surrounding areas, while thousands of Canadian soldiers arrived to try to contain the disaster. Relief aid poured in from Canadian and American cities. Canadian officials wondered if Langmuir had caused the Red River disaster.

Such a massive flood would have been a horrific unintended consequence of weather experiments. Rainmaking nearly always had been cast as a positive good—more water for crops. But now Canadian scientists felt that the Americans were playing with forces they did not adequately understand. On behalf of Canada's National Research Council, meteorologist J. L. Orr wrote his American colleagues to determine whether the two events—Langmuir's experiments and the Red River flood—might be connected. The enthusiastic rainmaking might have led to what Orr called "indiscriminate seeding" throughout the Southwest, and Canada was paying the price.

Two of Langmuir's most vocal critics, New York University scientists B. Haurwitz and Gardner Emmons, felt as though they had to defend him. They did not think Langmuir had succeeded at all, much less caused a storm in Canada. They tried to set the Canadians at ease. "In our opinion," they wrote unequivocally, "the Red River flood was beyond question an act of God." It did not help that Langmuir already had claimed to have statistical proof that his silver iodide cloud seeding experiments in New Mexico had caused heavy rainfall far away, in the Ohio and Mississippi river valleys. Haurwitz and Emmons wrote that Langmuir's statistical proof had been sloppy, that he had not used proper techniques. As far as they were concerned, he "had completely failed to prove his case." They did not believe that there was any connection between the New Mexico experiments and the Ohio and Mississippi River rainfall—and the case was even stronger against a connection to the Red River Valley disaster, much farther north. They assured the Canadians that the Red River Valley was not normally downwind from New Mexico. There were no links to Canada's catastrophic flood. They added: "unless you are willing to believe, as Dr. Langmuir does, that the introduction of silver iodide smoke into the atmosphere can alter, on a hemispheric scale, the basic patterns of wind and weather."[13]

Placated by this and other explanations, the Canadian National Research Council concluded that the disaster "resulted from natural, though abnormal, weather and that there existed no evidence that the flood was attributable to cloud seedings elsewhere."[14] But the incident spurred American meteorologists to more vocal opposition to Langmuir's claims of wide-ranging effects. In the *Bulletin of the American Meteorological Society*, MIT meteorologist Henry Houghton wrote of "over-optimistic statements" and "ill-advised" attempts at rainmaking, saying that large-scale effects of cloud seeding would be unlikely.[15] The whole affair served to harden meteorologists against the view that humans were capable of shaping the vast energies of the atmosphere.

Scientists outside the United States were torn about how to interpret the discrepancy between most meteorologists' conservative views and Langmuir's more outlandish claims. It was hard to dismiss work done by top American scientists working in concert with the military. Their track record was just too good. Geophysicist Edward Bullard advised colleagues at the British Ministry of Defence: "If anyone is really interested, I think the first step would be to go and see Langmuir. He has brought off several very good things and it would be unwise to dismiss what he says as nonsense."[16] Indeed British and Commonwealth scientists had been conducting experiments of their own. In East Africa, for example, meteorologists in 1951 and 1952 tried to control rainfall in the Kongwa region of Tanganyika by cloud seeding from hot-air balloons.[17] And some of the most successful rainmaking experiments took place in Australia. Nonetheless, the weight of evidence suggested to the British that Langmuir had blundered.

The many advocates of weather control in Britain, emboldened by Langmuir's claims of statistically significance success, had a difficult time getting government to take them seriously. Rainmaking came off as a flight of fancy, as the following exchange in the House of Commons reveals:

MR. ASSHETON: Has my hon. friend thought of the appalling responsibilities that would fall upon any Minister who had to decide whether it was to rain or not on a particular place?

MR. MOLSON: I have no doubt at all that this is a problem which will present itself at some time in the future, but at the present time we are still quite unable to make rain fall or to prevent it from falling where it does.

MR. MIKARDO: Will the hon. gentleman advise the Lord President that future experiments should be concentrated into periods when Test matches are being played?

MR. MOLSON: I am afraid that in the nature of scientific experiments it is difficult to limit experiments to the time when these sporting events are taking place.

MR. HOLLIS: Even though it may seem that there is a good deal too much rain in London and Nottingham, there are other parts of the country where there is not sufficient rain. If my hon. friend has any to dispose of, will he put some of it in my garden?[18]

Such jokes led only to ridicule for rainmaking research, not funding.

The British Isles soon were visited by entrepreneurial Americans who promised to change the weather. Irving Krick, heralded by the *Daily Mail* as the "King of Rainmakers," came to London in 1954 promising to increase rainfall in the Thames Estuary. Warning that global freshwater supplies were shrinking, Krick confidently claimed that he and his team could make it rain, despite the naysayers, and that he could forecast the weather six months in advance. The newspaper hailed him as the man with whom the generals had consulted prior to the Normandy invasion. One reporter added to his mystique with the following description: "Meeting him in his three-roomed suite, I was surprised when he asked me if it was snowing. I told him it was a fine, dry night. But as I left the hotel sleet was pelting down along the Strand."[19]

As in the United States, in Britain these rainmakers had few friends among professional meteorologists. Sir David Brunt, the most prominent of these professionals, heaped scorn upon the rainmaking enthusiasm in the United States. Because he was the principal government advisor on such matters, Britain held back its enthusiasm for weather control. Rainmakers such as Krick stretched their claims, meteorologists believed, persuading farmers to pay for their services. Indeed they had begun major businesses, heading to arid lands in Israel, Spain, and Italy and bringing small amounts of precipitation with them. They used statistics to show how their methods of cloud seeding produced conclusive results. Brunt and other meteorologists did not believe that these entrepreneurs could make enough rain to be economically important—other than to themselves. Despite occasional interest by military officers, members of Parliament, and even the prime minister, professional meteorologists routinely shot down suggestions for investing significant funds in rainmaking research. According to one official, the view could be summarized as such: "Trust the scientist and beware of people with something to sell."[20]

Rainmaking in the United States could not be halted so easily. As a way of adopting an air of scientific respectability, advocates of rainmaking transformed themselves into proponents of "weather modification." In a concession to these upstart scientists, military leaders, and hopeful farmers, US president Dwight Eisenhower appointed a high-level government committee to assess the question. Doing so lent weather modification the respect that it needed. The US military clearly was pressing forward. When scientists like Langmuir promised breakthroughs in manipulating the environment, military officers opened their wallets.[21]

In Britain, Member of Parliament Geoffrey de Freitas pointed to the American committee as a model for what Britain might do. He complained about the "music-hall joke" approach that British politicians thus far had used, treating rainmaking as a topic of ridicule. Weather modification was serious, he said in a 1954 parliamentary debate. Water and food shortages surely would afflict Britain in the coming years, and it was the government's duty to look into all solutions.[22] Moreover, de Freitas argued, Britain might be in a particularly advantageous position to use weather modification for war. A great amount of northern Europe's rain came from weather systems blowing first over the British Isles. "It is a terrible thing to contemplate," he said, "although it is no more terrible than the atomic bomb—depriving our European neighbours of rain in war for military purposes." Nevertheless, he said, it was the government's duty to explore the possibility.[23]

The disputes about rainmaking in the United States and Britain touched a nerve in the scientific community. They brought to light questions about tampering with the processes of nature. The rainmakers saw themselves doing a service—for the good of crops and possibly, as de Freitas suggested, for military strategy. Others feared unintended consequences, as in the case of the Red River catastrophe. But most meteorologists, working principally for weather agencies in the United States and Europe, hesitated to entertain the notion that human actions could have any discernible influence on the forces of nature. Man was simply too puny, compared with the vast energies of solar radiation, air masses, and storms. Unwilling to accept the claims of the scientific and entrepreneurial rainmakers, professional meteorologists held tenaciously to the view that far-reaching regional—to say nothing of global—effects of human actions were highly improbable.

Meteorologists thus had some experience defending this view—that man's powers were inconsequential—when it came under serious assault in 1954. For two and a half months, beginning on March 1, 1954, the United States government conducted a major series of hydrogen bomb tests, on the Bikini and Enewetok atolls in the Pacific Ocean. Although the United States had used the Pacific Proving Grounds previously, its tests had been limited to fission bombs, similar to the ones dropped on Hiroshima and Nagasaki during the war. It tested its first hydrogen bomb there in 1952, yielding an explosion nearly a thousand times that of the earlier bombs— measured in megatons rather than kilotons. Just over a year later, the Americans were back, ready to set off a whole series of hydrogen bombs. This was known as Operation Castle. The first shot, called Bravo, was the most widely known because of its role in contaminating the Japanese fishing boat *Fukuryu Maru* with radioactive debris and igniting the global debates about nuclear fallout. But in fact there were six explosions in the Pacific that spring, most of which turned out to be larger than expected, and all but one of which were measured in megatons rather than kilotons.

Revelations that the Bravo shot had been much bigger than expected— suggesting that scientists were not in control—led to questions about the hydrogen bomb's effects on global weather systems. Suspicious observers were emboldened by the warnings of chemist Frederick Soddy, the Nobel laureate who had gained fame in the first decades of the century with Ernest Rutherford by identifying the decay series of radioactive elements. Soddy believed that, just as factory smoke caused London's thick smog "pea-soupers," nuclear facilities "throw up many pounds of radium into the air every day. The atmosphere is ionized, and this is bound to affect the weather."[24] The flurry of hydrogen bomb tests in 1954, combined with es- pecially abnormal global weather conditions that year, coalesced into a widespread suspicion that the bombs might be disrupting weather and climate on a global scale.

Such suspicions emerged frequently in newspapers. Complaining about "every weather freak rolled into one disenchanted summer," Alan Dick of the *Daily Herald* opined that 1954 had been Britain's worst year for weather in living memory. It was a strangely cold summer, with tempera- tures on some August days dipping below those of the previous Decem- ber. He wrote of an uncommonly wet summer, not just in England but worldwide, with widespread flooding in Ceylon, India, North America, and in several European countries. Hurricane season in the United States had storms creeping much farther north than usual, and a massive typhoon struck Japan, killing some 1,600 people and destroying hundreds of ships. Dick wrote:

> Even meteorologists are puzzled. They used to say "The weather has always been funny. There have been other years like this." *Now they are not so sure.* Some say it could be atomic explosions. They recall that volcanic ash eruptions made a muddle of the weather in 1912, 1902, 1885, 1816, and 1784—so why not hydrogen ash in 1954?[25]

Neither the meteorologists nor the nuclear physicists gave credence to such speculation, but journalists continued to suggest it. One article included a map of the world, with text boxes revealing the strange weather patterns on every continent except Antarctica. In the center of the map, emerging from the Pacific Ocean, was a giant mushroom cloud with a question mark imprinted upon it.[26]

In the United States, the 1954 hurricane season indeed had been bizarre. It had not been the worst year for intensity or number of storms, but the three major storms to do serious damage to the continental United States all had struck the Northeast, rather than the Southeast or Gulf Coast. Such northerly landings were not unheard of, but to have three of them concentrated in one year might have suggested an unprecedented climatic disturbance. Meteorologists denied this possibility, though they did not know whether such northerly landings should be expected as "normal" in the future. The *New York Times* reported, "What this equivocal answer boils down to is this: that [storms] Carol, Edna, and Hazel did not visit the North because of any fundamental change in the weather or in wind patterns." The preferred explanation was that the prevailing westerly winds, which usually push storms east, were so choppy that the storms were able to head due north. What had allowed such northerly movement? "This last summer, for unknown reasons (but definitely not because of atomic bomb or hydrogen bomb explosions) the undulations have been choppy . . ."[27]

The professional meteorologists did not have the answers, but they adamantly refused to entertain any connection to the weapons tests. As powerful as such tests were, meteorologists insisted, they still were small compared to the forces of nature. Still, they could not ignore the anomalous weather. Aside from hurricanes, there were record numbers of tornadoes in 1953 and 1954. The United States had conducted 11 atomic tests, most of them larger than the Hiroshima bomb, at the Nevada Proving

Ground in 1953, as part of Operation Upshot-Knothole. D. Lee Harris, speaking for the US Weather Bureau at the annual meeting of the American Meteorological Society, admitted in 1954 that there seemed to be a coincidence between these tests and the record number of tornadoes in the United States in 1953 (532 total) and so far in 1954 (over 600). But he insisted that it was purely happenstance and that improvements in reporting were likely the cause.[28]

Harris and colleague Lester Machta soon published a more comprehensive analysis of the links between bombs and weather in the journal *Science*. Other than local events—like rainfall immediately following a blast—Harris and Machta wrote that nuclear tests had no conclusive effects on the weather. They acknowledged a conflict, however, between observation and theory. Especially for tornadoes, there had been a clear rise in the years of the Upshot-Knothole tests. But in a survey of meteorological organizations in the United States, Harris and Machta found that no one thought the explosions themselves had a serious effect. A few professionals admitted the possibility of other impacts—that radioactive debris could act as a cloud-seeding agent, or that the increased ionization of the air might disrupt the properties of the atmosphere, or that radioactive dust might block solar radiation. Harris and Machta wrote judiciously: "We cannot, with our present knowledge of meteorology, dismiss the remote possibility that the atmosphere is so unstable that some small impulse such as that given by an atomic explosion could produce a weather change that might otherwise never take place." But based on existing meteorological theory and the survey of meteorologists, they judged that the chances were quite small.[29]

Even the most conservative newspapers could not resist mentioning the allegation that nuclear tests had caused global weather anomalies. Britain's *Financial Times* noted soberly that the hurricanes and storms in the Americas and in East Asia had cost Britain in excess of $100 million. But it added that the weather had nothing to do with hydrogen bomb testing. Rather, as the American C. H. Smiley pointed out on the pages of *Nature*, the strange weather was likely due to strong atmospheric tidal forces. Smiley predicted that 1955 would be the final year of these strong forces and that they would be followed by four years in which, as the *Financial Times* phrased it, "the weather will be more friendly." The newspaper reminded its readers that even hydrogen bomb energies were minuscule compared with atmospheric tides.[30]

National weather service officials in the United States and Britain cast aside allegations of the unintended effects of their nations' weapons tests.

Sir Graham Sutton, director of Britain's Meteorological Office, wrote in *Nature* that the energy released in a hydrogen bomb was insignificant, equivalent to that of a small depression in the atmosphere.[31] Leading the US Weather Bureau's dismissive tone was the chief of its Scientific Services Division, Harry Wexler. In a 1955 statement before the US Congress's Joint Committee on Atomic Energy, Wexler relegated the whole question to the general human tendency—"from time immemorial"—to find causes for the weather in human actions. He observed that "the variety of weather changes is equaled only by man's inventiveness in trying to explain them." He pointed out that in recent years the Weather Bureau had noticed a "changing complexion" in the letters it received from the general public, indicating a sharp increase in concern about the large-scale effects of nuclear weapons tests. But as Harris and Machta had shown, Wexler advised the congressmen, there was no theoretical reason to expect such results, and the observational evidence was inconclusive.[32]

Wexler also chaired the committee on meteorology for the National Academy of Sciences' study of the biological effects of atomic radiation, which was published in 1956. Although the meteorological report was concerned principally with the problem of nuclear fallout, it repeated Wexler's earlier dismissive attitudes about weather, saying that "since the beginning of time" humans had looked for evidence that man was influencing the weather. As yet, Wexler's committee stated, no statistically significant changes in the weather had occurred in the past decade. As for the connection between nuclear tests and weather, they dubbed it simply "unlikely."[33] Responding to the repeated suggestions—not to say allegations—that nuclear testing was affecting weather systems, the World Meteorological Organization (WMO) convened its own group of experts to examine the question. Echoing the sentiments already expressed by meteorologists in the United States and Europe, the WMO noted that there was no conclusive evidence linking the admittedly strange weather to nuclear explosions. Both groups, the American one and the international one, attributed the rise in weather anomalies to better reporting.[34]

Not everyone was swayed by these reports, as authoritative as they were. "Why was the summer so bad?" John Davy of the *Observer* asked. "The most popular scapegoat has been the H-Bomb."[35] In Britain, *The Times* referred to the American report as "almost deprecating in its approach."[36] Within the government, high-ranking officials winced at how the Americans tried to make people feel foolish for even considering the idea. R. N. Quirk, the secretary of the office of the Lord President of the

Council, complained: "I was always rather put off by the pontifical way in which leading meteorologists dismissed as 'impossible' the popular suggestion that nuclear explosions might have an effect on the weather." To Quirk, who oversaw the government's efforts in scientific research and education, there seemed to be enough uncertainty to justify concern. Writing to science advisors within the British defense establishment, he cautioned against taking Wexler's word as gospel. After all, even if fission explosions in Nevada seemed insignificant, the much larger explosions in the Pacific might introduce enough extra radiation to the upper atmosphere to have the same kinds of effects as those caused by variations in sunspots. No one doubted that tiny changes in sunspot activity could cause storms, so why regard the persistent radiation from hydrogen bombs with such skepticism?[37]

Concerns about unintentional changes to the earth's weather and climate followed the ebb and flow of atmospheric weapons testing. Another year for anomalous weather worldwide was 1958. That was the year that President Eisenhower announced a moratorium on nuclear weapons testing, and both Britain and the Soviet Union respected it as a measure of good faith in the intensifying arms race. But before it could take effect, all three countries rushed to conduct as many tests as possible. As the latter part of its "Grapple" series of tests dating from early 1957, Britain made five tests of hydrogen bombs at Christmas Island, its Pacific test site. The United States alone detonated 35 bombs in the Pacific in 1958 and 37 in Nevada. In addition, the United States secretly conducted Operation Argus, a three-bomb series in the South Atlantic Ocean designed to test explosions at high altitude (about 300 miles high), using rockets launched from a ship.[38] The Soviet Union tested 34 bombs at its Novaya Zemlya site and in Kazakhstan, at its Semipalatinsk site, more than double its number of tests in 1957.[39]

Operation Argus—the series of high-altitude bomb tests secretly conducted in the South Atlantic by the United States—illustrated just how much human actions could affect the atmosphere. Although it was a secret test, the satellite used to collect atmospheric data had been launched as part of the International Geophysical Year of 1957–58. By international accord, all IGY data was supposed to be shared among all the participants. Had the US government continued to keep the existence of the project a secret past the data-sharing period, it would have broken the agreement. In the end, the *New York Times*, which had learned about it much earlier, published stories about it in March 1959, after some key officials signaled their desire to make it public.

On the front page of the *New York Times*, journalist Walter Sullivan broke the story first, revealing that the United States "drew a thin curtain of radiation around the earth," enveloping the entire inhabited area of the world "for a period whose duration is still secret." As Sullivan reported it, scientists were calling it the "greatest experiment of all time." It had started because of a discovery by State University of Iowa physicist James Van Allen, made from data collected by the first American satellites in early 1958. One particular instrument, a Geiger counter used to detect radiation, had appeared to fail at high altitudes. Van Allen predicted the existence of a massive belt of radiation that completely swamped the instrument. This radiation did not dissipate, but was trapped by the earth's magnetic field. Soon confirmed by other satellites, scientists began to call them the "Van Allen belts," or the "Van Allen radiation." Van Allen postulated that most of the radiation had come from the sun, perhaps released by solar flares and then trapped by the earth's magnetic field.

Operation Argus was not designed merely to observe these belts but to explode atomic bombs in them. Sullivan, who had covered most of the IGY stories for the *New York Times*, glorified it as a scientific triumph:

> What made the experiment particularly dramatic was that its results had been predicted. . . . It has been said that geophysics is a science "in which the earth is the laboratory and nature conducts the experiments." In this case the space surrounding this planet was the laboratory, but the experiment was conducted by man. The yield of each bomb was small, but it was enough to enable the scientists to follow the results with precision.[40]

The bombs had created artificial auroras, visible by airplane. They had also made the belts bigger. As Sullivan reported so cheerily, man now seemed capable of far-reaching experiments, using the entire earth and its surrounding space as a laboratory.

Van Allen, who had designed the Argus experiments, was hailed as a hero in the Cold War competition with the Soviet Union. If scientists were concerned about the radiation belt at all, it was because of the added danger of radiation exposure to humans who might soon travel into space. Published illustrations of the radiation belts showed them surrounding all of the earth except for the poles. *Time* magazine speculated, "Obvious conclusion: the space ports of the future may have to be in far northern Canada or Antarctica, where men can soar into space through the escape zones over the magnetic poles, thus eluding the lethal hazards of the Van Allen belt."[41] Soon *Time* put Van Allen's face on the magazine's cover, with the words "Space and the Radiation Belt." Because the Soviets had been the first to launch a satellite with Sputnik and to put a living creature, a dog, into space with Sputnik II, the United States was striking back with its own achievement. In a long profile of the scientist, *Time* reported that Van Allen never expected to find himself "a key figure in the cold war's competition for prestige."[42]

After years of scientists arguing that human actions were impotent in the face of nature's energies, Operation Argus provided evidence to the contrary. The radiation generated by the blasts had been trapped in the earth's magnetic field, spreading out and encircling the earth in a matter of an hour or more. This alteration to the composition of the earth's magnetic field might last for days, scientists speculated, but also could last for years. Here was irrefutable evidence that energies produced by humans could have a discernible, long-lasting effect on the atmosphere.

When the weather turned sour in the latter part of 1958, the irresistible connection to weapons testing returned. Hurricanes once again landed farther north in the United States, one missing New York City by a few hundred miles.[43] Newspapers called the year's weather quirky, puzzling, and baffling. Reflecting on downpours across the Atlantic, the *New York Times* reported:

> "Gorblimey, 'ow it rynes," said an elderly Cockney barrow boy in a sheltered doorway watching the downpour drench his fruit cart and drive away business. "It's all them 'oydrogen explosions, that's wot it is."[44]

Although meteorologists were in the habit of dismissing this possibility, Indiana University meteorologist George H. T. Kimble called it an "unanswered question."[45]

Reflecting on the apparent coincidence of the rise of bomb tests and of inclement weather, Canadian geography professor W. H. Parker wrote to *The Times* of London that "there has never before in recorded history been such a combination and concentration of intemperate conditions." He lamented that meteorologists treated with disdain the mere suggestion of a connection to nuclear weapons, lumping them in with earlier concerns about gunpowder and wireless telegraphy. Parker pointed out that Nevada atomic testing often had been followed by "lurid skies and thunderstorms" in Canada. He noted also that "very peculiar cloud formations" had been sighted both in Europe and in North America. Meanwhile the professional meteorologist, he inveighed, "has his eyes fixed on his synoptic charts and he is too obsessed with his isobars, which are expressions of effect, to consider causes." And yet the evidence of causation abounded: recent bomb tests had so affected the upper atmosphere that intercontinental wireless communication had been disrupted, suggesting to Parker a probable connection between weather disturbances and the radioactivity in the ionosphere. Radioactivity traveled far and wide, coming down not only as invisible "fallout" but as slightly radioactive rain. He asked: might radioactive clouds have a connection to the atmosphere's turbulence? Parker argued that the months prior to the moratorium had been unparalleled in the violence of weather worldwide.[46]

Predictably, Parker's letter provoked defensive commentary from leading meteorologists. It was true that recent heavy rains in England had "provoked some local emotion," the University of London's Gordon Manley wrote, but the recent variations in weather seemed perfectly in line with the normal range of events. Parker's grand claims, Manley wrote, were "nonsense." A former president of the Royal Meteorological Society, he took umbrage at Parker's characterization of meteorologists as dismissive and prone to ridicule. He contended that meteorologists were in fact devoted to "lives of pondering" and, unlike most people, had 300 years of recorded data to guide their views. As for the statement about "never before in recorded history," Manley suggested instead that never before had there been so much weather recorded at all. The recent rise in weather anomalies was likely due to increased reporting.[47]

Meteorologists such as Manley had begun by suggesting that the evidence was not conclusive, but in time they adopted a more adamant, hostile pose toward those who dared suggest a connection between weather variation and nuclear tests. These were acts of God, not man. Despite his defense of his profession, even Manley adopted ridicule as the favored tool. He wrote that of course there were lurid skies after an atomic test, just as the impact of bat on ball in a cricket match usually led to rain.

At least one meteorologist pointed out that such emphatic denials by the professionals probably were counterproductive. Writing in the *Times*, Peter Ball noted that "it is time that our school of meteorologists should take their heads out of the sand and, short of experiment or other *definite* proof to the contrary, give the benefit of the doubt to the worst possibility." There might not be enough evidence to make the link, but equally so, there was not enough evidence to deny the possibility. Why take such a definitive stand? Ball pointed out that meteorologists already believed humans were having an effect on the climate. The slight warming in polar regions over the past century, he said, was undeniable, and it most likely was a result of humans burning up fossil fuels and releasing carbon dioxide to the atmosphere. Why was it so hard to accept that another human activity might have an effect as well? Was it not possible that an increase in radioactivity would upset the norm in the upper atmosphere, "to cause a greater frequency of freak weathers, nay, cataclysms which might now be called 'physically impossible'—beyond the figment of imagination?"[48]

Others wrote in to *The Times* to offer thoughts on the matter, often expressing sympathy for Parker and distaste for Manley's arrogant and dogmatic tone. The shortest, and most pointed, observed simply: "Would it be too unkind if a plain man suggested that he could have more confidence in the dogmatic assertions of meteorologists if their daily forecasts were a bit more accurate?"[49]

The informal nuclear testing moratorium after 1958 momentarily eased the tensions surrounding the debate over extreme weather. In the meantime, France conducted its first nuclear test in early 1960, to the annoyance of the other nuclear powers, who were keeping to the moratorium. The following year, the Soviet Union too broke the moratorium and soon shocked the world with an extraordinarily large blast, dubbed "Tsar Bomba." Detonated on the large island of Novaya Zemlya, the bomb's magnitude was staggering, estimated at some 58 megatons. Even if the later downward revision of this figure is accepted, Tsar Bomba was equivalent to about 4,000 of the bombs that destroyed Hiroshima. Many times the size of any American test, it was an unprecedented display of power.

After Tsar Bomba, nuclear testing returned with a vengeance. As diplomats attempted to come to an agreement to cease such testing permanently, not only because of the possible health effects of fallout but also as a kind of arms control, atomic energy establishments ramped up their plans. In 1962, the year prior to the Limited Test Ban Treaty, the most nuclear testing yet occurred. The United States led the way with Operation Dominic, the most extensive program ever conceived. It included 105 nuclear tests, at both major testing sites (the Nevada Proving Grounds and the Pacific Proving Grounds), involving explosions in both the kiloton and megaton range. These included further high-altitude tests in space, affecting the Van Allen Belts—five blasts in all, this time in the megaton range. One of them, the Starfish Prime shot, created a sensation in Hawaii

as its flash filled the sky and hundreds of street lights lost power. The Soviet Union conducted 138 tests in 1961 and 1962, with one in 1962 about
half the size of Tsar Bomba—still much larger than any American test.

The winter of 1962–63 proved to be one of the most severe in recorded
history. An Arctic air mass chilled the East Coast of the United States. As
far south as Atlanta, Georgia, temperatures reached –2 degrees Fahren-
heit. In Kentucky the temperatures plummeted to –21 degrees. "Bitter winter weather," the *New York Times* reported, "plagued the nation . . . from
parched Southern California to the ice-jammed Niagara River." The river
under Niagara Falls was frozen solid for some 13 miles, forcing Canadians
and Americans to use icebreaker ships. Some areas of the Midwest saw
temperatures of –36 degrees.[50]

Reports of extreme weather came from cities throughout the Northern
Hemisphere. People in the town of Bari—on the "heel" of Italy—were
surprised to have ten inches of snow. Furious gales wreaked havoc on
ships in the Mediterranean. Boats were frozen into the Rhine River, and
most of Europe endured uncharacteristic levels of snow and ice. The cold
spell lasted from December through February, freezing rivers and crippling hydroelectric power stations. Slightly less cold weather did not
help—it meant snowstorms, rains, and floods. In the Far East, freezing
winds from Siberia brought large amounts of snow to Japan, leading to
the deaths of 20 people in an avalanche. Dozens of people died in what
The Times called "one of the worst snowstorms in Japan's history," leaving
entire towns and villages under 15 feet of snow.[51]

Just 11 days into the cold spell, the *New York Times* reported more than
800 deaths in Europe due to accidents, exposure, and asphyxiation. At an
airport near Bonn, Germans resorted to using military flamethrowers to
thaw the ice in early January.[52] Over the next month or so, Europe
descended into a veritable Ice Age. In Britain the season entered cultural
memory as the "Big Freeze of '63." It began snowing on Boxing Day
(December 26), innocuously enough, but then it kept snowing. The
Thames and other rivers froze over. Conditions were so poor that relief
operations often were hampered, and Royal Air Force helicopters simply
had to drop supplies into marooned villages.

The winter was so appallingly bad that it stretched the bounds of vari-
ability. The *New York Times* put it thus:

Weather, as the meteorologists say, is always abnormal since there
are no norms, but only averages. This winter, however, has thus far

been abnormally abnormal and already has made a place for itself in the records throughout the northern hemisphere. Spokesmen for the weather bureau insist that basic weather patterns have not really changed.[53]

But there were heretics who said otherwise. Irving Krick, the Caltech meteorologist who had turned into a famous rainmaker, attributed the intense weather to the Van Allen Belts. Although this belt of high-level radiation occurred naturally, its intensity had been increased enormously by the detonation of nuclear blasts at high altitude. Krick believed that this had a similar effect on the earth's weather as high solar activity such as flares and sunspots. The increased radiation in the Van Allen belts had intensified the Arctic storms and driven them farther south than usual.[54]

Although many disagreed with his conclusion, Krick was not wrong that American nuclear testing had significantly changed the amount of radiation in the Van Allen belts. The Atomic Energy Commission and the Defense Department admitted as much in 1962. They had not expected the July 1962 detonation to create such an intense and long-lasting amount of radiation. James Van Allen pointed out in August that the explosion had actually created a new belt, to complement the two that occurred naturally. Dubbed the "Little Van Allen Belt," it extended the field of radiation to lower altitudes. Initially predicted to fade within weeks or months, the Defense Department disclosed in September 1962 that the increased radiation in the belts was likely to persist for many years to come.[55]

By the early 1960s, it had become impossible to deny mankind's ability to make significant alterations to the physical systems in and around the earth. After nearly two decades of dismissing as fantastical the dreams of rainmaking and weather disruptions, scientists began to look seriously at weather and climate modification. It seemed possible, after all, for man to compete with the forces of nature. And yet meteorologists would continue to deny connections between bomb tests and weather. In addition, they argued fervently that the promises made by Krick, Langmuir, and others were spurious. The vast physical systems of the earth, they felt, were not easily changed.

The ability to alter such systems had become much more than an academic question. Because man's genuine impact on weather and climate seemed an unsolved puzzle, purposeful climate change assumed legitimacy as a research program for potential weapons systems. Like nuclear weapons, biological weapons, and radiological weapons, weather and climate control seemed to be very promising weapons of total war. Scientists working with military partners saw potential in using hydrogen bombs as triggers for momentous, cataclysmic events. This did not mean that they disagreed with meteorologists. Rather, despite imagining and planning catastrophes, they rarely saw these as permanent. The earth was resilient, they increasingly believed, giving mankind free rein to try extraordinary manipulations on a scale that was limited only by scientists' imaginations. This meant that, as in the case of biological weapons, the United States and its allies would need to find a place for environmental manipulation in their war plans. Doing so also compelled scientists to develop strong views about the extent of their homelands' vulnerability to environmental threats.

6

Wildcat Ideas for Environmental Warfare

This kind of warfare has the peculiarity that it could look like our image of nuclear war, or could be so subtle that the "weapons" and "battles" are hard to identify.
—Weapons Group, NATO Von Kármán Committee (1961)

As one who has witnessed the horror and the lingering sadness of war, as one who knows that another war could utterly destroy this civilization which has been so slowly and painfully built over thousands of years, I wish I could say tonight that a lasting peace is in sight.
—PRESIDENT DWIGHT EISENHOWER, in his farewell speech, January 17, 1961

THE YEARS BETWEEN the first hydrogen bomb tests and the Limited Test Ban Treaty in 1963 saw more than just increased anxiety about the effects of nuclear testing on weather. They also saw increased interest in large-scale, purposeful environmental modification. Most climate modification enthusiasts spoke of increasing global temperatures, in the hopes that this would increase the quantity of cultivated land and make for fairer weather. Some suggested blackening deserts or snowy areas, to increase absorption of radiation. Covering large areas with carbon dust, so the theory went, would raise temperatures. Alternatively, if several hydrogen bombs were exploded underwater, they might evaporate seawater and create an ice cloud that would block the escape of radiation. Meteorologist Harry Wexler had little patience for those who wanted to add weather and climate modification to the set of tools in man's possession. But by 1958 even he acknowledged that serious proposals for massive changes, using nuclear weapons as tools, were inevitable. Like most professional meteorologists, in the past he had dismissed the idea that hydrogen bombs had affected the weather. But with the prospect of determined experiments designed to bring about such changes, he warned of "the unhappy situation of the cure being worse than the ailment."[1]

Whatever one might have thought about the wisdom of tinkering with the weather in peacetime, the manipulation of nature on a vast scale for military purposes seemed to be a perfectly legitimate application of scientific knowledge. While planning a total war against the Soviet Union, every avenue begged for exploration. This chapter explores how the scientific advisors of America's key allies in NATO saw the alliance fighting in the future. Numerous ideas for creating catastrophic events through natural processes were presented, especially using hydrogen bombs as triggers. In these discussions, held as early as 1960, top scientists debated the fundamental environmental question—can humans have a long-term effect on the global environment?

The desire for novel military technology seemed especially urgent by the early 1960s. Although officially part of the International Geophysical Year, the Soviet Union's launch of Sputnik in October 1957 had clear military ramifications. Not only did it begin the space race but it also took the arms race to a new stage that included communications satellites and intercontinental ballistic missiles. The launch of Sputnik made the world seem smaller and made the most far-fetched visions of the future seem possible. The gee-whiz, Buck Rogers feel of the immediate postwar years returned. But this wave of technological enthusiasm was darker, because instead of coming on the tide of a war victory, it came as a foreboding new competition. For years the Americans had been preparing for the missile age, gathering data on the atmosphere and on the earth's gravity over the poles. The Soviets clearly had kept the pace. Sputnik served as a justification for a vast array of projects to use scientific knowledge to tamper with nature on a large scale.

Reinforcing the sense of urgency, President Eisenhower's special committee on weather modification submitted its final report in January 1958, just months after Sputnik's launch. The committee's chairman, retired Navy Captain Howard T. Orville, said at a press conference that he suspected that the Soviets already had begun a large, secret program on weather control. Despite routine dismissals of the idea throughout the decade by meteorologists, the high-level committee ranked weather control ahead of hydrogen bombs and satellites in military significance. Orville urged the government to support research on controlling large-scale weather systems, not just rainmaking. He further suggested that finding ways to manipulate the heat balance between the sun and earth might be the key to weather and climate control. The earth already had been heated up by man's efforts, by introducing carbon dioxide into the atmosphere through the burning of fossil fuels. This carbon dioxide helped to trap the heat and create, as the *New York Times* put it, a "greenhouse effect." It might be possible to harness this greenhouse effect. "If such steps are feasible," journalist John Finney reported, "then New York City might be put under a few hundred feet of ice or a few hundred feet of water depending on whether the temperature was raised or lowered."[2]

Rumors spread quickly about scientists in the United States and Soviet Union experimenting with unprecedented tools for controlling nature. Were the Soviets planning to dam the Bering Strait? Were the Americans able to steer storms? Naysayers pointed out that meteorologists could not even predict naturally occurring weather, so how could anyone control it? One author opined in the *New York Times*, "For would it not be foolish for anyone to talk of controlling an intricate piece of apparatus until he knew precisely how it worked?"[3] After the report of Eisenhower's special committee was made public, scientists in allied countries received strange, sheepish letters from their defense establishments, asking if the latest rumors about American research could be true. For example, a British Air Ministry scientific advisor, E. V. Truefitt, presented his countryman, oceanographer George Deacon, with "one or two questions which have come up in odd conversations." He called them "wild cat" ideas that he did not really take seriously, yet they appeared to be in discussion in the United States. Despite his instinct that they could not possibly be real, he felt obligated to run them by a competent man of science.

One of the ideas was to melt the polar ice cap by exploding nuclear weapons on it, thus raising the global sea level. The Soviets might be considering it, so the rumor went, to drown cities in the United States and Western Europe. Another idea was to change ocean currents or temperatures to interfere with an enemy's climate and food production. Truefitt had no idea how assess an ocean-initiated climate change, but he had made a rough calculation to determine what was needed to melt the polar ice cap. He believed that it would take about a million tons of fissile material to melt enough to raise sea level by 30 feet. "This is a large amount of fissile material whichever way you look at it," he wrote to Deacon, "and consequently my guess is that it is not the kind of project that even the Americans would embark on under the influence of Sputniks."[4]

The truth was that the immediate post-Sputnik years had a peculiar air, both of desperation and of opportunity. Doors were wide open to a range of technological possibilities. Nearly anything that was technically feasible made it to the highest levels of discussion. For starters, that meant revisiting the questions surrounding biological, chemical, and radiological weapons. But it also sparked discussion of the ambitious, the horrendous, and the quirky. Like wildcatters exploring for oil, American scientists grasped desperately around them, striving to find the next weapon of the future.

There were several post-Sputnik efforts to push the limits of the "possible," to explore exotic ideas that might prove decisive 5, 10, or 20 years into the future. Some actions to direct this scientific work were high profile and public. President Eisenhower created a science advisory committee to guide the course of American technology and ensure that the Americans did not fall behind the Soviet Union. This President's Science Advisory Committee (PSAC) also existed to rein in some of the wilder ideas, to avoid wasteful spending.[5] Other brain trusts, often dominated by physicists with expertise in nuclear affairs, sprang up behind closed doors to advise military establishments. One of these was "JASON," an elite group of scientists who got together during the summer months to assess major scientific and technological problems of military significance. Paid by government contract through several different bodies throughout its existence, "the Jasons," as they called themselves, were drawn from the cream of civilian academic science. Despite their outsider status, the Jasons gained the respect and trust of officials in the Defense Department and the armed services, and their advice often revolutionized military thinking during the nuclear era.[6]

Sputnik did not just spark new scientific projects, however. It also revolutionized military strategy, making it grimmer than ever. The American and Soviet air forces realized they were going to have to rethink the basic notion of national vulnerability. No longer could the Air Force's Strategic Air Command count on scrambling bombers and flying them over the North Pole. Most of the war's damage would have been done before bombers left the Western Hemisphere.

More than that, as a secret National Academy of Sciences group advised the Air Force in 1958, the range of possible wars soon would expand exponentially. Conflicts were going to become both more total and more limited at the same time. On the one hand, the United States was losing its ability to incapacitate enemy forces. In practice that meant that the most attractive targets all over the world would be centers of population—cities—rather than armies or airfields. Making an effective attack against enemy military forces seemed a dwindling prospect in an era when missiles could be put into hardened silos, mobile rocket units, or submarines patrolling the oceans. Cities, by contrast, would be ripe for plucking. "Weapon yields, delivery accuracies, and force level requirements for city destruction are modest," these scientists concluded, while attacking heavily fortified bunkers would require large and accurate payloads. That meant that finding ways of maximizing civilian death would assume an even greater importance than it already had.[7]

On the other hand, nuclear parity would make full-blown conflict less likely, meaning that all of the armed services would have to reorient themselves back to conventional warfare. As RAND Corporation game theorists had long feared, the atomic bomb was a wasting asset—and the window of opportunity to "win" decisively in a war against the Soviet Union had passed. By the late 1950s, the new orthodoxy in strategic thinking accepted that the Soviet Union was committed to avoiding a nuclear holocaust and that it intended to encourage "brushfire" wars instead. Small wars like those in Malaya and Korea would become more common. As the 1960s dawned, military strategists wondered about the fate of Vietnam, which the French had failed to hold. By treaty the country had split between North and South. Should the communist North Vietnamese invade, would the Americans consider using nuclear weapons? Some may have argued that nuclear bombs were America's answer to the human population imbalance against, say, people in China or Southeast Asia. But new studies at RAND had dismissed this possibility, showing that nuclear weapons would be ineffective against guerrilla forces in Southeast Asia and would visit enormous collateral damage upon friendly population centers. So the military would need to let go of President Eisenhower's preferred strategy of massive retaliation as America's basic posture.[8]

The Air Force would have to stop relying on aircraft designed purely to deliver nuclear weapons. Instead, it would need to find ways of fighting men, tanks, rockets, and airplanes—all without nuclear weapons. A decade earlier the Navy had bitterly opposed the Air Force's claims that the era of aircraft carriers and battleships had ended. Now it seemed that the Navy had been right. The new conventional wisdom, which President Kennedy (a former Navy man) soon would establish as the doctrine of "flexible response," was that the nations with the greatest range, flexibility, and cleverness in weapons systems would stand strongest. This meant conducting research on weapons at various levels of destruction up to and including nuclear bombs and being creative about their uses.[9]

It also meant combining modes of warfare across scientific disciplines. Geophysical and biological knowledge might be united, for example, in developing dispersal mechanisms for pathogens. In trying to achieve large area coverage, one might fall back on cloud-seeding techniques—with the important difference that the "seeds" would not be silver iodide to cause rain but pathogens to spread disease far and wide. For example, certain phenomena in air masses, such as "Polar Outbreaks" (thrusts of cold air from the poles toward the equator), seemed to have great potential for such seeding, especially given the Soviet Union's meteorological vulnerability from the north.[10]

The post-Sputnik national pall of gloom encouraged American scientists to explore unorthodox weapons, and they left no stone unturned. The US military forged ahead with research on weapons using radiation, particle beams, nuclear energy, and kinetic energy. The Army Chemical Corps even investigated the use of lysergic acid diethylamide (LSD) and cannabis as non-lethal, incapacitating agents. The National Academy of Sciences noted this approvingly in 1958 and suggested that the Air Force begin administering LSD to airmen as soon as possible, to judge whether to add it to the arsenal of chemical weapons.[11]

With so many wide-ranging ideas being vetted, NATO allies worried that the Americans were moving in too many directions at once. It was fine to support science in the United States and to speak grandly about possibly controlling forces of nature—but which ideas could be incorporated into actual NATO war plans? In 1960 NATO members agreed to convene a special group of scientists and military leaders to assess the long-term prospects of war. They wanted to know what would really be feasible by the 1970s, and what was just science fiction.

This kind of science forecasting was not just a matter of intelligent people guessing the future. By 1960 it had a distinguished history of shaping policy, particularly in some parts of the American military establishment. The Air Force, for example, understood in the 1950s that much of its strength relied on continuous research and development (R&D). Toward the end of World War II, General Henry "Hap" Arnold, commander of the then-Army Air Force, famously said that "for twenty years the Air Force was built around pilots, pilots, and more pilots. . . . The next twenty years is going to be built around scientists."[12] Throughout the Cold War, such brain trusts—in think tanks like RAND, secret groups like JASON, and many others—exercised a remarkable influence on policies.

When NATO tried, in 1960, to estimate the next 10 to 15 years of weapons, it enlisted the leadership of Theodore von Kármán, the grand old man of science forecasting. By then he was 79 years old. Born in Hungary, von Kármán had been one of the world's foremost experts in aerodynamics. He even had helped the Austrian military design aircraft during the First World War. In 1929 he came to the United States to head up an aeronautical laboratory at Caltech, helping to kick-start the aviation industry in southern California. Acting as scientific advisor to United States air forces during World War II, von Kármán had initiated a long-term study of air power that amassed some of the best brains in physics and aeronautics. The resultant report, *Where We Stand*, became a road map for postwar air power research. In subsequent years, von Kármán repeated this process with other studies, and in fact he chaired the 1958 secret committee advising the Air Force, under the auspices of the National Academy of Sciences. In 1960 he embarked on a study that would be the capstone of his long career: NATO's attempt to grasp the future face of battle over the entire earth.[13]

Known simply as the Von Kármán Committee, the new group included the chief scientific advisor of each national defense organization in the United States, Britain, Canada, France, and West Germany.[14] With several working groups of scientists under them, they ran the gamut of new weapons in an era of "total war." They included the typical range of military subjects, including aircraft, weaponry, and ships. But they also delved deeply into the implications of the global physical environment, particularly in light of the extraordinary size of thermonuclear weapons, the global reach of ballistic missiles, and the extent of global monitoring begun during the International Geophysical Year.

The buzzword of the IGY had been "synoptic." Taken literally, it meant observing more than one place at the same time—viewing together. The IGY's concept was to take a huge number of observations, spread out over a variety of geophysical disciplines and geographic areas, all within an 18-month period. Doing so would provide a portrait of the earth that was more true and comprehensive than anything ever attempted.

The Von Kármán Committee adopted the word "synoptic" too, but applied it to weapons. Weapons of a "synoptic scale" meant control and domination of whole physical systems. In military shorthand, the word synoptic called to mind vastness, encompassing large portions of the earth—or perhaps all of it. The IGY had brought this idea into military planners' field of vision. But while the IGY was concerned with synoptic-scale measurement, NATO was concerned with synoptic-scale manipulation.

Once they began to meet, the members of the Von Kármán Committee realized that they all agreed on at least one thing: the global observations initiated in the IGY would have to continue indefinitely. The geophysical factors of modern war involved knowledge of an operational environment—in other words, how would the sea, land, or air affect troops and ships? NATO forces needed to be able to operate in any kind of environment. If it was on planet Earth, NATO should be prepared to fight there and win.

In fact the US armed services already were developing environment-specific training centers to give American forces mastery of three classes of extreme conditions: polar, desert, and jungle. Given that the northern polar region was "the only large uncommitted area lying between the world's strongest antagonists," polar operations weighed heavily on defense planners' minds. Already polar and Arctic training centers existed at locations in Greenland, Canada, and in the state of Alaska. The United States also operated a desert warfare center in Yuma, Arizona. Still needed were centers approximating Mediterranean conditions and tropical ones.[15]

To take advantage of the apparent shrinkage of the earth due to ballistic missiles, NATO advisors also pointed out the need to revolutionize the field of geodesy—earth measurement. Mapmakers relied on data taken from a variety of oceanic or terrestrial expeditions, sometimes decades or more old. No one had seen the earth from space, much less taken accurate measurements based on satellites. Intercontinental ballistic missiles would require precision. But NATO literally did not know where the Soviet Union was. "On a world wide scale, we are not sure of the position of North America in relation to the Eurasian continent." Knowledge of anything in the Southern Hemisphere was even less accurate. The only decent data came from the Americas, Western Europe, Japan, and some of the former and current European colonial territories. The Soviets could target the West with accuracy, but the West could not do the same. Any kind of exact targeting of the Soviet Union would prove impossible before satellites could take comprehensive measurements. In the meantime, constant earth measurement from the air would prove essential. Fortunately, international scientific projects were providing that data.[16]

The IGY had convinced scientists and military planners of the usefulness of synoptic data collection. If done in real time, or close to it, data collection could be automated and collected over a large territory, perhaps even globally. Individual scientists might never analyze the vast amounts of data, but the data could be fed into computers in order to monitor and predict environmental conditions. Already the Americans were working on an anti-submarine warfare "environmental prediction system." It collected oceanographic information—to estimate sonar performance—and combined it with meteorological information to predict future oceanographic conditions.

Had the members of the Von Kármán Committee been military historians, there is little doubt about what they would have cast as the "decisive moment" in the history of global strategy. Time and again they called to mind the changes brought about by the advent of earth-orbiting satellites. It would prove to be, they believed, a dividing line between military eras. It promised total monitoring of the global environment, a vision of the future that was pervasive across the range of sciences and military operations. By 1970, these NATO advisors predicted, scientists would be able to identify and track thunderstorms as they occurred all over the entire earth and to keep the earth's radiation under constant surveillance. Old charts would be discarded, in favor of a constantly refreshing set of data beamed down from the heavens. Automated data systems would be necessary to achieve accuracy of measurement and improved forecasting. As the committee put it: "The concept of inaccessible geographical areas is no longer valid—observations over enemy-held, oceanic and uninhabited areas are as easily made as elsewhere." Reliance on existing charts and data, collected laboriously by error-prone humans, rarely uniform from country to country, seemed archaic. New methods of continuous, uniform data collection of the oceans, land, and space would provide the kind of mastery of the global environment that the Von Kármán committee envisioned.[17]

Aside from this unprecedented ability to forecast conditions and improve global accuracy, the NATO science advisors also predicted ambitious, large-scale manipulation of the environment. The brass ring of military geophysics was weather control. Scientists already had achieved modest results in increasing rainfall or dissipating fogs. But these successes required optimal conditions and certainly could not be projected over a large area or from a long distance.[18] But what about climate control?

In a 1956 *Fortune* article, mathematician John von Neumann had suggested that militaries would be able to make large-scale changes to climate. He pointed out various ways to alter oceans and seas. One was to blanket ice sheets with blackening agents, to absorb more light and melt them. If it could be done to Greenland, its ice sheet alone would raise sea levels by about 10 feet "and cause great discomfort to most world ports." Another scheme was to divert the Gulf Stream, which would severely change the climate of Northern Europe. Still another idea was to dam the Bering Strait. Such alterations would have clear, long-term effects on world climate. And these changes seemed possible.[19] Reflecting on von Neumann's predictions, the NATO group believed that an extraordinary tool lay in the hands of military planners: the hydrogen bomb. "It is perhaps true," the committee concluded, "that means presently within man's reach could be employed so as to alter global climate for long periods."[20]

Given the later controversy about the role of carbon dioxide in inducing global climate change, the focus on the hydrogen bomb might seem surprising. But the reason for this was simple. Advised by physicists, the defense establishments of NATO's strongest members believed that in order for "synoptic scale" weapons to be feasible, man had to achieve physical power that was comparable to nature's power. The only tool that seemed likely to provide that was the hydrogen bomb. Although professional meteorologists had insisted that hydrogen bomb tests had not created the extreme winters of 1954, 1958, and 1962, these military advisors were less adamant. They knew that the energies of nature were vast, but felt they might be shaped by man. It seemed that the Soviets were working hard on the problem. Canadian scientists repeated the oft-heard rumor that the Soviets were planning large-scale manipulation of the oceans, along with drastic modification of climate, by damming up the Bering Strait. The Canadians reasoned: surely the Russians had in mind the use of nuclear bombs?[21]

NATO scientists found the prospects of such power over nature intriguing. They called it *environmental warfare*. "This kind of warfare has the peculiarity that it could look like our image of nuclear war, or could be so subtle that the 'weapons' and 'battles' are hard to identify." The enemy might undertake a vast engineering project to change the climate of a whole region, "leading gradually to economic ruin and loss of strength." This could be done even without declaring war.[22]

Once again ecological vulnerability emerged as a crucial area in need of study for military purposes. The NATO science advisors did not yet understand their true vulnerability to what they called "living weapons." But new data were coming in. Since the late 1950s, American engineers had planned to use thermonuclear explosions to excavate a harbor in Alaska—a project dubbed "Plowshare." Beforehand they put together what today might be called an environmental impact statement and discovered that the effect on the Eskimos' diet might not be as negligible as originally assumed. For this and other reasons, the project was scrapped.[23]

But that knowledge had been useful for military thinking. Scientists had traced the pathway of radioactivity through the food chain. NATO scientists now used the example of the Eskimos' ecosystem to argue for more advanced knowledge of ecological warfare. Within that ecosystem, Eskimos lived interdependently with seals, otter, fish, caribou, and plankton. If the plankton were all killed, an Eskimo's ecological community would be utterly destroyed. "At best he would have to move," the group pointed out. "At worst he would die." This kind of thinking could be tailored to particular regions: "The people of Asia depend on rice and a very few other crops. Something like a lethal rice-rust or blight could make life in Asia much more difficult and perhaps untenable."[24]

As a weapon system, ecological links went further than killing—they also promised biological coercion. Destruction of the enemy need not be the goal. Getting rid of plankton, for example, would make the Eskimos' entire food system collapse and force them to be entirely dependent on food supplied from outside the region. To achieve this, toxic agents "may be developed to attack essential links in various ecological chains." The aim would be to shape an existing interdependent web along new lines, "to force the ecology to accept dependence on some crop or animal which cannot live at all in the homeland." Doing this would put the victim in an extremely disadvantageous position, "leading to a gradual loss of power and position and inevitable vassalage."[25]

Von Kármán died shortly after the first of his committee reports was completed. As colleagues remembered his contributions to aeronautics and to scientific advising, his death lent the committee's findings an extraordinary amount of authority within NATO. The reports had the air of a final act of service; the chairman's passing only augmented the committee's importance. With Von Kármán gone, the reports themselves were a foreboding, Cassandra-like vision of the future that military planners could ignore only at their peril. This was especially true of subjects that the committee felt it did not yet understand fully.

Environmental warfare had captured the imagination of the committee but the results had been unsatisfying. It seemed in keeping with the direction of science—toward global, synoptic-scale activities. Yet it was unclear how it might shape weaponry. The experience of the Von Kármán Committee established "environmental warfare" as a distinct concept, and it was not long before NATO reconvened the members to look into the subject more fully. They realized that there were commonalities between the work on geophysics and the ongoing work on radiological, biological, and

chemical weapons. Both involved alterations to the natural world with potentially devastating human consequences. Military technology seemed
on the verge of an unprecedented ability to tap the forces of nature on a
massive scale.[26]

Thus in late 1962, NATO summoned scientists and military planners
to Paris to hammer out what might legitimately come out of "environmental warfare" and what the long-term consequences might be. The man
who tried to fill Von Kármán's shoes was another Hungarian, nuclear
physicist Edward Teller, who joined the group as a "special advisor."
Known widely as the father of the hydrogen bomb, Teller already was
deeply committed to using nuclear explosions for massive earthmoving
projects, such as the construction of harbors. He also saw great potential
in developing novel uses of nuclear weapons in wartime. Along with
Teller, committee members were drawn from national defense establishments and from the US Advanced Research Projects Agency (ARPA).

The central question almost always remained the same: were natural
forces susceptible to human influence on a large, even global, scale? In
methodical fashion, these military planners broke down environmental
warfare into distinct spheres of possibility, corresponding with the layers
of the earth and its atmosphere as it extended into space: lithosphere and
hydrosphere (land and oceans), troposphere (lower atmosphere), stratosphere and ionosphere (upper atmosphere), and exosphere (outer space).
Some of the earlier "wildcat" ideas were quickly dispensed with as imprac-
tical, such as using hydrogen bombs to melt the polar ice caps. But other
wildcat ideas were feasible, particularly using nuclear weapons as triggers
for tsunamis in the oceans, or for altering the weather.

One only had to open a newspaper to see what natural catastrophes
could accomplish. In 1958, in Alaska's Lituya Bay, there was a landslide so
powerful that it carried the energy equivalent to a one-kiloton explosion.
In May 1960, a wall of water smashed the Chilean coast over a stretch of
several hundred miles, with wave heights of 5.5 to 13.5 meters. The Chilean
earthquake sent storm waves across a large area of the Pacific at speeds in
excess of 400 miles per hour. Even as far away as Hawaii, low-lying areas
were flooded. Thousands of Chileans were killed, and millions were left
homeless. Reporters described the relentless devastation:

> The quakes went on for all of the week, demolishing or damaging
> thousands of homes and other buildings, and burying some small
> communities under landslides. Whole villages were swept away by

tsunamis as high as twenty-four feet. The quakes were so violent that mountains disappeared, new lakes were formed and the earth's surface dropped as much as 1,000 feet in twenty-five miles. The worst quake, last Sunday, released energy of 240 megatons, equal to that of 1,200 atomic bombs of the type dropped on Hiroshima and far more than the 174 megatons released by all the nuclear explosions to date.[27]

Noting deaths all over the Pacific Rim, the *New York Times* reported that the Chilean earthquake "gave tragic testimony that in this age of the conquest of the atom and of triumphs in outer space man is still helpless against the vast and still largely unpredictable forces that frequently go berserk in his immediate environment—hurricanes, volcanoes and earthquakes."[28]

NATO saw it differently. Environmental cataclysms could become part of the alliance's arsenal, with the help of a well-placed nuclear explosion. The cascading effects of energy release from the existing instabilities of nature could be, quite literally, earth shattering. The power over nature was tempting: "The large engineering capability which is provided by multi-megaton nuclear weapons might open up the possibility of changing the course of ocean streams which are known to affect climate and continents." Narrow straits could indeed be dammed up, as some feared the Soviets planned for the Bering Straits. Peninsulas could be turned into islands, changing the patterns of water flow and mixing. With enough nuclear bombs, the sea floor in some areas might be reconfigured entirely.[29]

Even weather control seemed poised to make a quantum leap forward with the nuclear bomb as a tool. "Real weather control," NATO scientists argued, "would mean control of synoptic scale disturbances—the centers of high pressure and low pressure found on the daily weather maps." Such large-scale systems seemed inherently susceptible to influence, despite the huge energies required to do it. The sun imparted energy into the air masses constantly, but only some of it became kinetic energy. Most of the energy was stored, ready to be released. The results could be quite violent, as in the case of cyclones. A relatively small release of energy—say, a nuclear bomb—could trigger a much larger release of natural energy.[30]

One reason that such widespread and even long-term changes in the earth's systems seemed feasible—at least in theory—was the growing realization of how serious an effect humans already were having upon the upper atmosphere. High in the sky, major effects seemed well within

NATO's grasp. Nuclear explosions could create electron clouds some 70–90 kilometers up, disrupting high-frequency communication. One of the leading researchers on electron cloud disruption, Jerome Pressman, had been advising the US Army Signal Corps, the Air Force, and ARPA on this subject for years.[31] He told the rest of the environmental warfare committee that even a single nuclear burst could disrupt long-distance communication over a stretch of a thousand kilometers. If nuclear weapons were exploded in the atmosphere as a defense against incoming missiles, the range of this electron cloud would be vast indeed. High-frequency communication equipment and long-distance radar systems might be rendered useless.

Out in space—the exosphere—NATO saw great promise in the radiation belts that American and Soviet satellites had measured during the International Geophysical Year. The Van Allen belts were actually giant regions of charged particles trapped by the earth's magnetic field. They were sources of intense, persistent radiation that endangered any equipment or living thing in space. Although the Van Allen belts were natural phenomena, similar belts could be created artificially by exploding a nuclear weapon at an altitude of at least 400 kilometers. Large bombs at even higher altitudes would create an extraordinarily powerful radiation environment in space. The belts would cloak the earth, challenging any exit or entrance by missile, satellite, or spacecraft. Because the belts would be trapped by the earth's magnetic field, there would be holes in the radiation cloak at the north and south geomagnetic poles. Whoever controlled these entry points would have comparatively easy access to space. That would make the poles even more important as strategic regions.[32]

In fact, manipulation of the Van Allen belts already had begun. In 1958 the United States discovered that its high-altitude tests of "small kilotonnage" had created electron shells around the earth, about 60 miles thick. Because the operation in which these tests occurred had been dubbed "ARGUS," the creation of the shell became the "ARGUS effect." Just a few months prior to these NATO meetings, the United States detonated an even larger explosion at high altitude—the "Starfish" experiment. As Edward Teller reported, "this is the first time that the Argus effect was demonstrated on a really big scale." An immense number of electrons were caught in the earth's magnetic field and "are forming now a new Van Allen belt greater in electron density than any of the known Van Allen belts." He confided that the electrons had damaged the solar cells in American satellites.[33]

Despite their fascination with these weapons, the committee members struggled to overcome the possibilities that defied the logic of nuclear warfare. The military significance of triggering natural catastrophes was not readily obvious. "If the weapon can be exploded a few miles offshore, it can probably be delivered on, or close to, the target itself, and a far larger proportion of the energy available would be expended on the target and not on long lengths of unimportant coast line."[34] The same argument could be made against any effort to influence the flow of ocean currents and thus modify the world's climate. Why not just drop a bomb on a city? It seemed more logical.

On the other hand, there might be great value in environmental devastation in a total war. NATO advisors had already moved beyond "cities" as targets and had begun to imagine much larger swathes of territory. Aside from the blast and radioactive contamination, thermonuclear bombs could have wide-ranging horrific consequences. Disruptions of dams and levees would lead to widespread flooding. Drowning and starvation would result, posing a serious threat to those who managed to survive the bombs.

The most ghastly environmental threat was the prospect of large-scale fire. In *Whole World on Fire* (2004), Lynn Eden has written that military planners routinely ignored the consequences of huge firestorms caused by a nuclear explosion's thermal radiation. She suggests that this led nuclear strategists to underestimate the catastrophic effects of nuclear explosions throughout the Cold War. While war plans typically focused on blast effects,[35] not everyone ignored the totality of death and destruction from fires. Some military planners considered it part of environmental warfare. In the early 1960s, scientists and military planners at the highest levels of NATO faced a stomach-churning analysis that cast them as a way of arming the countryside against the enemy even when his cities were destroyed.

These fires would instantaneously ignite a huge area due to the explosion's initial thermal radiation, regardless of blast effects. Rather than just use bombs directly against cities, one could explode a large bomb of about 100 megatons high in the atmosphere, at about 80 kilometers. Doing so would maximize the amount of thermal radiation that would reach the earth. Such radiation would ignite flammable material instantly, over an area of nearly a million square kilometers. As a point of comparison, the largest recorded forest fire in the United States occurred in 1871 in Wisconsin and Michigan, which claimed 1,683 lives and spread over 15,000 square kilometers. Setting fire to forests, in an area of a million square kilometers, would pose intractable problems to an enemy. Outside the bombed-out cities, the countryside would provide no shelter, no food, and no hope of survival.

A fire from thermal radiation would differ from a typical forest fire because it would not need to spread—instead, the whole area would go up in flames at the same time. Oxygen would rapidly deplete, leaving any survivors suffocating to death. It would be impossible to run from it. Rushes of air would create firestorms with "strong winds of up to hurricane force," far more intense than the deadly firestorms created in German and Japanese cities during World War II. Edward Teller guessed that the energy released in a fire would exceed that of the nuclear explosion, roughly the equivalent of a thousand megatons. "This is the most violent and wide-spread environmental change which can be expected from a nuclear attack," he said.[36] If total war were the goal, fires from thermal radiation could achieve it on a continental scale.

These discussions, recorded for posterity in NATO meeting minutes, have a surreal feel to them. Scientists argued about whether hydrogen bombs were more effective as triggers of vast environmental events, or if they should just be dropped directly on their targets. Scientists quibbled over the extent of damage from a fire-raising weapon. Some doubted, for example, that hurricane-force winds would ensue. It was difficult to argue with the conclusion, however: "The immediate result would be beyond all experience." But some insisted that it would only "likely" be beyond all experience.

Such intellectualized detachment from human experience reached new heights when the long-term ecological consequences of nuclear weapons were imagined. The NATO group recognized that using nuclear weapons in this way might have severe consequences for the earth in the long run. But while acknowledging that the effect on weather and climate might be significant, scientists had little data with which to generate specific predictions. As for the devastation of the land, NATO was confident that a succession of vegetation "would sooner or later re-establish itself, and over a few decades there would be some ecological recovery."[37]

The only thing not in doubt in these discussions was that maximizing human death was the principal goal. Which was better, Teller and his colleagues asked—drowning villages along the coast, igniting the countryside with thermal radiation, or simply laying waste a city? Should humans be contaminated through the food chain, or beat into submission through ecological dependence? While praising the ingenuity of these wildcat ideas, Teller's own preference was to bomb cities. If death and devastation were the goals, he reasoned, why not keep it simple? Mammals, including humans, were more sensitive to radioactivity than insects, seed plants, or bacteria. It made little sense to attempt to contaminate man through these less susceptible organisms when the bomb would do the trick. "Thus the most economic way to attack populations with nuclear radiation," the committee concluded, "is to do so directly rather than through some element of their surroundings."[38]

For many in NATO, looking at the world as a zero-sum game between the nuclear-armed United States and the Soviet Union, environmental warfare seemed like an inefficient sideshow. As interesting as ocean manipulation and weather control might be, nuclear explosions would be required to produce them. In that case, presumably a real war would have begun, and the enemy could be bombed directly without resorting to exotic methods such as these. Even in the case of biological, radiological, and chemical weapons, changing the environment would be a more circuitous route than attacking directly.

In trying to imagine uses of environmental weapons, military analysts working with NATO confronted the same question that has stood at the center of environmental issues ever since: can human actions have long-lasting, detrimental consequences upon the earth? As an advocate of peacetime nuclear testing, Teller had reason to minimize the long-term impacts of human action, particularly nuclear fallout. He spoke at length to the committee about how some scientists had exaggerated these effects, and his point of view prevailed. The NATO committee concluded that the danger of sickness and disease from contamination "are no worse than the other hazards which would have to be faced by the survivors of a nuclear war." As for the long-term genetic effects upon future generations, the committee toed the pro-testing line that the ultimate effects on future generations could not be predicted with certainty.

Nevertheless, some on the committee were convinced that humans were capable of making large alterations to the environment. Throughout the Von Kármán reports were repeated references to unpredictable consequences of human action on the atmosphere. Increasing or decreasing the ozone concentration in the atmosphere was certainly possible, altering the amount of ultraviolet light reaching the earth. Deliberate creation of an ozone hole might confuse surveillance systems; deteriorate aircraft materials such as rubber, plastic, glass; and harm humans and crops. Less purposeful might be the introduction of chemicals from rocket fuel or other sources, resulting in "large inadvertent changes" in atmospheric properties.[39]

NATO concluded its assessment of environmental warfare with a warning that major changes might already be under way. "Much of the military planning of today assumes that the earth's atmosphere will remain substantially as it is," it wrote. Elaborate detection and surveillance systems were based on that very notion. But more and more booster rockets would traverse the upper atmosphere, depositing exhaust materials. "They may, within the near future, be sufficient in quantities to have a large effect," the committee concluded. The composition and temperature of the atmosphere, and along with them weather and climate, likely would change due to atmospheric pollution.[40] This warning undoubtedly sprang from Jerome Pressman's work on the effects of rocket trails, done for the Geophysics Corporation of America and funded by ARPA.[41] His work, some of it unclassified, would lead *New Scientist* writer Peter Stubbs to suggest in 1963 that there was "ample evidence that the amounts and types of contaminants that are likely to be ejected by the large rockets envisaged for future space programmes may radically change the environment of the layers surrounding the Earth. The modifications may extend to being world wide and of long duration and would clearly be substantial over large areas."[42]

Despite their belief that geophysical forces could be harnessed with nuclear explosions, several of these NATO scientists refused to entertain the notion that these environmental changes were anything but ephemeral. They would be wartime actions, justifiable in a total war against the Soviet Union, with only short-term consequences for man and the climate of the earth. Teller routinely emphasized the huge power differential between the forces of nature and the forces of man. Like the professional meteorologists, he had stiffened his resolve on this issue and was deeply skeptical—even dismissive—of ideas to the contrary. Yes, it would be possible to use nuclear weapons to make local changes to the earth's crust. Indeed, Teller encouraged creative uses such as constructing harbors. It might even be possible to use nuclear weapons to create ocean upwelling. But it was inconceivable to him that even a nuclear war could have a substantial and permanent effect on weather and climate. The intense fires would be brutal in the short term, but the energies were equivalent to what the sun delivered in the course of a day. Giant firestorms would devastate selected areas, but these were no different in scale from the large hurricanes that occurred as natural phenomena. These changes could ultimately be justified by the supreme need to stop the Soviet Union. In the final analysis, Teller and others insisted, even the most devastating change would not be permanent.

Teller and his like-minded colleagues built upon this notion and denied that even gradual changes to the composition of the atmosphere could be significant. This was a position that he had hardened over the years as he defended atmospheric nuclear testing. Addressing the NATO group, he said that even worldwide fallout would have negligible effects, because of the earth's ability to rejuvenate itself. The radioactive carbon-14 in the air technically should last thousands of years. However, Teller believed that within a decade all of it would exchange with the carbon dioxide in the oceans. He said that the radioactivity "will be precipitated by the calcium carbonate to the bottom of the ocean where it is outside the range of any living organism."[43]

In light of the Argus experiment, the fallout controversy, and the ill-fated Alaskan adventure, many others in government held less certain views. President John Kennedy stated openly his belief that American scientific experiments could have global consequences. He also was diplomatically astute enough to recognize that the rest of the world did not see the earth as America's scientific playground. In April 1963, the president secretly directed his cabinet to ensure that any future experiments with potentially large-scale impacts should be reviewed first at the highest level.[44] At an event commemorating the 100th anniversary of the country's most esteemed scientific body, the National Academy of Sciences, he also conveyed a warning about America's responsibility to control the effects of scientific study: "For, as science investigates the natural environment, it also modifies it—and that modification may have incalculable consequences, for evil as well as for good. . . . [S]cience today has the power for the first time in history to undertake experiments with premeditation which can irreversibly alter our biological and physical environment on a global scale." Kennedy chided the scientists, saying that every time they came up with a major invention, politicians had to invent new institutions to cope with them. That usually meant new international bodies. The ocean, the atmosphere, and outer space, he said, "belong not to one nation or to one ideology but to all mankind."[45]

The president was warning about the catastrophic consequences of human action—specifically, American scientists in concert with the military. His words suggested that America's military experiments had arrogantly tinkered with the global environment. But Kennedy was not just reacting to American (and Soviet) large-scale experiments. His words also reflected other stern warnings from his presidential science advisors and from others outside government that American practices were inadvertently altering or poisoning the environment. He urged scientists to continue their global vision but to train their eyes on the world's diminishing resources and to consider the earth's vulnerability. Land, water, forests, wildlife—all these needed protection, and measures to stop contamination of water and air were sorely needed. "The earth can be an abundant mother," Kennedy said, "if we learn to use her with skill and wisdom—to tend her wounds, replenish her vitality and utilize her potentialities." He called to mind the prophecy of doom issued a century and a half earlier by Thomas Malthus, who said that men's numbers would push past the limits of subsistence, condemning them to famine, poverty, and misery.[46] Such prophecies, renewed by the rhetoric of Cold War conflict and the expectation of global war, soon were rampant in discussions of the environment.

PART THREE

Gatekeepers of Nature

7

The Doomsday Men

KIRK: Bones, you ever hear of a Doomsday machine?
MCCOY: No, I'm a doctor, not a mechanic.
KIRK: It's a weapon, built primarily as a bluff. It was never meant to be used. So strong, it could destroy both sides in a war. Something like the old H-Bomb was supposed to be. That's what I think this is. A Doomsday machine that somebody used in a war, uncounted years ago. They don't exist anymore, but the machine is still destroying.
— *Star Trek*, "The Doomsday Machine," 1967

When President Eisenhower warned, in his 1961 farewell address, about the "military-industrial complex" and the "scientific-technological elite," many of his closest scientific advisers were shocked. Had they offended the president? Science was supposed to strengthen the nation, not threaten it. In his eight years in office, Eisenhower had supported science in innumerable ways—putting his political weight behind the International Geophysical Year, the creation of the National Aeronautics and Space Administration (NASA), and an array of technological developments from satellites to intercontinental ballistic missiles. Yet the president clearly was troubled. He had watched as civilians who had never seen combat rose in influence in military circles, professing to understand how to fight in the future. Prior to World War II, he said, America possessed strong businesses that had been mobilized for war. But now, there was a vast peacetime armaments industry, along with an immense military establishment being advised by top scientists. This was new to the American experience, the president warned. After praising scientists, he cautioned: "Yet, in holding scientific research and discovery in respect, as we should, we must also be alert to the equal and opposite danger that public policy could itself become the captive of a scientific-technological elite."[1]

When Eisenhower's successor, John Kennedy, reorganized the Defense Department around relatively young, civilian "whiz kids," many felt that

Eisenhower's predictions were coming true. Military analysts embraced strategic thinking from a scientific perspective, with an eye toward maximizing outcomes and efficiencies. Kennedy chose as his defense secretary Ford Motor Company executive Robert S. McNamara, who had served under General LeMay during World War II to maximize death from strategic bombing by using statistical analyses. Civilian contracting agencies such as the RAND Corporation rose further in prominence. RAND was the Santa Monica, California-based think tank (or "think-factory," as the *Times* of London called it) where scientists and military figures routinely had attempted to formulate strategic policies since the late 1940s. Scientists were not merely asked to do research or to develop technology but to plan global strategy. That encouraged civilian scientists to think of the whole earth as the playing field in a global conflict, to apply game theory to the Cold War itself. They applied models, quantitative analysis, and statistics to the scientific subjects of critical importance to understand how to survive such a conflict: radiation effects, geophysical forces, ecology, and many other disciplines.

In short, analysts were charged with predicting Doomsday. The 1960s were a decade of scenario building, as scientists tried to game out a third world war with an increasingly robust set of variables. The practice was infectious, and scientists used the same tools to imagine the future of the earth with—or without—a nuclear war. Military experts warned about the growth of population, of rampant industrialization, and of the growing vulnerability of America and its allies to infectious disease, crop destruction, and other environmental threats. Civilian scientists began to warn of imminent destruction due to unrestrained economic growth— the kind of growth that would leave millions to die of starvation and disease, especially in developing countries. Using computer models to make predictions, these doomsday scenarios fit snugly into what was becoming known as the environmental movement, pointing out the dangers of pollution, pesticides, and population growth. These often were just as dire as the models projecting a post-nuclear world. Environmentalists produced predictions and recommendations, and they created many enemies—especially among those who believed that environmental doomsday predictions played directly into the hands of the Soviet Union. Nonetheless, military planning and environmental prediction were rarely far removed from each other, as they asked the same questions, drew from the same data, and often involved the same scientists.

Military analysts approached doomsday predictions with a kind of scholarly detachment that many found appalling for such a grim subject. A classic example was RAND analyst Herman Kahn's seminal, ponderous 1960 tome *On Thermonuclear War*. The title suggested purely scientific or logical inquiry, as if it were akin to Aristotle's *On the Parts of Animals* or Copernicus's *On the Revolutions of the Heavenly Spheres*, but Kahn was trying to calculate the effects of a global cataclysm and to anticipate the millions of deaths—or "megadeaths," as he called them. Kahn presented numerous scenarios for hypothetical world wars, arguing the merits of deterrence and the necessity of gambling millions of lives. In making that gamble, Kahn wrote, one had to look at thermonuclear war as a legitimate and survivable future. To illustrate his point about deterrence, he introduced a hypothetical "Doomsday Machine," which could destroy all life on the planet.

Kahn's doomsday machine became an instant iconic image of the fateful course onto which the United States and the Soviet Union had put the entire earth. In a 1967 *Star Trek* episode, to use but one example, the doomsday machine was quite explicitly a planet killer, a giant worm-like robot that carved up entire worlds in order to feed off of them. As imagined by the television writers, the machine was simply a relic that continued to operate, an unintended consequence of warlike actions "uncounted years ago." Whoever built it did not even exist anymore, yet the machine continued to consume worlds. The television program became an opportunity to comment on the insanity of hydrogen bombs and the precarious nature of the Cold War. But the idea of Doomsday, or a doomsday machine, was not merely a matter of science fiction in the 1960s. It was an integral part of war planning and a powerful image for the vulnerability of the earth.

Kahn actually did not accept that nuclear weapons amounted to Doomsday. A nuclear war, he believed, would mean neither the end of existence nor the end of nations. Even with tens of millions of people dead, many would survive. Those who predicted the utter annihilation of the species were oversimplifying, he said, and ignoring the multitude of social and economic adjustments that humanity likely would make. Even Armageddon, he wrote, must have a sequel. One of his reasons for writing the book was to repudiate widespread claims that in a nuclear war, the survivors would envy the dead. Kahn and others at RAND had found that despite the quantitative rise in human tragedy, "the increase would not preclude normal and happy lives for the majority of survivors and their descendants."[2] In his zeal to show how real this sequel could be, Kahn resorted to seemingly matter-of-fact calculations about the genetic effects of radiation, to determine the years of recovery from nuclear war, dependent upon numbers initially killed. This ranged from one year (given only 2 million deaths) to 100 years (given some 160 million deaths). Like NATO projections, Kahn's imagined devastation was a temporary interlude—a brief chapter in the history of the earth and human race.

Although he had his admirers—a *New York Times* review said he "has had the singular courage to perform tough-minded and precise calculations"— Kahn faced immediate criticism or outright ridicule.[3] His book reflected a theoretician's worldview, and some found his calculations of megadeaths grotesque. That such an influential organization as RAND could recommend these projections to guide American foreign policy suggested that policy analysts had lost perspective. Boston University ethicist Paul Deats Jr. wrote that Kahn was preoccupied not with resolving conflict but with finding the most reasonable form of violence. In the pages of *Science*, Brookings Institution analyst Donald N. Michael wrote that Kahn's discussions of the post-nuclear world were "inadequate, incorrect, and glib to the extent that doubt is cast on the plausibility of his optimistic assumptions." There was little in *On Thermonuclear War*, he felt, to suggest that recovery could occur under a democratic government. A similar broadside came from a young historian Christopher Lasch, who wondered whether Kahn bothered to ask himself what exactly he hoped to see survive. The book had "a certain dream-like quality—great lucidity superimposed on fundamental confusion." At long last, he said, the world had reliable evidence of what kinds of work went on at RAND.[4]

The most withering critique came in the form of satire, particularly in the acclaimed 1964 film by Stanley Kubrick, *Dr. Strangelove: Or, How I Learned to Stop Worrying and Love the Bomb*. The film revolved around a tense nuclear standoff between the United States and the Soviet Union. The Americans have been unable to recall a nuclear bomber to the Soviet Union, which will automatically trigger just the kind of doomsday device described hypothetically in *On Thermonuclear War*, destined to destroy all life on the planet. Dr. Strangelove, America's director of research and development, claims to have commissioned a study of the doomsday device by the "Bland Corporation." Strangelove himself was a caricature—a brilliant yet mad scientist who formerly had worked under Hitler and now struggled to prevent his own body from making the Nazi salute. Though obviously fictional, Dr. Strangelove seemed to be a jab at key scientists who had come to exercise enormous influence in political and military circles. Among these were RAND fixtures John von Neumann and Herman Kahn, former Nazi rocket scientist Werner von Braun (who had become the director of NASA's Marshall Space Flight Center), and the "father" of the hydrogen bomb, Edward Teller.

These men were new kinds of experts tailored for the nuclear age. Gone was the deference to military officers' experience; here to stay was the belief that scientists could plan for, and determine the outcomes of, future world wars. Seeing the entire earth as the field of battle, systems analysts plotted the outcomes of myriad scenarios in which the United States and Soviet Union employed the latest technologies of destruction. Theirs was a world of total war. Global catastrophe was the bread and butter of their intellectual lives. Kahn extolled the virtues of theory over experience, modeling and simulation over hard-won military lessons. This attitude had many manifestations: game theory, operations research, systems analysis, even cybernetics—in which actors attempted to interact with, learn from, and ultimately outwit an opponent. These were, as one historian has put it, the Manichean sciences. Like the ancient Persian philosophy of good and evil, these sciences cast the world as a struggle between two opposing forces and developed solutions based on actions and reactions.[5] They fit the bipolar geopolitical worldviews of the United States and Soviet Union beautifully. Analysts at RAND offered not only quantitative projections but also claimed to offer dispassionate and objective advice. Who could argue against it? After all, no military figure could claim to have fought a thermonuclear war.[6]

The totality of conflict envisioned by Kahn and others translated into the most dire scenarios, as human beings played with technologies of increasing magnitude—leading to unpredictability, instability, and global catastrophe. The idea of a life-killing, even planet-destroying doomsday device proved to be an irresistible metaphor for humanity's capacity to wound itself through the natural environment. That capacity was invariably linked to the hydrogen bomb. Its scale defied the imagination and produced seemingly inhuman calculations of casualties on the order of hundreds of millions.

Thinking about the fate of the earth, and especially the humans living on it, in terms of global vulnerability, translated into similar projections—but without the hydrogen bomb. How vulnerable were humans to the vagaries of catastrophic change? The meat of RAND's work was in predicting the future—"gaming" it—to attempt a quantified assessment of the most important variables they could imagine. Already by the mid-1950s the analysts at RAND and other think tanks had ceased limiting themselves to nuclear catastrophe. The connection between national security and the earth's vulnerability extended much further. Dire warnings about population pressures, for example, came in secret reports about national insecurity long before they were popularized by the Stanford biologist Paul Ehrlich, whose 1968 *The Population Bomb* became a runaway best seller. A decade earlier, in the immediate post-Sputnik anxiety, the Air Force had received similar advice.

Under the auspices of the National Academy of Sciences, longtime RAND advisor Theodore von Kármán had chaired a committee that in 1958 told the Air Force to take a broad view and to assess America's vulnerability by examining the ways Americans lived and how it opened the nation up to grave dangers. It gave its most candid assessment of these dangers in a report on the looming biological crisis. Because of population growth, the balance of global resources was destined to shift to the "backward" countries of the world. Food shortages would become acute, and even the greatest advances of science and technology would almost certainly fail to keep up. "The non-white peoples," the academy committee warned, "will gain in relative numbers in relation to the whites. Natural resources, being finite, will be hard pressed by increasing exploitation." Technology surely would help to stave off disaster, partly through food research but mostly by promoting contraception. In 1958, von Kármán's group warned, some 64 percent of Americans lived in cities—compared to about 40 percent at the turn of the century. Urban development was happening at a staggering pace, facilitated by President Eisenhower's brainchild—the federal interstate highway system. The new highways were estimated to consume 1.5 million acres of land—"an area greater than 50 San Franciscos." According to academy estimates, land was being taken for construction at the rate of 3,000 acres per day.[7]

Why issue such warnings about biological vulnerability, pollution, and urbanization to the Air Force? The academy viewed these as national security issues of deep significance in the global Cold War. The scientists warned the Air Force that the American way of life had become rather complex and the land increasingly crowded. People all across the country had become dependent upon an array of intertwined systems of transportation, communication, and food distribution. America had become exceptionally vulnerable to military and natural disasters. Power failures and road accidents already paralyzed human activity and economic productivity for hours at a time. What if this were extended to larger areas, for longer periods? A new disease, a shortage of food, or a loss of electrical power could have disastrous consequences. "The extreme vulnerability of a crowded, technological, advanced nation to enemy attack is obvious."[8] In the struggle against the Soviet Union, such environmental weaknesses had to be taken into account—urbanization, pollution, scarcity of water. If the maxim of war was to know thy enemy, surely the Soviet Union could see that America's affluence and increasing dependence upon technological systems were planting the seeds of its own destruction.

Outside of government, scientists also pointed to impending doom. One of them was plant physiologist Barry Commoner, working under the banner of the American Association for the Advancement of Science (AAAS), the organization that published the most prestigious scientific journal in the United States, *Science*. At the height of the fallout controversy in 1956, the AAAS had created a group to assess the social aspects of science. Led by Commoner, the group was convinced that scientific advances were creating problems for society and that scientists ought to be involved in the political solutions. Four years later, that group was more convinced of this than ever. It cited the uncertain effects of radiation, pesticides, food additives, population growth, and weather modification. The group also suggested that the governmental pressure for scientific "achievements" in the United States' geopolitical race with the Soviet Union was slowly beginning to erode scientists' integrity, giving rise to pettiness and "unseemly" assertions of priority.[9] In 1964, the AAAS Committee on Science in the Promotion of Human Welfare launched an unsparing critique of the recent erosion of scientists' backbones in recent years. In its report, "The Integrity of Science," Commoner's group lamented how fully major scientific projects had been corralled by geopolitical aims.

The main thrust of Commoner's argument was that the United States paid too little attention to the potentially negative consequences of its large-scale projects. He cited not only the widespread environmental damage due to pesticides but also the vast experiments conducted for military and scientific purposes, such as the nuclear explosions in the Van Allen belts. Such experiments had far-reaching consequences for huge parts of the world, yet scientists working for the military leaped into them with little hesitation and without consulting the rest of the scientific community in the United States and the rest of the world. The report stated that rigorous scientific justification and methods often fell by the wayside in favor of military aims, and the results rarely were opened to full scrutiny to those lacking proper military clearance.[10] Later that year Commoner called the radioactivity from atmospheric nuclear tests the "greatest single cause of environmental contamination of this planet."[11]

The irony was that, despite the arrogance and overconfidence that Commoner saw in these military actions—and in the war projections conducted at RAND—scientists working for the US armed services were deeply absorbed in trying to answer questions of the earth's vulnerability. The military conducted experiments, such as nuclear tests, but were not unaware of the resultant environmental consequences. Planners of nuclear tests were insensitive to many of these consequences, to be sure. But military organizations had been trying to identify environmental weaknesses for many years, either to exploit them or defend against attack. Commoner was absolutely right that there was no limitation of scale. Scientists had, without discernible hesitation, helped the Atomic Energy Commission or armed services to explode hydrogen bombs in the oceans, underground, and in space, not just to test yields but also to observe the consequences upon the natural environment. NATO, for one, took a special interest in environmental warfare in the early 1960s, hoping to explore the means of manipulating earth systems on a synoptic scale.

Scientific explorations in environmental warfare already were forging conceptual links between catastrophic war and catastrophic environmental change. Some of the ideas were encapsulated in a 1968 book *Unless Peace Comes*, edited by Nigel Calder, former editor of the *New Scientist* magazine. In it a variety of scientists and military planners wrote on an array of strange subjects—ostensibly representing the future of war and the fate of life on earth. Reflecting on recent wars in Algeria and Vietnam, French general André Beaufre wrote that even with the most sophisticated technology, it was impossible to control all of the terrain—a major power became "a lion attacked by mosquitoes." In the end, he contended, the mosquitoes will win. The use of increasingly powerful weapons made matters worse, "subjecting the general population to almost inhuman stresses." Such warfare began to look very much like a war *against* the population. Another contributor, the Yugoslav historian and former military officer Vladimir Dedijer, warned that the technological superpowers often focused too readily on the threat of worldwide nuclear war, ignoring the more likely kinds of conflicts to occur, and he predicted that large powers overconfidently would get drawn into unwinnable smaller conflicts. Guerrilla fighters usually matched the will of the population. While

Europeans and Americans thought big and lost, indigenous populations thought small and won.[12]

Such voices against global thinking, and against harming civilians, were relatively muted compared to the other contributors to *Unless Peace Comes*, who focused on large-scale disasters and the impending total war against the Soviet Union. Harvey Wheeler, the author of the acclaimed novel about an accidental nuclear war, *Fail-Safe* (1962), wrote of how the coming revolution in computing would give armies unprecedented power of command and control to manage large conflicts. This, he warned, would militarize society. William Nierenberg, the director of the Scripps Institution of Oceanography (and previously ex officio member of NATO's Von Kármán Committee), wrote that the nations of the world "have added possession of the oceans as an objective," through the mastery of vast submarine strategic systems and the exploitation of minerals on the ocean floor. Others wrote of the potential to weaponize LSD, a psychedelic drug then taking college dormitories by storm. A kilogram or so of LSD, a pair of French scientists cautioned, was "sufficient to render temporarily schizophrenic the entire population of London. . . . The whole population of a country could be poisoned by spraying LSD solutions over large areas, which seems technically possible today." Similar claims, certainly not new, were made about biological agents. Swedish microbiologist Carl-Göran Hedén surmised that weapons soon would escalate to the scale of nature and bring untold perils for humankind. "Future conflicts are likely, in short," he wrote, "to breed weapons modeled upon nature's own ecological system."[13]

The ultimate expression of the earth's vulnerability and manipulability came from Gordon MacDonald, a geophysicist at the University of California, Los Angeles. No neophyte on matters of military geophysics, MacDonald was a member of the President's Science Advisory Committee and participated in several classified military studies for the JASON group. In a chapter called "How to Wreck the Environment," he explicitly linked military research on exploiting the natural environment to global concerns about catastrophic environmental change. He acknowledged, but dismissed, some of the fears expressed at the dawn of the nuclear age about the effects of nuclear weapons on the earth. For example, he repudiated former vice-presidential candidate Estes Kefauver's statement that nuclear testing could knock the earth off its axis by several degrees. Yet he admitted that scientists in concert with the military were "slowly overcoming the gap between fact and fiction regarding manipulations of the earth's physical environment." Then he went on to recount many other examples of changes in human ability to manipulate the environment for harmful purposes.[14]

As an extreme example of such effects, MacDonald wondered if lightning could be induced to strike in a controlled, repetitive way, in enemy territory, to disrupt the enemy's brain functions. He mentioned that electrical activity in the brain was concentrated at certain frequencies. Laboratory experiments with flickering light suggested that it was possible to interfere with normal brain frequency, to induce unpleasant sensations or impair performance of everyday activities. MacDonald said that this or other perturbations in the environment could produce changes in human behavior. The relationship between man and his environment was subtle and deeply vulnerable to manipulation. He took it as an article of faith that even if these weapons seemed abhorrent, they most certainly would be developed in time.[15]

What struck MacDonald was not the quirkiness of the weapons he described but their global and catastrophic nature. The most ambitious and troubling modification schemes, he wrote, affected not just enemy territory but the earth as a whole. Like most defense scientists, MacDonald believed that humans were relatively powerless in the face of the enormous energies of nature. That meant any real manipulation would have to occur in the areas of instability, where the earth's potential energy lay trapped and ready to be unleashed—as in the case of the earth's crust under strain built up from centuries of plates trying move against each other. Although he devoted some discussion to the artificial inducement of earthquakes and of weather control, MacDonald was particularly interested in existing mechanisms for global catastrophe. Most military research pointed in the same directions: climate change and ozone depletion.

To really change the climate, defense scientists reasoned, one would have to tamper with the earth's heat budget. Just as any household has a budget for income and expenses, the earth takes in a certain amount of energy from the sun, and then sends it back out again. Some of it gets trapped in the atmosphere. Since the late nineteenth century, scientists had been speculating about ways to alter the heat budget, to keep more heat in. The Swede Svante Arrhenius proposed in 1896, for example, that a relatively small change in the atmosphere's composition might actually have an impact on the global heat budget. Scientists such as Guy Stewart Callendar argued in the 1930s that human beings were intervening in the climate by burning up fossil fuels, adding carbon dioxide to the atmosphere.

The ability of the earth to regulate itself, compensating for such increases by the ocean's absorption of excess carbon dioxide, remained an open question. Most of these early commentators had emphasized that global warming, as we call it today, would have been a positive outcome, increasing the availability of arable land and holding off future ice ages.[16]

Climate change for military purposes, similarly, would necessitate some creative thinking on how to change this heat budget. There was no shortage of creative thinkers in military circles in the 1950s and 1960s, and scientists at RAND already had proposed the basic tool: blackening large expanses of ice. Doing so probably would have been prohibitively expensive—after all, one might need millions of tons of soot to blacken enough ice to be worthwhile. But in theory, blackening the ice would prevent some energy from reflecting back out into space, which would increase the earth's temperature. That escalation would have a cascading effect on other ice areas, melting them and further decreasing the reflective surface area of the earth, making the earth hotter.

MacDonald was rather skeptical about this option, mainly because of the cost and logistical difficulties. Instead he believed that a different mechanism would hold the key, namely, physically moving ice rather than melting it. Drawing on a theory about the origins of the ice ages by New Zealand scientist A. T. Wilson, he suggested that ice sheets in polar regions might be induced to slide further into the ocean by some well-targeted nuclear blasts. Under the influence of gravity, these gigantic blocks of ice would surge into the water, possibly creating massive tsunamis but— more important—extending the reflective surface of the earth. More heat would escape, and the earth would get colder. People living in most of the temperate zones would have to survive in arctic conditions.

Was all this purely science fiction? MacDonald did not think so. He saw extraordinary changes in modern meteorology, brought on by sophisticated mathematical models, aided by computer technology for accomplishing the myriad calculations, and the constant influx of data from instruments, especially satellites. Together, the whole earth could come under scientific inquiry, comprehension, and control.

Another means of accomplishing catastrophic change would be to alter not the reflective surface of the earth but the composition of the atmosphere—again with an eye toward altering the earth's heat budget. "If a nation's meteorologists calculated that a general warming or cooling of the earth was in their national interest," he wrote, "improving their climate while worsening others, the temptation to release materials from high-altitude rockets might exist." There was no doubt that it was possible, he believed, because it was already happening on a small scale due to burning of fossil fuels. More catastrophic still would be tampering with the quantity of ozone in the atmosphere. The thin layer of ozone blocked most of the sun's ultraviolet radiation from reaching the earth. Without the ozone, the full force of the sun's radiation "would be fatal to all life— including farm crops and herds—that could not take shelter." Therefore vulnerabilities in the ozone layer might be exploited, creating temporary holes in it, to shower an enemy with lethal doses of ultraviolet radiation.[17]

Reviewers of *Unless Peace Comes* skipped over the warnings about fighting wars against guerrilla movements and focused instead upon the frightening portraits of vulnerability. If the authors were to be believed, it would be possible to poison whole regions, even if only to produce a general state of psychotic delirium in the population. And the ever-present threat from biological weapons would only increase with time because of changes in ways of living: increasing urbanization, centralized sources of food and water, and air conditioning. With growing population would come decreasing strength, not just because of food shortages but also because of the risk of quickly spreading disease.

These concerns about synoptic-scale weapons and worldwide environmental change dovetailed with other influential commentaries on the potentially disastrous consequences of the close collaboration between science and the military. The American historian Lewis Mumford compared modern states to the pyramid builders of ancient Egypt: the all-powerful pharaohs who created a well-oiled "machine" made of skin and bones to do stunningly complex and enormous construction projects. "Does anyone suppose that either atomic bombs or intercontinental rockets would have been brought into existence within a single decade except at the command of an all-powerful state, bringing to bear the financial and scientific resources of a vast community in the closed totalitarian situation of war?" He warned that technology often provides an illusion of convenience and freedom, but that it can enslave people too.[18]

A similar critique came from French scholar Jacques Ellul, who complained in 1962 that man was letting himself be driven by technological mastery over nature:

> The possibility of action becomes limitless and absolute. For example, we are confronted for the first time with the possibility of the annihilation of all life on earth, since we have the means to accomplish it. In

every sphere of action we are faced with just such absolute possibilities. . . . And here I must emphasize a great law which I believe to be essential to the comprehension of the world in which we live, viz., that when power becomes absolute, values disappear.[19]

Ellul was blunt: such power eliminates the boundary between good and evil, threatening a catastrophic end to all life. Technology represented more than this or that invention; it was the whole apparatus of society, compelling humans along certain paths, often unconsciously. At the end of those paths lurked something forbidding, enslaving, and dire.

A common thread in this critique was that science and technology gave man godlike powers of destruction while fundamentally weakening his defenses. Man had become dependent upon the very systems that made him powerful. Historian Lynn White Jr. argued in the journal *Science* that medieval Christianity encouraged human mastery over nature, as if the earth were created specifically for man's purposes. The "ecologic crisis" had finally come:

> When the first cannons were fired, in the early 14th century, they affected ecology by sending workers scrambling to the forests and mountains for more potash, sulfur, iron ore, and charcoal, with some resulting erosion and deforestation. Hydrogen bombs are of a different order: a war fought with them might alter the genetics of all life on this planet. By 1285 London had a smog problem arising from the burning of soft coal, but our present combustion of fossil fuels threatens to change the chemistry of the globe's atmosphere as a whole, with consequences which we are only beginning to guess. With the population explosion, the carcinoma of planless urbanism, the now geological deposits of sewage and garbage, surely no creature other than man has ever managed to foul its nest in such short order.[20]

White's vision was not just a critique of pollution; it was a warning about global destruction.

Critiques of the relentless pursuit of technological power firmed up the academic backbone of a kind of catastrophic environmentalism already discernible in the discussions of epidemic disease, global food shortages, and worldwide nuclear fallout from the 1940s through the 1960s. The best-known critic was Rachel Carson, the science writer who brought worldwide attention to the problem of indiscriminate pesticide use (especially DDT) in *Silent Spring*.[21] Looking at Carson's work more broadly reveals her long-time focus on the staggering vulnerability of the earth and the humans living upon it. There is a hint of this in the preface to the 1961 edition of her best-selling *The Sea Around Us*. In the 10 years since its first publication, Carson wrote, human knowledge of the oceans had increased tremendously, due to major oceanographic expeditions, submersible dives, and the long-range explorations by nuclear submarines under vast expanses of ice. Scientists during the International Geophysical Year had started a grand epoch of ocean exploration and measurement. Like other scientists of her time, Carson marveled at the changing worldviews of the oceans. Where once there was permanence, now there was change. "Even a decade or so ago it was the fashion to speak of the abyss as a place of eternal calm, its black recesses undisturbed by any movement of water more active than a slowly creeping current, a place isolated from the surface and from the very different world of the shallow sea." That view had been replaced by one of movement and rapid change, Carson wrote. Such dynamism in the sea suggested not only the workings of nature but also the potential manipulations by man.[22]

Carson particularly worried about the unintended consequences of humanity's technological decisions. Just as critics of atmospheric nuclear testing voiced concern about the dangers of fallout, Carson pointed out how naïve it was to assume the oceans could absorb the byproducts of the nuclear age, namely, radioactive waste. "In unlocking the secrets of the atom, modern man has found himself confronted with a frightening problem—what to do with the most dangerous materials that have ever existed in all the earth's history, the by-products of atomic fission."[23] While critics of fallout worried about the concentration of strontium-90 in the bones, Carson pointed out that radioactive isotopes concentrated in marine organisms. "What happens then," she asked, "to the careful calculations of a 'maximum permissible level'? For the tiny organisms are eaten by larger ones and so on up the food chain to man."[24]

Rachel Carson's writings awakened some readers to mankind's ecological vulnerabilities. Her discussion of the food chain questioned the viability of human beings in a contaminated landscape. She warned that humans should not assume that the sea is eternal and unchanging. And yet the lesson was not that the sea was being harmed but rather that there would be unintended and negative consequences for man. "It is a curious situation that the sea, from which life first arose, should now be threatened by the activities of one form of that life. But the sea, though changed in a sinister way, will continue to exist; the threat is rather to life itself."[25]

The same message is evident in *Silent Spring*, which focused on the problem of the food chain. Carson had been inspired by reading English ecologist Charles Elton's 1958 *The Ecology of Invasions*, which had warned about pesticides as well. Elton's principal concern was not the preservation of wildlife for its own sake but rather in security for humans and their products. He argued for biodiversity (he called it the conservation of variety) to decrease the vulnerabilities in nature—to make the natural world "more safe for wild life, more interesting, and also more secure for the farmer, forester, and fisherman."[26] Simplifying ecological communities, by using deadly chemicals, was the worst course of action in protecting one's plot of land from invasive pathogens, insects, and animals.

The responses to *Silent Spring* were in some ways predictable—pesticide companies loathed her—but surprisingly, one of Carson's staunch supporters was the President's Science Advisory Committee (PSAC), then represented by the first rank of mainstream American science. PSAC argued that pesticides might be making America's natural environment weaker and more vulnerable. Had Americans contaminated themselves? In response to *Silent Spring*, British defense scientist Sir Solly Zuckerman sent his American colleagues a humorous exchange in the House of Lords over "the story of the cannibal in Polynesia who now no longer allows his tribe to eat Americans because their fat is contaminated with chlorinated hydrocarbons." The US Department of Agriculture went to battle with PSAC scientists over *Silent Spring*, trying to persuade them to withdraw their endorsement, or even to say unequivocally that food produced in the United States was safe.[27] But PSAC stood firm.

Much of what is today considered pro-environment literature, in the 1960s and 1970s, was in fact human survival literature. "Nature bats last," Stanford biologist Paul Ehrlich was fond of saying. Like Rachel Carson, Ehrlich became an icon of the environmental movement, especially because he routinely employed the language of global crisis. His worldview was like that of Thomas Malthus, whose early nineteenth-century *Principles of Population* set forth the grim law of nature—populations increased much faster than food supplies, and nature ultimately corrected overpopulation with famines, diseases, and wars. Ehrlich, who had been shocked at the poverty and sheer numbers of people he had seen on a trip to India, predicted a dire fate for all the world's people. Populations grew, and humans continued to make matters worse by fouling their own nest with environmental degradation. In his 1968 *The Population Bomb*, he identified the root of the crisis as the sheer number of people.

Ehrlich's worldview was survivalist, drawing inspiration from many of the same sources as had Elton, such as Fairfield Osborn's best-selling 1948 book *Our Plundered Planet*.[28] On the one hand he seemed simply to lament the loss of wilderness for ethical or aesthetic reasons: "Our population consists of two groups; a comparatively small one dedicated to the preservation of beauty and wildlife, and a vastly larger one dedicated to the destruction of both (or at least apathetic toward it)." On the other hand he predicted not simply the loss of natural beauty but famines, plagues, and wars of extermination.

In his work, Ehrlich had much in common with those who tried to game World War III and plan for surviving it. In *The Population Bomb* and elsewhere, he introduced fanciful scenarios about the future state of the world, though Ehrlich's were embellished with political predictions. In one titled "Eco-Catastrophe!" he wrote of a fictional President Edward Kennedy declaring a national emergency, calling out the National Guard to harvest California's crops. In this scenario, "even the president of Union Oil Company" began to voice concern about the decline in bird populations due to DDT spraying. Ehrlich's vision of 1973 was the perfect storm of environmental cataclysm:

> Rodents swarmed over crops, multiplying rapidly in the absence of predatory birds. The effect of pests on the wheat crop was especially disastrous in the summer of 1973, since that was also the year of the great drought. Most of us can remember the shock which greeted the announcement by atmospheric physicists that the shift of the jet stream which had caused the drought was probably permanent. It signaled the birth of the Midwestern desert. Man's air-polluting activities had by then caused gross changes in climatic patterns. The news, of course, played hell with commodity and stock markets. Food prices skyrocketed, as savings were poured into hoarded canned goods. Official assurances that food supplies would remain ample fell on deaf ears, and even the government showed signs of nervousness when California migrant field workers went out on strike again in protest against the continued use of pesticides by growers. The strike burgeoned into farm burning and riots.[29]

That's when, in Ehrlich's doomsday scenario, the fictional president called in the National Guard to do some harvesting.

In the midst of Ehrlich's various dire predictions was a manifesto about man's fundamental rights within the natural world. He listed 11 rights: to eat well; to drink pure water; to breathe clean air; to live in non-crowded shelter; to enjoy nature's beauty; to avoid regimentation; to avoid pesticide exposure; to enjoy "freedom from thermonuclear war"; to limit families; to educate children; to have grandchildren. Some of these "rights" seemed uncontroversial. The one that provoked an outcry was the right to limit families. In *The Population Bomb*, he encouraged parents to give their kids an intra-uterine birth control device (IUD) to take to "show and tell" at school. He encouraged Catholics to register stern disapproval to their priests about the church's stance against contraception. He prodded them to complain about positive treatments of large families in the media and of "mother of the year" awards to women who had lots of kids. Of course, he told his readers to set an example by not having more than two children.[30]

Worries about the global population *bomb* did not replace concerns about a catastrophic nuclear war but reinforced them. Ehrlich and like-minded scientists routinely pointed out that technology had given humans enormous capacity for destruction, and hydrogen bombs were the ultimate tool leading to self-extinction. Because population pressures would lead to war—initially in the developing world but ultimately everywhere—nuclear holocaust was all but inevitable. The crisis would be global, and the war would be total. The consequences would involve all the postwar obsessions—disease, famine, war, and death. *The Population Bomb* predicted the coming of the Four Horsemen of the Apocalypse.

Although he made no theological claims (other than to mention the Four Horsemen), the inventions in Ehrlich's scenarios were similar to those of fundamentalist Christian "End Times" literature, which connected current events to predictions in the Bible of the end of the world. In fact, another best seller of 1970, Hal Lindsey's *The Late Great Planet Earth*, was exactly that. It was a surprising hit, published by a major press and appealing to an audience far broader than the usual clientele in Christian bookstores. Like Ehrlich, Lindsey was writing about the fate of the planet. Lindsey believed that the 1948 establishment of the state of Israel had set off a string of events that had been predicted in the book of Revelations—the final chapter of the Christian Bible, which lays out a vision for a clash between good and evil, the second coming of Jesus Christ, and a thousand years of peace prior to the final day of judgment. Lindsey explicitly juxta-posed his book with those of scientists, believing that God already had provided answers to the "basic and visceral questions of man." He wrote, "There are other places men search for answers: philosophy, meditation, changing environment, science. Please don't misunderstand me, all of these are good if used properly. However, if we are to be absolutely honest, if we are to use our intellectual integrity, let's give God a chance to present His views." At first blush *The Population Bomb* and *The Late Great Planet Earth* may seem worlds apart in their political aims or motivations, but there are striking similarities—a sense of doom and a sense that humanity was on the brink of a global catastrophe.

This is not to say that environmental doomsayers were evangelists for Christianity. Ehrlich had read Lynn White and agreed with him whole-heartedly. For White, the root of ecological crisis could be found in Judeo-Christian values—namely, that man had mastery over nature. Ehrlich advised looking elsewhere, to the non-Christian East perhaps, or perhaps to the hippie movement, which embraced Zen Buddhism, physical love, and disdain for material wealth. "They may not have *the* answer," Ehrlich wrote, "but they may have *an* answer. At the very least they are asking the proper questions." But where White was looking at these values as a cause of the problem, Ehrlich never lost sight of his own culprit: overpopula-tion. At the root of his worldview was the belief that the fouling of the human nest would ultimately harm man rather than nature. Nature, after all, batted last. "For, as I hope I have convinced you," he wrote in *The Population Bomb*, "even though we would like to dominate nature, it still dominates us!"[31]

Apocalyptic stories were not new, and the threat of nuclear war had already given birth to numerous incarnations of the end of the world in fiction, film, and comic books. But the doomsayers of the late 1960s and early 1970s, like Ehrlich, returned power to nature. Whereas many post-nuclear novels, such as Walter M. Miller's 1960 *A Canticle for Leibowitz*, put characters into desolate, charred, and contaminated landscapes, now Mother Nature was armed and dangerous. For example, Michael Crich-ton's 1969 best seller *The Andromeda Strain* had an extraterrestrial micro-organism infect people and drive them insane, creating a global crisis. Although the disease came from outer space, a military satellite had cap-tured it while collecting specimens for biological weapons research. It was the same kind of mysterious, David versus Goliath death that killed off the alien invaders in H. G. Wells's 1898 story *War of the Worlds*. Such scenarios were revitalized by the predictions of global nuclear conflagration and environmental suicide in the late 1960s. Destructive environmental effects were sometimes invisible. As in Rachel Carson's *Silent Spring*, one had to stop and listen. The global spread of pathogens became a trope of the science fiction and horror genres, leading to numerous films and television variants. To give but one example, the young horror writer Stephen King published a story in 1969 called "Night Surf," about a group of survivors of a deadly virus called Captain Trips. A decade later the virus resurfaced in his massive novel *The Stand*, in which Captain Trips kills off 99 percent of the world's population. The human world fell away as the natural world flexed its muscles.

What separated Crichton, King, and others from Ehrlich was belief. Fact versus fiction. *The Andromeda Strain* was a frightening vision of what could happen and of how vulnerable people really were. But Ehrlich's vision was more than a warning—it was a prediction shared by other environmental activists. At the first Earth Day celebration, held simultaneously in college campuses across the United States in 1970, many students carried signs that indicated not merely environmental consciousness—saving wilderness, cleaning up pollution, preserving wildlife—but rather more dire statements about the death of the entire earth. A photograph of the earth, taken from space in 1968, provided the iconic image of a vulnerable planet seen for the first time from a different vantage point. "Earthrise," it was called. Such photographs of the whole earth ended up on student placards all across the country on Earth Day. A photograph of a young man carrying one such placard, with the simple descriptor "R. I. P. 1990 A.D." has itself become an iconic image for Earth Day and the environmental movement.

In the midst of these worries, Barry Commoner was dismayed to discover that most of the young people who participated in the first Earth Day in 1970 had no conception that the movement was rooted in scientists' declining integrity and the unintended consequences of technology. He saw scientists such as Paul Ehrlich, with his emphasis on population and shared resources, as obscuring the larger issue. The problem was the intensive use of technology, such as the over-use of fertilizers and pesticides, the conversion of the prewar car into today's high-powered monsters, and the increased use of detergents. What struck Commoner about them, and what ultimately brought him into conflict with Ehrlich, was that the scale of these technologies was increasing faster than population—the use of inorganic nitrogen fertilizer was up some 40 percent since the war.[32]

Environmentalists could not agree on why they saw disaster coming, and they bickered among themselves. Ehrlich accused Commoner of "numerical sleight of hand," exaggerating the impact of technology. And Commoner criticized Ehrlich for trying to force consensus upon the environmental movement. But there was at least one commonality. Catastrophe was on its way, and it had to be stopped. Next to one exchange between them in the pages of the *Bulletin of the Atomic Scientists* stood an advertisement placed by the World Association of World Federalists. It pictured a map of the earth, transposed upon an apple with a bite taken out of it. "It's your earth," the ad proclaimed, "if you care enough to save it!"[33] Environmentalists had many different ideas about what the problem really was, but they agreed on matters of scale: it was global and cataclysmic.

One of the mouthpieces for catastrophic thinking was the new magazine *The Ecologist*. Founded in England in 1970 by Edward Goldsmith, it was not devoted to detached studies in ecology but rather espoused the principal idea of ecology—the interconnectedness of all living things within the environment. As a special issue, it issued *A Blueprint for Survival* in 1972. It contained a hodge-podge of environmental warnings: overreliance upon technology, the ecological consequences of pesticides, rising unemployment, gaps between rich and poor countries, social discontent and, ultimately, wars, famines, and diseases. It emphasized that the present mode of industrial life was not sustainable, pointing out the sharp disparity in energy consumption between the industrial and developing worlds. Its main point was that growth had its limits and that a reduction in consumption would make the global economy more sustainable.

Blueprint for Survival had perhaps a greater impact in Europe than in the United States. Not only did the UK Green Party, founded in 1973, base its political platform upon it, but also it provoked a hostile reaction from prominent British scientists—particularly John Maddox, the editor of *Nature*, the most significant scientific publication in Britain. Maddox warned about the "doomsday syndrome," the tendency to believe that science and technology would lead to disaster. Recalling Herman Kahn and his doomsday machine, he said: "There is no reason to believe that the problems we are concerned about now cannot be dealt with in the same way as the nuclear problem." To him, that meant balancing the pros and cons, and working out politically and economically reasonable solutions to each issue. He criticized environmentalists for conjuring up catastrophic scenarios. All this accomplished, he believed, was to create panic.[34]

Maddox saw environmentalists as shrinking violets who feared technology and lacked confidence in the Western, market-oriented economy. Just as the West should not back down against the Soviet Union in the face of nuclear war, he believed, Westerners ought to have more confidence in their economic and political systems' ability to confront any given challenge. It was the path to salvation, not the road to ruin. Scientists' predictions of large-scale change were encouraging extremists to insist on momentous alterations to standard practices. Most environmental issues were not earth-shattering, global problems, Maddox contended. "Environmental pollution is not so much a threat to the global environment, and the existence of the human race," he wrote, "as a demonstration of the need for the vigorous application of social instruments, laws and taxes, which are as old as society itself."[35]

Academics of all kinds emerged to defend *Blueprint for Survival*, and the framework Maddox had created for the debate stuck—was the ecological crisis really a doomsday scenario? Sociologist Hilary Rose said that "scientists had only begun being a little disillusioned with science when some of their toys registered the possibility of holocaust, with the development and use of atomic weapons." She looked 20 years into the future and imagined a world similar to the one of Aldous Huxley's 1932 novel *Brave New World*, with euthanasia councils and sterilizations of people with low IQs. She derided Maddox for his complacency, suggested that he might found *The Pangloss Journal*—a reference to a character in Voltaire's eighteenth-century satire of optimistic philosophy, *Candide*. Pangloss, having witnessed a catastrophic earthquake, having contracted syphilis, and having been enslaved—and having witnessed worse horrors happening to those around him—still believed fervently that all was for the best.[36]

Maddox expanded upon his ideas in a 1972 book *The Doomsday Syndrome*. He labeled Ehrlich and his ilk the "false prophets of calamity." Doomsaying was a particularly American phenomenon, he believed, rooted in the fallout controversy and continuing with Rachel Carson's complaints against American farmers. He disliked Carson's imputation, however, that pesticides were elixirs of death destined to poison the whole environment and cause cancer in the process. Americans were quick to make their problems seem like global ones. It was part and parcel of the same worldview, Maddox believed, and he put the concerns about fossil fuels into the same category:

One bizarre calculation, for example, is that carbon dioxide from the burning of fossil fuels—coal and petroleum—accumulates in the atmosphere so as to trap increasing amounts of solar energy and thus, in due course, to transform the climate of the earth.[37]

Maddox found the notion to be one more ludicrous point on the continuum of environmentalists' and some scientists' false prophecy. He felt that if Americans saw DDT as a problem, they ought to address it—in the United States. He railed against what he considered extreme environmentalism, with its dangerous global social remedies. He opposed Ehrlich's recommendation that American foreign aid should be withheld from countries that did not expressly commit to stabilizing their populations. "One of the most pernicious dangers of the extreme environmental movement," Maddox argued, "is that it will create such a sense of imminent catastrophe that the will to use the humane institutions of civilized communities will be undermined."[38]

The Ehrlich-Maddox clash was one of many on environmental conflicts, and it made for great political theater. *The Observer* sent science correspondent Gerald Leach to interview and "cross-examine" several of the most outspoken figures on the food crisis, the energy crisis, and the growth crisis. It advertised the segment as "The Great Doom Debate." The series included a logo with a depiction of the planet with the words "Spaceship Earth." Was man on the brink of starvation, or were new cereal crop hybrids a sign that science and technology could solve the problem? Were vast changes in the social system necessary to meet energy needs, or should nuclear power be given a chance? Had humans lost the power to guide a society with explosive growth, or was there hope in international relations? These were cast as issues of planetary significance. *The Observer* asked: "Have the prophets of doom overstated the case? Have they overlooked the recuperative powers of technology and simple common sense? What are the real dimensions of the problem? How much time is there left in which to tackle it?" *The Observer* pitted each against an esteemed opponent with a diametrically opposing view, setting up a series of environmental cage-fights for the pleasure, and presumably the education, of its readership.[39]

While the Ehrlich-Maddox debate set the stage for scientific animosity, the Club of Rome instigated a study that soon would establish a permanent battleground on environmental questions and created a compelling tool for predicting future catastrophe: computer simulations. One of the most internationally minded of the new environmental bodies, the Club of Rome has been described variously as an activist organization or an international think tank. It was really a loosely defined association of dozens of influential businesspeople, scientists, and politicians. Its founder, the Italian businessman Aurelio Peccei, drew distinct parallels between the nuclear story and the environmental one. Mankind had made a "colossal investment in genocide" by funding the development of nuclear weapons, he wrote in 1971. Because of that, political action to prevent a global catastrophe had become international in scope. Similarly, humankind now confronted a "growth syndrome," having overexploited and polluted its environment so much that future generations were destined to live in desperate conditions. The threat to man was man himself.[40]

The Club of Rome's "catastrophic" environmental worldview drew directly from the expertise of American military planners. At a conference in Lake Como, Italy, Aurelio Peccei happened to encounter a man who would give the Club of Rome a powerful, authoritative, and extremely controversial voice in environmental affairs. That man was Jay Forrester, who in the 1950s had helped design the US military's massive automated defense system for all of North America. He was part of what scholars refer to as the postwar revolution in the management sciences, resulting from the need to oversee and operate large complex organizations. Although some big corporations already had been working on these issues—notably telephone companies—the US armed services took them rather seriously during the early Cold War and helped to launch a robust field of study: operational research.[41] By the late 1960s, Forrester had begun to apply command and control concepts from the military to social realms. The Lake Como conference, which happened to be on the topic of urbanization, brought these strange bedfellows together and immediately they began to see the potential of applying large-scale computer modeling to global environmental problems.[42]

The connection between war planning and environmental modeling was not as strange it might appear at first glance. Many of the pioneers in environmental modeling were inspired by concepts in conflict resolution and geopolitical issues. In fact, some of the same people worked on both topics. Seminal works on conflict resolution written and published in the late 1950s and early 1960s imagined the earth as a closed system with finite numbers of inputs and outputs. Game theory developed into "decision theory," providing policy makers with powerful tools for making choices. Some analysts, including economist Kenneth E. Boulding, started an academic outlet, the *Journal of Conflict Resolution*, to publish the latest developments in economics and international relations coming from universities and think tanks like the RAND Corporation. In his 1962 book *Conflict and Defense: A General Theory*, Boulding predicted that the current international system was going to plunge the world into the worst kind of disaster. In the mid-1960s he characterized the earth as a knowable, manageable closed system—"spaceship earth." He criticized the prevailing "cowboy economy" that encouraged risk and recklessness rather than wise management. He also wondered about the permanent alterations to the earth. "We are already producing irreversible changes in the atmosphere which are causing alarm to meteorologists," he wrote. "It is clear also that we know very little about what we are really doing, that we do not understand the earth at all well, and that the earth sciences, even the physical sciences, are shockingly backward."[43]

Jay Forrester became, with Boulding, a powerful link between studies in global conflict with the Soviet Union and the projections of environmental catastrophe. During World War II, Forrester had helped to develop electric and hydraulic servomechanisms—automated devices that regulated machines in response to feedback—to improve the accuracy of radar controls and gun mounts. He then moved into digital computing and designed a method for storing memory based on magnetic core technology. He pioneered the design of electronic flight simulators before finally taking on a project of much larger scope. In the early 1950s, the prospect of war with the Soviet Union seemed to imply extremely short reaction times, either with strategic bombers or (later) with intercontinental ballistic missiles. This made automated, feedback-oriented defense systems seem more important than ever, and Forrester was instrumental in developing the Semi-Automatic Ground Environment (SAGE) air defense system for North America in the 1950s (it remained in use until the early 1980s).[44] This system was the basis for the North American Aerospace Defense Command (NORAD), tucked away from nuclear attack inside of Cheyenne Mountain near Colorado Springs. With the SAGE system, which linked a network of radar stations to a network of computers, the United States tried to prepare itself to detect and quickly intercept incoming bomber or missile attacks from the Soviet Union. These computer systems, and those like them, were designed to be reactive, capable of processing large inputs and anticipating future outcomes.[45]

By the time he came into contact with the Club of Rome, Forrester had become a professor of management at the Massachusetts Institute of Technology. Extending his military research, he had worked with programmers to develop a computer simulation to help businesses respond to fluctuations in inventory, demand, and personnel—this was the beginning, he later recalled, of the field of system dynamics. But he soon thought bigger, expanding his studies to urban problems, to help officials see the impacts of policies such as building low-cost housing. That is what brought him into contact with Peccei. None of this marked a clean break from his earlier work. Forrester approached problems as systems to be managed—a gun mount system, a business enterprise, a city, or the defense of all of North America.[46]

Soon Forrester's outlook got even bigger, returning to the global outlook of his earlier work on SAGE. This time, however, he would attempt to predict the future of the earth. Effusive in his enthusiasm, Forrester argued that the human mind itself developed models, which it used to guide human action and work toward creating laws. But we could not predict the future, mainly (he said) because of inadequate models. "The problem is not a shortage of data," he proclaimed, "but rather our failure to understand the laws and behavior patterns determining the implications of the data." Computers, he and other believed, were going to change that.[47]

Based on conversations between Peccei and Forrester, the Club of Rome asked MIT to do a comprehensive assessment of the planet, using the latest sophisticated computers to do calculations of population trends, resource use, production of food, and fuzzier variables such as quality of life. These problems, as *New York Times* science reporter Walter Sullivan put it, evidently were "too tough for a mere brain."[48] Forrester conducted a preliminary study and soon put a more sophisticated one in the hands of Dennis Meadows, a young assistant professor of management and system dynamics. Meadows's team consisted of some 17 members who attempted to plug in as many variables as they could imagine and develop a sophisticated portrait of potential futures. The title of their group was all-encompassing: "The Project on the Predicament of Mankind."[49]

Forrester's results gave the human race just a few decades more before the world environment would reach the crisis level—he had produced, as one headline put it, "A Computer Curve to Doomsday."[50] Reactions to his book, *World Dynamics*, exceeded his wildest expectations. Forrester later described it:

It was running through editorial columns of mid-America newspapers, it was the subject of prime time documentary television in Europe, it was debated in the environmental press, the zero population growth press, and the anti-establishment underground student press. And, if you don't like your literature on either the establishment right or the establishment left, then right in the middle of the political spectrum, it had a full-length article in *Playboy*.[51]

All this was the public splash made by *World Dynamics*, an environmental tract written by one of the inventors of the SAGE defense system.

That reaction, according to Forrester, "seemed to go up another factor of ten" after the publication of a second study called *Limits to Growth*, written by Meadows's group and hastily published by the Club of Rome to precede a major United Nations conference on environmental issues in Stockholm.[52] The book proposed a series of "World Models" based upon the computers' complex calculations. More sophisticated in its approach and more popularly written, *Limits to Growth* had a wider appeal than *World Dynamics*. The message, however, contained the same "scarifying predictions," as one journalist put it, including massive increases in death rates over the next half century.[53]

The modeling advocated by Forrester and his protégé Meadows were not far removed from the kinds of models used by the RAND Corporation to game out catastrophic scenarios. Kenneth Boulding later wrote: "It is hard to deny Herman Kahn's status as a major prophet of our times. He is certainly no Jeremiah. That role is clearly occupied by Jay Forrester and his fellow doomsters. . . . Perhaps he is more of an Ezekiel, with his wheels within wheels, a vision of machinery."[54] Where Kahn and his ilk saw logic in the mechanisms of the world, Forrester saw a cataclysm. Dennis Meadows continued to advocate more attention to long-range forecasting based on computer simulations, urging fellow scientists to develop "a social radar function" that could predict the future long enough in advance to allow institutions to change if necessary. "If an ocean liner takes 5 miles or more to change course," he wrote, "one cannot successfully steer it on the basis of information only about obstacles a few hundred yards ahead of it." Scientists previously had seen social systems as beyond the realm of prediction. But now computers could handle complex models, he believed, well enough to predict the future.

But not all was harmonious in the world of environmental prediction. Such interventionism smacked of socialism. Economists emerged to defend the Western market system. One modeler, Yale's Martin Shubik, ridiculed the MIT work in the pages of *Science*. Compared to the models being formulated at RAND, Shubik believed, the MIT work apparently was wildly inadequate to account for real social change. Forrester ignored social behaviors and the variety of economic decisions people made. He thought Forrester had been swept away by the political trendiness of environmental issues and compared him to Soviet agronomist Trofim Lysenko, who had used to his political power to send his enemies to the gulag and undermine the entire field of genetics. Shubik rather snidely suggested that unless members of the Club of Rome "regard themselves as nothing more than a fancy wine-tasting and entertainment society," they ought to sponsor less naïve science.[55]

The weaknesses in MIT's computer model approach—derided by one journalist as "computer fetishism"—emboldened economists to speak out.[56] Yale economist Henry C. Wallich wrote in *Newsweek* that the calls to limit economic growth were a sign of the "intellectual instability of our times" and that it amounted to an effort "to stop America dead in her tracks."[57] Peter Jay, the economics editor of *The Times*, for example, flatly rejected *The Limits to Growth*, saying, "Mankind is in no kind of general ecological peril whatever. Nor are there any reasons to think that continued economic growth will make mankind's age-old problems any worse than they are. The recent spate of contrary scares rests on nothing more than a tissue of schoolboy howlers of logic and fact cloaked in portentous, but specious, computerized models."

For economists, it was easy to find *The Limits to Growth* downright offensive. The MIT analysts seemed to think that plugging such variables into equations was a new phenomenon. Economists had been grappling with predictive problems for centuries. *Limits to Growth* had cast these very difficult problems aside and made bold predictions anyway, claiming that the feedbacks of supply and demand had been handled in their calculations. These supposed calculations themselves had not been published, however, but apparently had been presented at an MIT conference on computer simulation. University of London economist Wilfred Beckerman's reaction bordered on the apoplectic:

This is like my publishing a scientific book, showing the world will soon come to an end on account of increasing instability of subatomic particles and mentioning, en passant, that in order to reach this result it was necessary for me to overcome the little problem of the Heisenberg uncertainty principle, but that I would not actually bore readers with the details of how I did this. If they were really interested they could read about it in a paper I presented to a conference of the railwaymen's branch of the YMCA.[58]

Another Yale economist, William D. Nordhaus, said that Forrester and his MIT colleagues had shown "some lack of humility," given the poor record of humans in predicting the future.[59]

The conflict over *World Dynamics* and *Limits of Growth* would set the terms in environmental disagreements for decades to come. Both sides of the debate were rooted in studies of how to plan for the next world war or to outmaneuver the Soviet Union. Receptiveness to doomsday scenarios—Kahn's post-nuclear world, Ehrlich's population bomb, or Forrester's economic collapse—depended on one's views about the global Cold War. While Forrester and Meadows had felt confident enough to predict disaster, their critics emphasized man's ability to adjust to any change and the ability of price fluctuations to moderate trends. These were not merely academic disagreements. One side said the West was doomed because of its rapacious, unsustainable practices. The other side said the West was healthy because of its reliance on market mechanisms rather than state planning. In the latter view, the Soviet Union was far more vulnerable to environmental challenges. With such high-profile discord, the question of global doom had a polarizing effect upon the environmental movement. While scientists and economists bickered in journals and newspapers, the real fight had just begun in the arena of international relations. One might have expected the US government to side decisively with the economists who defended the Western economic system. Nonetheless, the greatest doomsday man of all would turn out to be Richard Nixon, president of the United States.

8

Vietnam and the Seeds of Destruction

*Mankind already carries in its own hands too many of the
seeds of its own destruction. By the examples we set today,
we hope to contribute to an atmosphere of peace and understanding between nations and among men.*

—US President RICHARD NIXON, 1969, upon
renouncing any American use of biological weapons, even
in retaliation, and any first use of chemical weapons

THE ANCIENT HISTORIAN Tacitus once recounted a Caledonian leader
heaping scorn on the Roman legions: "To ravage, to slaughter, to usurp
under false titles, they call empire; and where they make a desert, they
call it peace."[1] These words resonate when glancing at aerial photographs
of the pacified countryside of South Vietnam, a US ally. Pockmarked,
cratered, defoliated, its rich forests appear sprayed to death by chemical
herbicides and its people and wildlife laid waste by daisy-cutter bombs
and napalm. In the pursuit of military and geopolitical aims, ostensibly
to prevent nuclear war and to defend allies, Americans wielded enormous
power to transform the natural world, and they used that power with little
hesitation.

The great irony, or perhaps hypocrisy, was that in parallel with such
scenes, Americans were the loudest advocates of global environmental
consciousness in forums such as the United Nations. It was not only environmentalists who warned that the world faced global environmental
catastrophe. Even the US government explicitly endorsed this view, precisely when Americans were trying out environmental manipulations on
an extraordinary scale in Vietnam as they fought a decade-long war.

American scientists, politicians, and activists approached environmental problems in the same way they approached other Cold War crises. Just
as war planners imagined a future total war, environmentalists prophesied
the entire planet in peril. The US government deftly used this rhetoric to

its advantage. Rather than ignoring warnings by scientists about environmental harm, American statesmen during the Nixon years deftly used these warnings in the diplomatic struggle against the Soviet Union. At the same time, Americans and their allies implemented many of the plans formulated by scientists and their military partners in previous decades. The United States fought a war in Vietnam that tried out crop destruction, massive herbicide spraying, and rainmaking, while Americans preached, in international settings, against others who treated the environment shabbily. President Nixon even attempted to turn NATO into a forum for responsible joint action on environmental issues. This chapter examines the political creativity of the United States and its allies as they shaped the environmental movement and tried to outmaneuver the Soviet Union, all the while lending extraordinary legitimacy to fears of global environmental vulnerability.

The way the Americans conducted themselves in Vietnam was a logical outcome of scientific research and war planning over the previous two decades. The Joint Chiefs of Staff struggled in the 1940s with how best to utilize knowledge of the natural world in fighting a global war against the Soviet Union. How could nature's pathways be exploited? What was the military use of poisoning food chains, for example? The JCS had determined by the 1950s that many of the new weapons—notably crop destroyers—were best suited to smaller conflicts. After all, spraying the entire Soviet Union would present impossible logistical problems. Historians have noted the many parallels between what the British accomplished in Malaya and what the Americans attempted to accomplish in Vietnam, particularly the strategic hamlets campaign in South Vietnam.[2] The effort to relocate Vietnamese villages away from sources of communist influence was similar to what Gerald Templer had done in Malaya in the early 1950s. Templer too had employed herbicides and crop destruction as part of his campaign to deny sustenance to the communist forces and force them out of their sanctuaries.

But institutions often have short memories. Their employees move on or retire, and new ones possess little or no historical knowledge. Many at Porton, Britain's biological and chemical warfare research headquarters, had forgotten that these American efforts in Vietnam had been their ideas in the first place. The British experience in Malaya had already demonstrated that crop warfare and defoliant spraying could be effective in small-scale wars and in limited geographical settings. Younger British scientists at Porton regarded the American interest in defoliants for anti-guerrilla operations as a new phenomenon, and they pushed to create a similar British defoliant program. Older hands reminded them that the Americans were new to the game and that the British Army already had learned to appreciate the convenience of destroying vegetation to uncover roadways and to eliminate enemy crops. By looking to Americans for inspiration, one official wrote, "the [British] Army does itself and its advisors less than justice."[3]

Still, the scale of the American program was unprecedented. By the end of the 1950s, scientists at Fort Detrick had screened some 12,000 chemical compounds and had created a large network of scientists, industry consultants, and contractors. These chemicals became leading candidates to fulfill the Kennedy administration's desire to find new "techniques and gadgets" to employ in US counterinsurgency operations in Vietnam. Trying to prop up the anti-communist regime of South Vietnamese dictator Ngo Dinh Diem, Americans started experimental spraying as early as 1961. Diem was so impressed that he endorsed a much larger spraying campaign. So the US Department of Defense called upon the scientists at Fort Detrick to ramp up plans for massive jungle spraying along major roads, near enemy encampments, and on crops.[4]

The decision to start such a campaign provoked a little soul-searching in Washington, just as it had in London a decade before. The State Department pointed out that the British had already used chemical herbicides and defoliants in Malaya. Crop killers, American officials realized, had the potential to backfire, killing the wrong crops and generating resentment among the South Vietnamese people. This hesitation proved to be short-lived. In November 1961, President Kennedy personally approved the start of Operation Ranch Hand, the codename for the US Air Force's herbicide campaign. The next year, under pressure from Diem, Kennedy allowed spraying food crops.[5]

Fort Detrick welcomed Diem's enthusiasm for this new gadget. In 1962, it invited industrial firms to submit contract proposals for expanding the screening of chemical compounds. Typically, spraying operations used a traditional chemical mixture of roughly equal parts 2,4-dichlorophenoxyacetic acid (2,4-D), and 2,4,5-trichlorophenoxyacetic acid (2,4,5-T), the same mixture used to control weeds. But scientists at Fort Detrick wanted to put hundreds of additional compound combinations to the test, to identify the right mixtures for specific plants. Crops such as sweet potato and manioc, for example, were broad-leafed plants, whereas rice and corn were narrow-leafed. It might be possible to fit the chemical more closely to the plant, to

decide which plants should live and die in Vietnam. Among those to conduct chemical trials were Dow Chemical Company, Pennsalt, Ethyl Corporation, and Monsanto Chemical Company. Combining Fort Detrick's own
screening program, those done by corporate researchers, and the actual
spraying in Vietnam, American scientists acquired an extraordinary amount
of data on the properties of a vast range of herbicides. British scientists marveled at it, wondering how they "could usefully compete with a project carried out on this scale."[6]

The United States courted British participation as well, in the hopes of
finding the right chemicals for specific jobs. Those who liaised with the
Americans were high-profile British experts in ecology such as Oxford
plant physiologist Geoffrey Blackman. Blackman had considered himself
a "pure ecologist" in his early career but during World War II had delved
deeply into questions of national security and agricultural defense—a preoccupation he did not abandon during the Cold War. He conducted plant
hormone research and studied the effects of herbicides, and he developed
a coterie of researchers at Oxford who advised Porton and occasionally
visited the United States' chemical and biological weapons research headquarters. Oxford ecologists had advised the British Army in Malaya, and
now they tried to help the Americans develop something new in Vietnam.[7]
At dozens of universities in the United States, leading scientists participated willingly in the quest to find out each plant's specific vulnerabilities.
By the end of the decade, this widespread participation would become the
target of universities' anti-war protest movements.[8]

Despite these efforts, the actual chemical compounds used in the war
in Vietnam remained fairly static. American planes sprayed millions of
tons of various combinations, most commonly a mixture of 2,4-D and
2,4,5-T known as Agent Orange, which was just as effective in killing
underbrush in Vietnam, Laos, Thailand, and Cambodia as it was in killing
weeds back home. Agent Purple (also a combination of 2,4-D and 2,4,5-T)
was employed against crops, as was Agent Pink (made of different compounds of 2,4,5-T). These could be sprayed directly by soldiers on patrol
who encountered small plots, or mixed with fuel oil and sprayed over large
areas by low-flying aircraft or helicopters.[9]

In fact Agent Orange and Agent Purple were not "defoliants" but were
herbicides; a true defoliant causes leaves to fall but does not kill the plant
or tree. British officials raised this point constantly as they debated their
own plans for defoliant research in the 1960s. They pointed out that the
Americans had chosen effective killers of plants, not defoliants. Like the

Americans, British researchers hoped to find a true defoliant—but neither did. Instead, despite a tremendous amount of money spent on screening chemical compounds as defoliants, the Americans in Vietnam used the same ones already commercially available for killing weeds.[10]

Why did the British have this requirement about not killing trees? By the late 1960s, anti-war protests had spread in Europe. The British government stood accused of "knowingly contributing" to American offensive actions by sharing research on chemical weapons. Porton scientists avoided defending or endorsing American policy and hoped to deflect criticism by working on "true" defoliants. They said defoliants stood on better ecological footing than herbicides, and in fact better than any conventional alternative. Preventing ambushes was a perfectly legitimate military objective, they argued, and no one would complain if this were accomplished by chopping down— or burning down—trees. But doing so would be far more damaging in the long term than simply defoliating the trees for a short time. Thus the research at Porton was not supposed to be herbicidal. One official advised his colleagues in talking with the press to "emphasize as often as necessary the difference between defoliation and crop destruction." Scientists at Porton argued that reasonable people would see defoliation as the responsible alternative to herbicides—and that it would be politically acceptable.[11]

This turned out to be a vain hope, as the term "defoliant" soon earned an association not only with killing trees but also with harming humans, and few differentiated between defoliants and herbicides. Agent Orange, for example, was clearly a herbicide, yet often newspapers identified it as a defoliant. Although it was supposed to be non-toxic to humans, disturbing reports emerged in the late 1960s that a particular contaminant found in it—known as dioxin—caused birth defects in rats. Agent Orange soon became the center of controversy about birth defects in humans, leading to its ban in 1971.[12]

New York Times writer Anthony Lewis saw the term "defoliation" as part of an American pattern of using technical terms to conceal reality:

> Defoliation as a word has an abstract, Latin ring. It does not instantly make us visualize primitive mountain villages cut off from their local rice and roots, or miles of lifeless mangrove swamps. It might focus our minds to think of the Florida Everglades suddenly dead, or the Blue Hills of Virginia brown and bare.

To Lewis's mind, Americans hid reality behind these abstract concepts. Americans expressed shock at the mass murder of an entire village by

US soldiers, yet gave little pause to chemical spraying or carpet-bombing. The greater part of the war's horror, Lewis argued, was Americans' habit of concealing these human sacrifices from the world—and from themselves.[13]

Even leaving aside the death toll from fighting, or even the human cost of Agent Orange as a carcinogen, the environmental balance sheet of the war in Vietnam was staggering. A team of scientists led by Harvard biologist Matthew Meselson concluded that 15 percent of the entire countryside had been saturated with chemicals. Of Vietnam's life-sustaining mangrove forests, at least a fifth had been "utterly destroyed." About half of the mature hardwoods near Saigon were dead. Longtime *New York Times* journalist Walter Sullivan commented that photos of "parts of the delta region between Saigon and the sea look as if they had been devastated by a nuclear attack."[14] Department of Defense spokesman Jerry W. Friedheim countered ineffectively, arguing that the aftermath of nuclear bomb tests at Bikini looked quite different from the sprayed delta near Saigon. Although Meselson argued that the mangrove trees were not growing back, Friedheim claimed that it was too premature to say whether they would regenerate over the long term.[15]

Much of this devastation took place in South Vietnam, the country American troops were there to protect. In addition to using chemical sprays, military commanders tried to transform Vietnam's landscape using big bombs and powerful machines. Intense concussion bombs called "daisy cutters," designed to clear football field–sized areas, blasted through the countryside. The Rome Plow, a kind of bulldozer developed in Rome, Georgia, worked to level and clear vast areas. "Every day from dawn to dusk, between 100 and 150 huge plows are making flat wastelands," American ecologist Arthur Westing observed in 1971. These measures to deny hiding areas to the enemy had consequences—not just in wildlife habitat loss and farmland destruction, but also in encouraging erosion, loss of topsoil, and flooding.[16]

New revelations in the 1970s amplified this image of wanton, large-scale environmental destruction. As early as 1967, the US Army knew that its crop-killing schemes were having little effect on the food sources of enemy soldiers. Scientists at the RAND Corporation had correlated data on spraying with data on soldiers' rice rations, based on interviews with captured North Vietnamese soldiers. They concluded that although the spraying was not hurting soldiers, it was having a tremendous effect on the livelihood of civilians in South Vietnam. The Army rationalized that the continuing spraying harmed "sympathizers." Clearly, civilians had been drawn into the spraying campaign on a massive scale. The United States was using chemicals in a grand starvation campaign against any Vietnamese people who might be sympathetic to the enemy's cause or who might simply live near enemy operations. The Department of Defense declassified this and other studies around the same time Meselson's group revealed their findings, and soon the American Association for the Advancement of Science called upon the US military to halt spraying. The *Washington Post* called this move a vote of "no confidence" in the president's statement that spraying was being phased out.[17]

The Vietnam War became a crucial part of public discussions of environmental catastrophes. Meselson had revealed that over 4,000 abnormal births had been recorded at Saigon Children's Hospital from 1959 to 1968. In one highly sprayed region, Tay Ninh, the rate of birth defects was 64 per 1,000 (compared to 24 per 1,000 in another part of Saigon).[18] The British weekly, *The Observer*, provided an unambiguous headline: "US Spraying Devastates Vietnam." It stated the conclusions baldly: the United States had destroyed enough crops to feed 600,000 people for one year; it would take decades for plant life to recover and for animals to repopulate the area; the spraying might be responsible for the rise in stillbirths and unusual congenital problems in infants. More to the point, it seemed clear that the White House had known about these problems but made the decision to phase out the spraying only after the Meselson study had made them public.[19] Critics began to call American actions in Vietnam "ecocide."[20]

President Richard Nixon tried to restore the government's image with a series of bold, even stunning, political gestures. His strategy was to acknowledge, not deny, the power of modern science to devastate the entire world and to warn of environmental catastrophe. His first move was the most surprising of all, especially to scientists working at Fort Detrick. He announced in 1969 that the United States was going to abandon its offensive biological weapons program. He then reopened debate about ratifying the Geneva Protocol of 1925, which banned the first use of chemical weapons. That the Senate had refused to ratify it for over four decades did not deter him. Nor did the fact that the United States already was engaged in a war that used chemicals—not just herbicides but also riot control agents—on a massive scale. There was little consensus about whether these violated the Protocol or not. Indeed the British in Malaya had concluded that crop destruction probably did violate it; in their case they justified it on the grounds that they were merely advising and equipping the Malayan government in its domestic problems, making the international implications moot.

Shutting down the biological weapons program, after three decades of intense research—and military gnashing of teeth about how to integrate them into war plans—may have seemed like a rash move. On the other hand, biological weapons research had become a rallying point for political protest. It had been some 15 years since the government had done a comprehensive review of biological weapons—not since the advent of the first hydrogen bombs. Given the reliance on nuclear weapons, biological weapons seemed like a major political liability without a clear military justification. In addition, a series of scandals related to chemical weapons suggested a comprehensive review of chemical and biological weapons might be in order. In 1968, scientists at the Dugway Proving Ground in Utah had botched a test of the nerve gas VX, and a toxic cloud killed more than 6,000 sheep grazing nearby. Then in 1969, newspapers reported that the Army had been secretly transporting leaky chemical weapons across the country, putting them on ships, and sinking them at sea in an operation known as Project CHASE ("Cut Holes and Sink 'Em"). The Army seemed to lack not only control of its experiments but also a sense of responsibility. These scandals, along with the ongoing criticism of herbicide spraying in Vietnam, led Secretary of Defense Melvyn Laird to conduct a major policy review shortly after the Nixon administration took the helm in 1969. A subsequent scandal in Okinawa, during which American soldiers were accidentally exposed to sarin nerve gas, raised serious questions about whether the United States should be deploying chemical weapons overseas.[21]

The United States was not alone in wondering whether this whole class of weapons caused more trouble than it was worth. The United Kingdom in 1969 tabled a draft treaty banning biological weapons, having recently experienced some unpleasant political repercussions from its activities dating back to World War II. The British attempted to decouple biological weapons from chemical ones, to avoid the sticky issues associated with their ally's unpopular war in Vietnam. But then the Soviet Union jumped on the bandwagon, and Foreign Minister Andrei Gromyko spoke before the UN calling for a major treaty banning both kinds of weapons and destroying existing stockpiles. Others began to insist that the 1925 Geneva Protocol banned the sorts of agents used by the Americans in Vietnam—herbicides and riot control agents such as tear gas—and 12 nonaligned countries drafted a resolution affirming it. Reports from other international bodies, including the World Health Organization, emphasized the widespread and indiscriminate effects that biological weapons would have upon civilians. All of this made Nixon's policy review more urgent than ever, and the political wisdom of cutting these weapons loose even clearer.

Many leading scientists backed Nixon's decision to abandon biological weapons. Stanford geneticist (and Nobel Prize winner) Joshua Lederberg believed man's warlike nature had to be contained through social institutions. "Biological warfare should be carefully set apart," he wrote in the *Washington Post*. He believed that these weapons were not only of dubious military use, with unpredictable consequences upon soldiers, cities, and even the users, but that also their closeness to medical research "conveys the most intense perversions of the human aims of science." Worst of all, however, was that infectious agents posed a threat to the whole species. Mutant forms of viruses, he wrote, "could well develop that would spread over the earth's population for a new Black Death."[22] Biological weapons, he and others would argue, were not tied to any particular global strategy—unlike nuclear weapons—so why not ban them?

The notion, advanced by Lederberg, that biological weapons constituted an intense perversion of science, motivated others to pressure academic scientists to break ties with classified military sponsors. Given the pervasiveness of the American scientist-military partnership, breaking these ties seemed impossible. In one case at the University of Pennsylvania, scientists had begun collaboration with the Department of Defense more than a decade earlier, amid the Korean War germ warfare accusations. Now these academics were taking the heat: one headline read "Germ Warfare Brews behind the Ivy." Penn chemist Knut Krieger led a team of researchers on an array of chemical and biological warfare projects. When in 1966 students discovered that one of these was on rice diseases, the research gained an unshakable association with the war in Vietnam.[23] Were America's universities trying to kill off Vietnamese peasants?

Initially, Krieger and the university administration had hoped the scandal would blow over. After all, the Pentagon had contracts with dozens of American universities. But the protests did not dissipate, and soon Penn's president, Gaylord Harnwell, tried to find ways of removing these contracts from the university. He argued that the issue had polarized faculty, distracting them from their work and creating "a great deal of emotional disturbance." Some of the faculty had threatened to wear gas masks to that year's graduation ceremonies. The university's trustees soon decided unanimously that this kind of research had no place on their campus, and they moved to terminate the contracts.[24]

Biological weapons research fed into protest movements in Britain as well, with Porton scientists constantly under fire for their secret work. There was a particularly embarrassing case that amply demonstrated that a relatively small amount of a dangerous agent could have devastating and long-term consequences upon the natural environment. This was the case of Gruinard Island, known to biological weapons researchers as "X-Base." Located in the far north of Scotland, just off the coast, Gruinard Island had been requisitioned in 1942 by the British Ministry of Supply for anthrax trials. As the experiments progressed, the two square kilometer island became contaminated with anthrax spores, and researchers had to abandon it. Fully expecting anthrax to persist for many decades to come, the ministry purchased the island in 1947, posted warning signs to keep away, and visited it annually to collect soil samples. The whole operation continued under strict secrecy. Even today Gruinard Island does not exist on many maps.[25]

By the 1960s, Gruinard Island had become an albatross around the government's neck. Complaints and protests arrived routinely from a dizzying array of groups: "bodies devoted to peace and disarmament, by preservation societies, individual bird-watchers and ramblers, and holiday makers." Most of these hoped to return the island to recreational use. The UK Ministry of Defence tried in 1964 to convince Scotland's Department of Agriculture and Fisheries to explore ways to decontaminate the island, but officials there had little interest—why should it take on such a responsibility, especially when the land was itself of negligible value? Besides, no one knew how to decontaminate it. Anthrax contamination, for all intents and purposes, lasts forever.

Around 1965 the British government reconsidered its policy of secrecy about Gruinard Island. The general public did not know exactly what the Ministry of Supply had done there or what kind of contamination existed there. In the 1940s some local farmers had been compensated when their animals had been infected with anthrax; corpses of their sheep had washed ashore on the mainland. The annual inspections of Gruinard could not be hidden in such a sparsely populated area, because the teams had to stay in local hotels and depart from the nearby jetty in plain view of all. "It would seem that we are only deluding ourselves if we maintain that the current security classification has any meaning," one official complained. If they went public, at least they could put the word "anthrax" on the signs, which they thought would keep people away.

Coming clean about Gruinard Island, Porton openly stated what the contamination source had been and what the expected duration might be. Instead of its ideal scenario, the Ministry of Defence got negative widespread publicity in major newspapers. After the 1966 inspection of the "forbidden island," the *New York Times* reported British scientists saying "the island may remain infected for 100 years."[26] The decision to declassify matters related to the island had done nothing at all to change its status, except to put it more fully in public eye.[27] That gave British politicians, like their American counterparts, even more reason to dissociate themselves from these weapons.

The 1971 American debates about the Geneva Protocol differed in a remarkable way from those of the past. Previously, arguments had focused on military strategy and moral issues related to the humaneness of the weapons. One of the oft-cited tracts in favor of chemical weapons, British biologist J. B. S. Haldane's 1925 *Callinicus*, pointed out that chemical weapons were no worse in moral terms than conventional weapons. Haldane and many others had argued that both chemical and biological weapons could be morally superior if they were designed to incapacitate rather than kill. But now, scientists also made explicitly environmental arguments. These pointed out the need to prevent the destruction of the landscape and highlighted man's capacity for bringing about his own ruin by initiating catastrophic change. Testifying before Congress, Yale botanist Arthur Galston observed that man had a great Achilles' heel:

> For man lives in this world only by the grace of vegetation. He is totally dependent on and cannot substitute for that thin mantle of green matter living precariously on the partially decomposed rock we call soil. . . . In view of the present population of about 3.5 billion people on earth and the estimated doubling of the population every thirty years, it ill behooves us to destroy with profligacy the ability of any part of the earth to yield food for man's nutrition, fiber for his clothes, wood to build and heat his houses, and other useful products too numerous to mention.[28]

This was a view that opposed the specific actions in Vietnam, any future use of herbicides in war, and yet made it a global issue. Indeed Galston and others used the Agent Orange controversy to promote much broader environmental warnings.

The destruction of Vietnam's landscape began to take on paradoxical symbolism. For well-meaning scientists like Galston, what Americans were doing in Vietnam stood for what humans might do all over the world, to humanity's detriment. In the midst of a global environmental crisis, much-needed foliage and produce were disappearing. Yet in making this point, they distracted debate away from the situation in Vietnam. The scientists' critique stood apart from protestations about the war. It was not about the Vietnamese themselves, but about the whole earth and all of its inhabitants. This is not to say that vocal scientists like Meselson, Westing, and Galston were unconcerned about the Vietnamese people whose environment had been laid waste. But their rhetoric generalized the problem and began to call for universal bans upon any kind of warfare that could wreak such environmental devastation.

President Nixon was astute enough to understand that biological and chemical weapons were only one part of the criticism leveled at the United States for "ecocide" in Vietnam. The controversy about herbicides had linked the military research on exploiting knowledge of nature with the mounting question of the earth's vulnerability. Nixon himself was not immune to concerns about the natural environment. Less than a month after being sworn in as president, he visited the beaches of Santa Barbara, California, covered in crude oil from a rig's blowout offshore, which had devastated the area's wildlife. The spill galvanized environmental activism in California, Nixon's home state, and stimulated Nixon's own environmental agenda. In fact, despite the president's mixed reputation for understanding and caring about environmental issues, many of the key pro-environment national developments came during his presidency, including the creation of the Environmental Protection Agency.[29]

More than any president before or since, Nixon explicitly reinforced the view that the entire earth was at risk due to human activities and that mankind stood at the brink of its own annihilation. He did so on military questions, on environmental issues, and especially on subjects that mixed the two. Nixon also played an enormous role in promoting a global vision of environmental change, one that acknowledged the environmentalists' rhetoric of catastrophe and drew from the deep well of military work on exploiting nature to maximize human death. He expressed candid and rather pointed views about the earth's vulnerability and humanity's fragility, reinforcing the notion that humans could not only bring about serious changes in the natural environment but that doing so could have devastating consequences for humans all over the world. As he put it, humanity held in its hands the seeds of its own destruction.

Had Nixon achieved some sort of green enlightenment? Undoubtedly he was concerned about environmental problems, but the energies and political capital he expended in addressing these require a different explanation. In his pursuit of diplomatic détente with the Soviet Union, and in continuing America's global Cold War struggle with that country, Nixon found the rhetoric of global catastrophe to be extremely useful. It informed his surprising decision to unilaterally ban germ warfare and ultimately to negotiate a treaty with the Soviets. He used it to justify a new push to finally ratify the 1925 Geneva Protocol banning the first use of chemical weapons. He used it to assert a leadership role in the new UN "global brain" on environmental matters. He would also use it to argue for a major non-nuclear disarmament pact banning environmental modification. All of these were wise diplomatic moves for Nixon. In the case of the weapons treaties, they required little sacrifice because the only catastrophic weapons that actually mattered to Nixon—nuclear weapons—were studiously ignored throughout all of these actions.

To accomplish his diplomatic goals, Nixon tried to control—and even lead—the global environmental movement. With widespread criticism of its conduct of the war in Vietnam, the Nixon administration took pains to ensure that leadership in global environmental affairs did not fall into other hands. Already there were threatening contenders. Motivated by a strong opposition to the Vietnam War and an increasing attention to environmental problems, Sweden had taken a first step toward establishing a body under the United Nations specifically oriented toward environmental issues. The Swedish government successfully called upon the UN to sponsor a major international environmental summit and even offered to host it.

From the American perspective, Sweden was one of the most dangerous competitors for environmental leadership. Its prime minister, Olof Palme, had been an outspoken critic of the Vietnam War since the Americans escalated it in 1965, and the Swedish government was unwavering in its opposition to American actions there. The US government had already demanded in vain that Sweden apologize for one-sided speeches given by high-ranking officials. Sweden had hosted a major anti-war event in 1967, the Bertrand Russell International War Crimes Tribunal, which even the French—rarely shy from asserting an independent path from the Americans—had refused to host. The tribunal heard evidence of alleged American atrocities against civilians, but heard no evidence against America's foes. It was such a one-sided affair that even Swedish newspapers predicted that the country would be perceived as the center of anti-Americanism in Europe. Palme later walked side by side with North Vietnamese diplomat Nguyen Tho Chanh in a protest rally numbering some 5,000 people. Sweden then shocked the United States by offering housing and government pensions to Americans soldiers who deserted.[30] Relations between the two countries plummeted. Next the Swedes had called for the first international environmental meeting to be held in Stockholm, which promised to have an anti-American theme unless Americans stepped in to lead it.

Although the global consequences of environmental change were still highly controversial within the United States, the Nixon administration played up the earth's vulnerability, the global environmental threat, and the need for a global solution. Nixon wanted the United States to play a leading role in creating a global body. He had powerful reasons for doing this. One was the looming threat that UN-wide environmental discussions would merely become vehicles for criticism of the Vietnam War. The other was a public relations contest with the Soviet Union. It proved to be in American interests to nip criticism in the bud and to embrace catastrophic environmentalism. Nixon went so far as to promise to provide millions of dollars to finance the activities of a new United Nations body that would coordinate these global solutions.

In a surprising move that revealed a great deal about his focused, East-West approach to international politics, Nixon initially attempted to promote environmental issues through the North Atlantic Treaty Organization. In his first year in office, he pressured NATO into creating a Committee on the Challenges of Modern Society, specifically to address issues that were symptomatic of technologically advanced, industrial societies. It would include the hot-button issues of the day, covering not just pollution but also traffic, road safety, and unemployment. At least in its rhetoric, the new NATO group tried to tackle what leading environmentalists had identified as the malaise of unfettered growth. While some sectors of NATO were exploring the finer points of environmental warfare, the new committee claimed it wanted to save the earth. The New York Times proclaimed, "NATO Joins the Fight to Save the Environment," pointing out that the alliance would try to "face the ecological consequences" of industrial life and stave off the doomsday scenarios offered by Ehrlich, Commoner, and others.[31]

Although some were skeptical of this new mission for NATO—even at NATO Headquarters it was referred to blithely as "the environmental thing"—Nixon's critics were downright horrified. Nixon seemed to be hijacking a peaceful global movement to improve the conditions of life and coupling it with a nuclear-armed military alliance. At the very least, did that not send the wrong message to the rest of the world?

To Nixon, on the other hand, it was the natural move. NATO countries could coordinate with each other more easily under the alliance, and it might provide a natural outlet for collaboration with the Soviet bloc. One of Nixon's principal strategies in the Cold War struggle with the Soviet Union was to develop multiple points of discussion between superpowers. Rather than simply get bogged down in the same old questions of nuclear disarmament, why not improve one's negotiating power by linking it with other issues—such as scientific cooperation, economic aid, human rights, and even environmental issues? In time, such "linkage" would become a hallmark of the Nixon diplomatic approach.[32]

Within the alliance, Europeans resented this use of NATO because it diverted attention from local and regional problems and made "the environment" conform to the large-scale vision of the president. Europeans had their own environmental problems, and they often disagreed among themselves. One French diplomat complained to a British colleague that he thought the environmental committee was supposed to be a group of experts and that the Americans in particular were turning the environment into a mere vehicle for East-West dialogue.[33] German diplomats felt obligated to support the pet projects of the Americans but saw NATO's Committee on the Challenges of Modern Society as pointlessly repeating work better suited to existing bodies.[34] The British put it bluntly, "we do not like the CCMS, which is too susceptible to United States pressure, particularly from White House empire builders. We shall be stuck with it for good if it becomes the main channel for East-West environmental work—and have little control over its activities."[35] The British were rather vocal—behind the scenes—in criticizing Nixon and his environmental envoy Russell Train for trying to enforce a global vision for environmental action.

The Soviets at first seemed serious about environmental cooperation. The Soviet government began to mimic Nixon's actions, upgrading environmental issues to a high status—which meant that instead of sending scientists to international meetings, it sent diplomatic delegations. This made questions of representation impossible to avoid, and environmental issues soon became casualties of the Cold War impasse on the question of recognizing East Germany as a nation. The Soviets eventually withdrew from the 1972 Stockholm conference, compelling most of the Warsaw

Pact countries to pull out too. Although this was widely perceived as a major failure for global collaboration, it served American interests perfectly. The Soviets no longer were serious contenders for leadership in whatever global body might emerge from the conference.

What worried American allies was that the geopolitical momentum seemed to favor a new international "brain" to coordinate environmental action. NATO countries insisted on finding a way to prevent the body from being hijacked by the Soviet Union or by countries of the developing world. One key indicator was a workshop on the international management of environmental problems, held in the summer of 1971 at the Aspen Institute for Humanistic Studies, in the United States. Drawing together scholars; some government officials from Britain, France, Germany, and Sweden; and members of the Stockholm conference secretariat, the Aspen workshop produced a series of recommendations for global effort. It embraced the United Nations as the vehicle for action and rejected the notion that cooperation could succeed on a purely East-West basis but had to include the participation of the global South.[36] Although it did not go so far as to recommend a new agency, it did encourage a special unit or secretariat to coordinate global action. The US State Department suggested setting up a global environmental fund to which the United States would contribute about $100 million.

With free-flowing cash, the United States hoped to buy leadership in the new global brain, simply by being its principal benefactor. Some European officials abhorred the idea of a special fund, or even a global brain.[37] In a speech at the University of Sussex, the chief scientist at Britain's Department of the Environment, Martin Holdgate, was very critical of the Aspen workshop. He called it "a masterpiece of global generalization without adequate awareness of the national—like a building in which the architect begins by designing a roof and omits specifications of the walls by which it is to be supported or the function of those who are to work within its shelter."[38] The biosphere may be a unit, he said, but most environmental problems were local, national, or regional, not requiring clunky international organizations and global action. But as another British official, Eldon Griffiths, complained, "our determination to deal with this problem on a regional basis in the first instance is not really in accord with the Americans' more global philosophy."[39]

The NATO allies thus had to contend with a clash of worldviews. On one side were those who preferred pragmatic local and regional actions to address specific environmental problems. This had been the approach favored on the pages of *Nature* by its editor John Maddox. On the other side were those who favored global action, on the grounds that the world confronted a universal crisis that could be handled only if everyone worked together. In the end, NATO chose the global approach even though its members explicitly disagreed with it, because together they accepted that NATO consensus could be useful in relations with the Soviet bloc and with the countries of the developing world.

Nixon was savvy enough to see the handwriting on the wall. Environmentalism was going global. The United States could embrace it, and hope to control it, or oppose it, letting others take the helm. Reluctantly, the British, the French, the Germans, the Belgians, and in fact all the NATO allies supported the Americans in their attempt to buy control of the new global environmental body. A few NATO countries created an informal "Brussels group" to help define their genuine interests in environmental politics and guide global activities.[40] This still required liaison with the United States but circumvented the White House in favor of State Department diplomats, who struck European diplomats as more experienced and reasonable. If a global body were unavoidable, Britain insisted that industrialized Western European countries first should establish consensus among themselves rather than leave all the diplomacy to Nixon.[41]

European diplomats, particularly the British, held their noses as they embraced the global vision of environmental action. But they were confident that the formation of the secret Brussels Group would protect their interests. The Brussels Group was even narrower than NATO's already exclusive membership: it was comprised of the United States, Britain, France, Italy, the Netherlands, Belgium, and West Germany. They agreed to keep in touch with Maurice Strong, who headed up the plans for the Stockholm conference, and said "we should not be deflected by his grumbling that we were working in a 'secret group.'"[42] This secrecy mattered: the Brussels Group believed that the substance of environmental agreements had consequences, that each nation had its own interests, and that the allies ought to negotiate with each other first. So, on a small wooded estate outside Brussels, the Château du Val Duchesse, key allies began to outline the steps they could make in unison in any international forum, in the face of pressure from either the Soviet Union or the countries of the developing world.[43]

Gaining control of global environmental action meant that American and European diplomats had to embrace the rhetoric of those who warned of environmental catastrophe. The US State Department soothed the allies' tempers by promising true negotiations within NATO, in return for solidarity on general principles in international venues. State Department envoy Christian Herter believed in "the power of the purse" because new environmental work would be financed from this voluntary pool of funds, and thus it actually would control spending. Europeans only agreed to the American vision on the condition of a strong commitment to the consensus of Cold War allies. Their governments would need to control their delegations, "so that at least the leading industrialized countries who provide most of the funds would speak with one voice in the Agencies." A core alliance-based position would be essential on all major environmental issues, and, as one British official added, "we must be careful when expanding the group not to include awkward bedfellows."[44]

Historians may look back at the Stockholm conference and the subsequent UN Environment Programme as a successful effort by the United States and Western Europe to address environmental issues on a global basis. But the most important issues for the United States were to ensure that it kept a leadership role vis-à-vis the Soviet Union and to avoid environmental action becoming a mouthpiece for criticism about the Vietnam War.[45] Under other leadership, the UN group might have begun to criticize the United States and its allies on many other fronts too. America's European allies agreed with these aims but also wanted to avoid having their voices drowned out by the rising voice of developing countries, including many former colonial territories. In other words, they embraced global environmental action with self-interested cynicism. In Britain, Foreign and Commonwealth Office bureaucrat Frank Wheeler observed that despite the pleas for global action, the genuine international discussions would be confined to the occasional "skull session" between trusted friends.[46]

Those friends would soon begin negotiating a major treaty across Cold War lines that tackled head-on the human ability to arm nature on a global scale. This time, the phrase "environmental warfare" would emerge from secret NATO meetings and enter public consciousness. As the great powers tried to decide whether to ban environmental manipulations for military purposes, the lines between civilian and military research blurred even further, initiating a lasting controversy about whether human actions could push the earth to the brink of catastrophe.

9

The Terroristic Science
of Environmental Modification

*This is an era in which there has been a lot of para-or-
pseudo-scientific extrapolation. And most of this extrapolation has been of a terroristic or brain-washing kind. We
are threatened with the melting of the polar ice-caps. . . .
We are threatened with the exhaustion of the oxygen re-
serve in the earth. . . . We are threatened with cancer. . . .
We are threatened with hunger. We are threatened with
emphysema. We are threatened with poisons. We are
threatened with numbers; such numbers that there will be
less than elbow room, not on earth, but in our little already
half-scuttled spaceship.*

—BRAZILIAN AMBASSADOR MIGUEL OZÓRIO DE
ALMEIDA, addressing the United Nations,
November 29, 1971

BY THE EARLY 1970s, the average reader of newspapers would have been
exposed to a dizzying array of information about the environmental perils
facing the world. In 1972 *The Times* (Britain), *Die Welt* (West Germany), *La
Stampa* (Italy), and *Le Monde* (France) published a joint report on the environment to sort out fact from fiction. The general public had learned a new
watchword—ecology—and it seemed that mankind was himself a kind of
invasive pest. Citing the MIT studies instigated by the Club of Rome, these
newspapers warned that unless mankind changed direction in population
growth, consumption, and pollution, painful disruptions "will be forced
upon it by the agency of disaster within the lifetime of those now living."
But did doomsayers take this too far? World-ending, apocalyptic imagery,
these newspapers reported, had the potential to obscure real issues. There
was something about ecology peddlers that was "too much like revivalist
preaching" to convince sober scientists.[1]

Already countries of the developing world had begun to perceive global environmental action as a hypocritical rich man's game. The rhetoric of the industrialized countries—the main sources of pollution—emphasized global catastrophe, seemingly in order to tie the hands of poor countries trying to improve their economies. The United States fought an immensely destructive war while its scientists played with computer models and warned that the rest of the world needed to stop having so many children. Because global solutions seemed to suggest limits on national autonomy and (especially) on economic growth, commentators from developing countries began to characterize American science as "terroristic" and "brainwashing."

In the years to come, that terror was coupled with the international discussions about large-scale environmental modification for military purposes. Had scientists working with military sponsors in fact found ways to cause human death over large areas, using natural processes? At first glance, it seems that they had: for several years the United States negotiated with the Soviet Union to ban not just biological weapons, but weapons of environmental modification. However, many Western scientists saw the superpower talks as pure Cold War politics, not genuine arms control negotiations. They believed that the weapons being banned remained firmly in the realm of science fiction. Journalists' and politicians' efforts to play up the dangers of environmental warfare deepened the skepticism of those already wary of grandiose claims about global change. That left unanswered the question among scientists and laypersons alike—what were the real possibilities of large-scale, human-induced environmental change?

At the UN General Assembly, the Brazilian delegate Miguel Ozório de Almeida lampooned what he called the "para-or-pseudo-scientific extrapolation" given by American and European scientists about environmental dangers. "We are threatened with the melting of polar ice-caps, the consequent increase in sea levels and the wholesale drowning of some of the largest cities and capitals in the world." These were the same risks that scientists claimed were part of Soviet and American military arsenals. But now the world was being frightened into blaming themselves? The Brazilian complained that such statements had caused the price of real estate to escalate to higher elevations in Rio de Janeiro. He was particularly critical of the audacity of environmentalists to complain about the depletion of the Amazon rain forests—which absorbed a great deal of carbon dioxide— as if it were the responsibility of Brazil to compensate for the North

American and European excesses. He went on to list supposed threats, all based on scientific extrapolation of a "terroristic or brain-washing kind": cancer, hunger, emphysema, poisons, and numbers of people "not on earth, but in our little already half-scuttled space-ship." He mocked the "body of ecologists who have been free to escalate their threats and adopt an apocalyptic approach to public opinion." Brazil's approach, he claimed in contrast, was to set aside over-dramatization and utilize "a little bit of good old common-sense."[2]

Skepticism in the face of doomsaying ran deep within the United Nations, where civil servants grew weary of American scientists' scare tactics. Even the idea of creating a new UN agency, on the grounds that environmental problems were global in scope, seemed to require a catastrophic mentality. Although UN Secretary-General U Thant suggested that a new agency might be just the right remedy, his words were met with, as one journalist put it, "quiet dismay in UN circles."[3] One example was an early planner of the Stockholm conference, Swiss engineer Jean Mussard. He had played an active role in the creation of the European Center for Nuclear Research (CERN) and had directed the European Space Research Organization, but was not known for his environmental anxieties. Interviewing him from his office at UN headquarters in New York, journalist Kathleen Teltch was surprised to hear him describe the smoke coming from Long Island factories as picturesque. He sat smoking a pipe, which he jokingly called his own contribution to pollution. He was actually quite sympathetic to poorer countries that said they wanted pollution—because pollution meant industry. He warned that the dire predictions of catastrophe by scientists and politicians were undermining serious environmental efforts. "Too much scare talk," he said, "can have its bad effects. People get bored." A longtime participant in international organizations, Mussard was skeptical of a global solution to environmental problems and dismissed the idea of creating another a new agency as a typical UN solution.[4]

Mussard was not alone in feeling beaten down by the rhetoric of global crisis and the prophecies of doom. *Los Angeles Times* environmental reporter Bryce Nelson wondered whether it did any good to warn about catastrophe. In a 1971 essay review of six recent books—S. P. R. Charter's *Man on Earth*, Michael Hamilton's *This Little Planet*, Jean Dorst's *Before Nature Dies*, James Ridgeway's *The Politics of Ecology*, Alexander B. Adams's *Eleventh Hour*, and Gordon Rattray Taylor's *The Doomsday Book: Can the World Survive?*—Nelson observed that the tone of gloom and doom was so pervasive that it was difficult to avoid the impression that the world was beyond hope. "Anyone who might read six recent ecological books in one concerted effort," he wrote bleakly, "would feel so overwhelmed with problems that he might go out and chop down a few trees, shoot an endangered species or take a long drive in his polluting automobile just to obtain therapeutic relief."[5] Similarly, a contributor to *Science News* complained in 1972 that modern-day utopian visions had abandoned the message "heed us and life will be better" and replaced it with "heed us or the human race cannot survive."[6]

The UN found a new man to organize the Stockholm conference who was less cynical and UN-weary, Canadian businessman Maurice Strong. *The Times* described him in late 1970 thus: "Mr. Strong is an activist. The UN system, like the Amazon rain-forest, feeds largely on its own decomposition. It suffers from an epidemic of documentation. The calendar of meetings and symposia and seminars is as thick as the Bible. Stockholm 1972, Strong believes, could and should be different."[7] But Strong knew also that employing the language of crisis could provoke a backlash of cynicism. He tried to take a moderate line, saying that there were considerable differences of opinion among scientists about the severity of the environmental problem. Doom might—or might not—be imminent. But he did not believe complacency was an option. "We need subscribe to no doomsday threat to be convinced that we cannot—we dare not—wait for all the evidence to be in. Time is no ally here unless we make it one."[8]

Meanwhile major newspapers and magazines gave prominent coverage to environmental issues. Science correspondents routinely reported issues related to pollution and other ills, and the *Washington Post* even gave journalist Claire Sterling the specific task of reporting periodically on "the damage being done to the planet Earth" and the global efforts to address it. Sterling began with an air of crisis, reporting breathlessly prior to the Stockholm meeting:

> Scientists still aren't sure how much carbon dioxide we can inject into the atmosphere before heating it up enough to melt the polar icecaps, how much smog can cut off the sun's rays without bringing a new Ice Age upon us, how many germs per cubic centimeter of water we can swallow and live, how much better or worse off the human race would actually be for using or banning DDT.

Perhaps Stockholm itself would set the stage for drawing up "planetary environmental codes."[9]

As the United States government tried to take the helm of this global movement, its global vision had some long-range effects, not simply the creation of the American-financed United Nations Environment Programme. Nixon matched his rhetoric not with massive environmental reforms on an international scale but by making a show of banning weapons associated with global environmental devastation and manipulation. Many of the weapons systems developed after World War II seemed to violate America's posture as a leader in global environmental awareness, without adding significantly to America's strategic position vis-à-vis the Soviet Union. The most obvious example of this was biological weapons, which Nixon swiftly denounced, using the most dire language about risking the destruction of all humanity. The Nixon administration took the initiative, banning germ warfare in advance of an agreement. Rather than deny the possibility of catastrophe, Nixon embraced the idea.

If American scientists were acting like "terrorists," as the Brazilian ambassador claimed, the US government played up that terror by pointing to the decades-long research in environmental manipulation. In addition to banning biological weapons and pushing ratification of the Geneva Protocol, Nixon turned his back on climate modification. As recently as 1965, the director of America's National Center for Atmospheric Research in Boulder, Colorado, William Orr Roberts, had tried to associate weather and climate research with preventing rather than causing catastrophic change. Control meant management, and the recent development of numerical modeling for weather prediction seemed to empower the atmospheric sciences to take a more realistic managerial view of the earth. Roberts observed, "In a world beset by drought, severe storms, and a population explosion which requires management of natural resources, people become impatient." But true weather control, Roberts cautioned, was far off, if possible at all. Still, scientists were engaged in a large-scale study to build a model of the atmosphere, taking into account enough variables to predict future weather and climate conditions, and for testing schemes for modification and control.[10]

In just a few years, however, large-scale weather tampering appeared as much a symptom of environmental problems as their solution. One clear signal was in the fate of Project Stormfury, a series of experiments on large-scale hurricane seeding begun in 1962, as a joint effort of the Navy and the Department of Commerce. A new technology— satellites—allowed tropical storms and hurricanes to be spotted long before they reached landfall. Stormfury researchers believed that they could dissipate these massive storms. If clouds on the outer edges of a storm could be seeded by aircraft, this might cause the "eye" to widen and thus decrease wind speed. Though taken over by the civilian National Oceanic and Atmospheric Administration (NOAA) in 1970, Stormfury continued to enjoy the patronage of the Department of Defense because of clear military implications of dissipating, strengthening, or steering hurricanes. But Nixon's budget for fiscal year 1974 simply cancelled support for the project at NOAA and the Department of Defense. Although the project continued to exist until 1983, it devoted most of its efforts to cloud seeding in Florida. After sending a plane into Hurricane Ginger in 1971, the project stopped seeding hurricanes. There were not enough "ideal" hurricanes in the Atlantic Ocean for the experiments, and moving to the Pacific Ocean would have entailed far too many diplomatic problems if the scientists were accidentally to send a storm over a foreign country.[11]

Why the sudden shyness about weather control? Over time, weather modification would fall from grace, due in part to the rise in concern about climate change and the possibility of unintended modification. It became what one scholar describes as "a technology contested in multiple ways."[12] Perhaps most important in the early 1970s, weather modification had acquired an unshakeable connection to the war in Vietnam after the June 1971 publication of a secret history of the war prepared by the Department of Defense. Leaked to the press by RAND economist and game theorist Daniel Ellsberg and published in installments on the pages of the *New York Times* and other newspapers, the report became known colloquially as the Pentagon Papers. The documents revealed how four successive American presidents escalated the war in Vietnam. It revealed scores of misleading or false statements, such as Johnson's 1964 campaign promise not to widen the war—made after he already had planned to do just that. The highly inflammatory documents also entangled President Nixon, because in vain he used every legal means at his disposal to stall publication in newspapers.[13] Among the Pentagon Papers' many revelations were some surprising efforts to alter the physical environment for military purposes, not just with herbicides but also through weather modification.

In terms of weather control, the Pentagon Papers revealed, Stormfury was just the tip of the iceberg. In addition to cloud seeding of hurricanes, the Americans had become pioneers in military applications of rainmaking. In Project Popeye, American planes attempted to lengthen the monsoon season in Laos and Vietnam to keep the Ho Chi Minh trail muddy and hamper the ability of the North Vietnamese to move supplies and men. Despite the uncertain consequences for surrounding areas, American scientists had been working with the military to bring as much rain to these supply lines as possible.[14]

After the revelations in the Pentagon Papers, many scientists wished to go on record as having been opposed to weather modification, particularly for military purposes. The policy-minded scientific organization, the Federation of American Scientists (FAS), wrote to the president in early 1973 asking him to disclose past and present activities using weather as a form of warfare. The group's scientists, numbering around 4,500, tried to stress that it did not need to be a partisan political issue—after all, the alleged rainmaking along the Ho Chi Minh trail had been initiated during the Johnson administration, so Nixon would bear no responsibility for it. Indeed the FAS spokespeople on the issue were two men with politically moderate credentials—Herbert Scoville Jr., who had been deputy-director of the CIA under Eisenhower and Kennedy, and Gordon MacDonald, the geophysicist who not only had been an original member of Nixon's own Council on Environmental Quality but had also worked with the Institute for Defense Analyses. Thus the FAS wisely chose two men who had credibility not as activist scientists but as Washington insiders—in defense, intelligence, and science.[15]

As in the case of herbicides, these critics extrapolated from what actually had occurred in Vietnam and called to mind a problem of global scope, with catastrophic consequences. They implied that American scientists and military leaders were playing with forces they could not control. The focus on rainmaking implicated all of the "wildcat" ideas on environmental warfare, which NATO had studied in the early 1960s and MacDonald had written about in *Unless Peace Comes*. In his letter to the president, FAS chairman Marvin L. Goldberger warned that the United States was setting a dangerous precedent:

There are many different kinds of geophysical warfare which, if they were to be engaged in by ourselves and by opponents, would be to the clear disadvantage of mankind. The use of weather modification as a weapon of war is an opening wedge to the use of climate modification, the inducement of earthquakes, and other still more terrible methods. We see geophysical warfare as a "Pandora's box" to which the seemingly inoffensive weather modification may be the disastrous key.

The general public, Goldberger wrote to Nixon, had a right to know what the US military had done.[16]

Was the United States going to attempt an international treaty to ban yet another class of weapons unrelated to nuclear arms? Taking in these events, the British Embassy was not overly worried that Nixon would give in to these critics. Although it was disturbing to see establishment scientists and officials speak out so forcefully, particularly Gordon MacDonald, they guessed that "no landslide is likely to be caused by the stones that he threw."[17] Irresistible quips ensued about the possible reaction: disarmament negotiations were "passing through the doldrums"; meteorological warfare will "fail to raise a storm"; and "even a mild flurry is only a remote possibility."[18]

Despite their wit, the British could not have been more wrong. The political pendulum had swung decisively against military weather modification. Senator Claiborne Pell reinforced the FAS request by calling upon Nixon to disclose all related American activities in Southeast Asia, pointing to the dangers posed "to our own country, and indeed to all of humanity" by the unbridled development of geophysical weapons.[19] By mid-1973, the US Senate passed a resolution to seek a treaty banning its use in war.

Nixon played the subject of environmental warfare precisely the way he had played biological weapons. If it was not a crucial part of America's geopolitical posture, why not ban it in as public and grand a way as possible? Why not play up the ability of scientists and the military to harness the powers of nature and destroy all of mankind? Certainly there was no reason to play down their catastrophic character. Agreeing to ban these kinds of weapons would make Nixon appear responsive to public outcry, environmentally conscientious, willing to talk with the Soviets, and capable of coming away with a real international treaty.

By this time scientists were taking seriously the likelihood of human-induced climate change, giving the military possibilities more urgency. Edward Teller and NATO advisers had concluded, a decade earlier, that humans could produce energies to trigger the forces of nature but had doubted permanent changes would ensue. Meteorologists had insisted throughout the 1950s and '60s that even hydrogen bombs could not alter weather systems. But other scientists—using modeling techniques and computer simulation—were revising their views about the cumulative effects of altering the atmosphere's composition. Many of them were taking seriously the predictions being made since the end of the nineteenth century that burning fossil fuels could lead to widespread warming.

Even the hard-line naysayers, professional meteorologists, had come around to the view that tampering with the chemical composition of the atmosphere could alter its average temperature. Data collected since the International Geophysical Year seemed to confirm the long-suspected accumulation of carbon dioxide. In a 1972 *Nature* article, the director of Britain's Meteorological Office, John S. Sawyer, warned of the "Greenhouse Effect" due to trapped carbon dioxide. He predicted that a 25 percent increase in carbon dioxide, projected to occur by the year 2000, would amount to an increase in temperature of 0.6 degrees Celsius. (He turned out to be close: the global surface temperature between the 1970s and 2000 would rise about 0.5 degrees Celsius. This made Sawyer's projection, as one author put it later, "perhaps the most remarkable long-range forecast ever made.")[20]

Sawyer was not alone in his calculations, but he saw the preoccupation with catastrophic change to be counterproductive. Because the Americans were obsessed with the specter of military environmental change, they were putting climate change into diplomatic discussions in the same way they had done with nuclear disarmament, linking it with world-ending cataclysm. While linking climate change to catastrophe, he felt, the Americans were ignoring the real issue: nuclear weapons. Despite the grand gestures of the United States and the Soviet Union, purposeful climate modification was a weapon that nobody actually possessed and probably never would possess. Compared to nuclear weapons, he felt, the global significance of military weather or climate modification was laughable. Sawyer still believed that humans could not compete with the forces of nature and certainly could not control them. Advising his government's diplomats, he was adamant that there was "no scientific justification for the assumption that any alterations of weather or climate can be produced by artificial means with sufficient magnitude or with sufficient reliability to be of military significance."[21]

Global environmental cataclysm became the subject of bickering across Cold War lines, to the disgust of many scientists, including Sawyer. Unlike the agreements to ban atmospheric nuclear tests, there was no way to tell whether any alleged weather or climate modification had been caused by man or by nature. Sawyer saw only a future of "fruitless discussion and wasteful effort," sapping away scientists' energies and taking time away from their legitimate studies of climate and weather variation. At best, they were politicians' way of distracting people from the nuclear weapons that posed a genuine threat to humanity.[22]

Although Sawyer's government listened to him carefully, British disarmament experts kept their options open. If waging weather warfare "might affect the ecological balance of the entire planet," it raised the same fundamental issues evoked by other weapons classed as weapons of mass destruction: nuclear, chemical, and biological.[23]

Arms control specialists at the United Nations explicitly took up the issue of weather and climate modification in 1974, when Undersecretary of State Inga Thorsson of Sweden raised it at the Conference of the Committee on Disarmanent (CCD). Of independent mind and spirit, Thorsson distrusted the superpowers' commitment to disarmament. Too often, Thorsson later would write, the superpowers just negotiated with each other and ignored the international community.[24] In the case of weather and climate control, Thorsson made a forceful case that the UN ought to get involved even if there were no immediate risks of such weapons being used. She cited the Outer Space Treaty and the Seabed Treaty, which banned the placement of nuclear weapons in these areas—even though doing so was beyond present capabilities.

So the UN was to keep a "watchful eye" on weather and climate modification. Thorsson spoke of human ambitions to improve the weather and of human influence on the climate as a whole. "We are warned," she said, "by environmentalists that caution should be exercised in these and other activities with possible bad direct or indirect effects on climate, on which future human life depends." Thorsson did not mention Vietnam and did not suggest that past efforts had been successful. She prudently avoided any language that could be refuted or denied by any government. Instead, she proposed taking measures to prevent it happening in the future. She also separated out weather modification from climate modification, a step that opened discussions to include a wide variety of environmental alterations. Soon the delegates began talking about "environmental warfare," using the term analyzed more than a decade earlier by NATO military planners.[25]

What was environmental warfare? One arms control specialist admitted to not understanding the difference between weather modification and environmental warfare, except that the latter seemed to include a variety of "less probable technologies—making holes in the ozone layer; melting ice-caps; manufacturing earthquakes (some with the added frill of a tsunami), and, last but not least, fiddling with lightning in such a way as to enhance low frequency electrical oscillations in the atmosphere and thereby interfere with the alpha activity of the brain!"[26]

Having already embraced the rhetoric of global environmental catastrophe, the United States government committed itself to negotiating and signing a treaty condemning environmental modification. As in the case of biological weapons and the UN Environment Programme, the Nixon administration was determined to shape international discussions rather than allow others to take the lead. Secretary of State Henry Kissinger tried to define environmental warfare in ways that would leave considerable room for maneuver. For example, the Americans still wanted to keep enough loopholes in the treaty to allow military actions of actual significance. Fog clearing, for example, technically tampered with the environment for military purposes to make runways accessible to military aircraft. Bombing dams, surely a time-honored tradition in warfare, devastated the natural environment. But these would not be banned. Most important of all, no environmental modification treaty could include nuclear weapons, despite their central role in nearly all previous military assessments of tampering with synoptic-scale forces.[27]

With such loopholes, banning environmental warfare seemed completely pointless. American allies went along with it, carried forward only by geopolitical inertia. "So far as we can see," one British Ministry of Defence official concluded, "climate and weather modification are unlikely to become effective 'weapons of war' and many of the techniques are in the realm of science fiction." Another put it more bluntly, saying "discussion of this subject on the diplomatic net seems well set to aggravate the already acute world paper shortage!"[28]

The subject rapidly turned into Cold War theater. Just as Nixon and Kissinger tried to open loopholes, the savvy Soviet negotiators tried to close them up. Negotiations turned into contests to use the threat of global environmental cataclysm to greatest diplomatic advantage. The Soviets put environmental warfare on the agenda of the UN General Assembly. The proposed subject: "Prohibition of action to influence the environment and climate for military and other purposes incompatible with the maintenance of international security, human well-being and health."[29] Its vague reference to "military and other purposes" promised to take in many more activities than the Americans might be willing to ban. In fact, the Soviet Proposal on Environmental Warfare (referred to by Western negotiators as SPEW) could have been interpreted to rule out anything, including nuclear warfare.

The problem with banning environmental warfare was one of pure logic: didn't all war have an impact on the environment? Didn't the fundamental threat of the Cold War—nuclear warfare—promise environmental devastation on a global scale? Even conventional warfare—using techniques such as "dam-busting," an often-cited example—harnessed the powers of nature. The contours of debate followed a peculiar path that attempted to distinguish between these clear cases of environmental harm and what might legitimately be banned under a new treaty. Questions abounded, and arbitrary lines emerged, connecting and separating weapon systems. Would the creation of artificial acoustic fields under the sea constitute environmental modification? Navies—themselves instruments of war—would be doing it, but using the sea as a medium rather than itself as an instrument. What about the uses of live biological organisms, such as locusts and aphids, not covered in the existing biological weapons treaty? These would cause serious environmental damage—as indeed had occurred in the late 1940s, when the East Germans and Czechs accused American planes of deliberately infecting potato crops with Colorado beetles.[30]

As diplomats chewed over these questions in the summer of 1974, environmental issues must have occupied only the tiniest part of the US president's attention. Although American diplomats had been deeply enmeshed in bilateral talks in Moscow through the summer, including the subject of environmental modification, at home Richard Nixon's presidency was imploding after the Watergate scandal became public. He faced the possibility of impeachment by the US Congress and on August 9, 1974, resigned.

The chaos following Nixon's resignation proved a perfect opportunity for the Soviet Union to seize the leadership role in making environmental modification a serious disarmament issue. It was not long before the Soviet position, authored by seasoned diplomat Victor Israelyan, appeared on the pages of the state-sanctioned journal *International Affairs*.[31]

The Soviets drew deeply from the well of catastrophic rhetoric in American newspapers. Soviet commentators routinely pointed out the attempts to modify the environment during the Vietnam War, but they also widened the threat to include all planetary life. Israelyan mentioned that the "foreign press" increasingly published stories about the efforts to influence the environment:

At first sight, some of these ideas appear to be altogether fantastic. But it cannot be ruled out that the possibility exists of implementing a number of methods described in the press. It is well known that there is an ozone interlayer in the upper layers of the atmosphere, which plays an important role in protecting life on Earth from the Sun's ultra-violet radiation. Some scientists believe that, by using appropriate methods, "holes" in the ozone shield of the Earth can be created in this interlayer, so as to intensify the penetration of rigid ultra-violet radiation on some sectors of our planet. As a result, every form of life in these areas can be destroyed and the entire territory will be turned into a desert.[32]

Israelyan went on to describe the use of low-frequency sound waves, which could bring about the "complete derangement of the human psychics," by provoking feelings of dejection, fear, panic, horror, and despair. Such sound waves might be capable of causing heart attacks or even death. Citing "Western periodicals," Israelyan pointed out that sound waves could be used against ships—and indeed entire flotillas of ships.

It was obvious that, like Nixon, Soviet leaders had found reasons to embrace the idea that global environmental catastrophes might be imminent. Atmospheric electricity could be harnessed, Israelyan said, to suppress mental activities for long periods—or even to harness the power of lightning. The ice of the Arctic and Antarctic could be melted with low-yield nuclear bombs. If detonated at depth, these bombs would create a water cushion between the ice and the mainland rocks. This way, vast chunks of ice would simply slide into the sea, creating gigantic waves "which could wipe off the face of the Earth many coastal cities and entire areas." Underground nuclear explosions could instigate mayhem in a number of ways, from starting a tsunami to setting off a string of earthquakes.[33]

None of the projects or concepts mentioned by Israelyan came from Soviet sources, and certainly none made reference to actual Soviet military projects. All of it was lifted from the "foreign press," especially American and European newspapers, and transcriptions of earlier US congressional hearings. Israelyan emphasized American military applications and contrasted them with the Soviet Union's supposedly peaceful research on rainmaking. It was a typical propaganda piece. But it signaled the Soviet Union's embrace of a catastrophic vision of global environmental change. Israelyan's language was dire: artificial earthquakes could trigger chain reactions and send the earth into the same convulsions it must have felt when it first formed. His conclusion was unambiguous: "Influence on the human and geophysical environment for military purposes constitutes a grave threat to life on Earth."[34]

As diplomats shuttled back and forth between Washington and Moscow, trying to figure out exactly what they wanted to ban, a few scientists tried to speak out against the entire undertaking. Banning environmental warfare, some said, distracted people from the true conclusions of postwar research on global vulnerability—namely, the gradual alterations due to peacetime activities. The rhetoric of American and Soviet negotiators lacked scientific credibility, creating an aura of cynicism about any large-scale environmental change. Again a leading voice was the British meteorologist John S. Sawyer, who was deeply involved in developing ways to detect the steady rise in global temperatures from the "Greenhouse Effect." He stated that researchers were only now developing models to predict what changes might occur if, say, the ice cover in the Arctic were removed—but this, he said, was a far cry from studying how to bring it about. It was highly unlikely that any scientific group—including those in the United States and the Soviet Union—could predict the consequences of a deliberate attempt to modify the climate of any area. The climate "is not easily affected," he argued, requiring any tampering to be on a scale far beyond human capabilities.[35]

Most of the diplomats did not take purposeful climate change much more seriously than Sawyer did. But the ENMOD (Environmental Modification) negotiations had taken on a life of their own, as both superpowers embraced global doomsaying in order to pursue diplomatic aims. Even the Soviets, who had developed a laundry list of potentially grave threats to the earth from environmental modification, could not always discuss them with a straight face, as the following account reveals. It involves Admiral Tom Davies, an assistant director of the US Arms Control and Disarmament Agency, and Evgenii K. Fedorov, the head of the Soviet Union's own hydrographic and meteorological service:

> Fedorov had loved to expatiate on the military potentialities of the activities in the Soviet list; whereas his colleagues had smiled behind their hands and evidently regarded him as a "nut" on the subject. Davies had had to show that military uses did not actually exist. They had taken the Russians down to Florida, in order to brief them on the lack of success in seeding hurricane clouds under the National Oceanic and Atmospheric Administration's Project "Storm Fury."

It is difficult to imagine Soviet delegates snickering about one of their own if they really took these threats seriously. But whether Fedorov indeed put so much stock in the military applications, or was directed to play up the dangers, is unclear. But the Americans clearly did not believe in them, despite the public political rhetoric that widespread, long-term, severe changes to climate were within reach.[36]

The list of genuine military requirements in environmental warfare was actually quite short: dissipating fog and cloud cover and rainmaking. Despite some promising signs that seeding hurricanes might someday yield interesting results, military leaders held little faith in the modification of "synoptic systems," meaning large-scale systems. As one NATO document summarized the situation, "we do not understand the processes involved in these systems sufficiently well to have any knowledge of how we might possibly influence them." At best, scientists might learn through numerical simulations where a system's areas of instability might be—with this knowledge, "the input of a small amount of energy may have a considerable effect on the further development of the system."[37] This euphemism—the input of a small amount of energy—referred to thermonuclear detonations, which no one expected to be banned.

Despite widespread cynicism, the governments of both the United States and the Soviet Union made a point of playing up the dangers to the earth as they tried to lend significance to their high-profile negotiations. The Soviet Union seemed entirely committed to signing an ENMOD treaty. Party Leader Leonid Brezhnev, in advance of the 1975 Supreme Soviet elections, delivered a speech that not only reinforced his country's commitment to détente but also stated his personal desire to see the world's major powers ban new kinds of weapons of mass destruction.[38] As for the United States government, it was on a roll, having signed the Biological and Toxin Weapons Convention in 1972 and having reopened discussion of the Geneva Protocol on chemical weapons. Gerald Ford's presidency continued what Nixon's had started. On April 8, 1975, Ford issued an executive order banning the first use of herbicides in war—turning his back on America's environmentally destructive policies in Vietnam. Two days later, the United States officially deposited its ratification of the Geneva Protocol—50 years after first signing it.[39]

The fact that the two Cold War rivals quite publicly advocated for a treaty made global environmental change seem more real to some while hardening skepticism of knowledgeable insiders to any talk of catastrophe. The Americans' and Soviets' preference for talking first between each other, rather than hashing out their positions at the United Nations, made the mysterious weapons even more terrifying. Actually the reason for the head-to-head talks was that the Americans wanted to get the Soviets to agree to some basic principles so that the treaty language could not be interpreted as a ban on nuclear weapons or on research. These direct discussions were interpreted by journalists as secretive, quiet talks designed to fly under the radar of the international community. *The Guardian* interpreted this darkly, stating that "at present only the Super Powers have the means to develop this kind of warfare."[40] This was a striking contrast to the overall feeling among government officials that these talks were intended simply to keep the lawyers and diplomats busy on a subject that had nothing to do with the Cold War's main attraction, namely, nuclear war. To them, environmental warfare was science fiction.

Belief that the superpowers could cause widespread, catastrophic change to the environment gained considerable ground in the years surrounding the ENMOD negotiations. For example, readers of *New Scientist*, a magazine geared toward a scientifically literate audience, learned in 1975 of the effects of removing the Arctic Ocean's ice cover—"changing our climate, either by accident or by design." Quoting the work of the University of Washington's L. K. Coachman, the magazine pointed out that the formation of ice in the Arctic might be halted if the Soviets were to divert the rivers of Siberia. By decreasing the amount of freshwater reaching the sea, the salt content in the upper layers of the ocean would increase, making it more homogeneous with lower layers and allowing faster mixing with warm water. By rerouting the rivers, the Soviets could stop the formation of ice in as little as a decade, keeping northern ports open and improving the Russian climate.[41]

Soviet participants in international meetings continued to emphasize the catastrophic consequences of human action. They worried about tampering with the ozone layer, which could expose large areas to punishing doses of ultraviolet light—effectively destroying organic life. They also worried about large-scale meddling with cloud cover, or with the evaporation of the ocean, on the grounds that small changes in temperature could lead to major changes in the weather. The Soviets also mentioned the destruction of vegetation, of irrigation systems, of changing the atmosphere's radiation balance by injecting dust into it, and of melting glaciers by coating them with soot. Already the Soviet Union had experimented with this last idea, they claimed, with some success in melting river ice.[42]

Newspapers reported the minutiae of diplomatic meetings with relish. In an article titled "How to Make Weather a War Weapon," the British

Daily Telegraph listed seven ways of tampering with the environment, using information drawn from the disarmament deliberations:

Dispersing cloud or fog
Generating fog and clouds with chemicals
Inducing violent hailstorms
Generating or directing big storms
Making rain or snow
Stimulating volcanoes
Burning vegetation on a large scale

From this list the newspaper speculated about steering hurricanes, using forces of nature quite beyond those of nuclear weapons to wreak havoc on enemy cities. It whetted readers' appetites about climate change— evidently possible by melting ice caps, changing the direction of rivers, and diverting ocean currents. "The climatic changes this would produce," the newspaper predicted, "could result in a major disruption of food production, changes in the ecological balance, increasing erosion and destruction of forests."[43]

Bucking such sensationalism, the *Financial Times* instead chose dry hyperbole: "Is the current British drought a cunning Warsaw Pact plot?" one writer asked in 1975. "Is the recurrence of poor Russian harvests the result of the Americans depleting the Soviet ozone layer, so letting ultraviolet rays shrivel the Russian corn belt and boosting U.S. sales?" The conservative paper relegated such ideas to the realm of "pure Jules Verne fantasy."[44]

Diplomatic negotiators nonetheless began to home in on the meaning of catastrophic environmental modification. They tried to identify activities that were "widespread, long-lasting, and severe." The first two dealt with scope, both in geography and in time. But the third designator, "severe," was explicitly anthropocentric: were significant numbers of humans affected? (See Table 9.1.)

Ironically the Soviets and Americans found more common ground than they expected. They were united in their rhetoric of catastrophic change, and they wanted the treaty to specify the kinds of environmental damage, so that they would not be subjected to a constant barrage of criticism over what they considered trivial environmental harm. The major negotiations ended up being with the "non-aligned" countries, led by Mexico and Argentina, who feared that the superpowers were designing a

Table 9.1 Possible Maximum Effects of Environmental
Modification Techniques

Widespread	Long-lasting	Severe	Activity for Hostile Purposes
*			Fog Dispersion
*			Cloud Dispersion
*			Fog Generation
*			Cloud Generation
**		*	Rain and Snowmaking
*		*	Hailstone Generation
*		*	Lightning Control
*			Changing Electrical Properties of Atmosphere
*			Generating Electrical Fields in Atmosphere
**			Changing Ionosphere
	*	*	Stimulating Landslides
*		**	Generating and Directing Storms
**		**	Generating Tsunamis
**		**	Generating Earthquakes
		**	Stimulating Volcanic Eruptions
**	**	**	Radioactive Material in Sea
**	**	*	Destruction of Forests
**	**	*	Modification of Permafrost
**	*	**	Diminishing Ozone Layer
**	**	**	River Diversion or Pollution
*	*	*	Changing Parameters of Ocean
**	**	**	Climate Modification

Widespread: (*) More than some square kilometers, less than hundreds; (**) More than hundreds of square kilometers

Long-lasting: (*) More than some months, less than some years; (**) More than some years

Severe: (*) Some humans affected; (**) Significant numbers of human affected

The table is adapted from an informal working paper submitted by a delegation of experts from the Netherlands, summarized for the British delegates, August 7, 1975, UK National Archives, FCO 66/825.

cosmetic treaty designed with large loopholes—which they were. In addition, the Americans faced a lawsuit from a coalition of environmental groups claiming that the treaty violated the US Environmental Protection Act. In fact it was in violation: in all their negotiations, diplomats never thought to generate an environmental impact report, one of the key requirements of the Act. These hurdles delayed the date of the official treaty. But the Mexicans eventually relented, leaving in the specifications that the treaty banned environmental warfare only if the effects were widespread, long-lasting, and severe. The case against the US government was thrown out of court because it had been filed improperly. So both the Soviets and the Americans were ready to sign the treaty, along with more than 30 other nations, when it finally was opened for signature in May 1977.

Presiding over the treaty ceremony was UN Secretary-General Kurt Waldheim, which was supposed to reflect not only the treaty's global reach but also the fact that many others played a hand in its formulation. The treaty document itself was to reside at the United Nations, rather than in Moscow and Washington. It was a minor detail, but to the UN it suggested a growing global responsibility for disarmament and for the environment. Like so many commentators of the era, Waldheim invoked the language of ecology to describe international relations. The environment, he claimed, was symbolic of global interdependence. "Politically we are a divided world," he said at the treaty's signing ceremony, "environmentally we are one world. . . . In the last few years it has become evident that advances in science and technology will permit man to change climatic conditions or otherwise change the dynamics, composition or structure of the earth or outer space."[45]

Despite the nearly three dozen initial signatures and the facilitating role of the UN, the treaty was clearly a Cold War document. The Soviet Union sent its minister of foreign affairs, Andrei Gromyko, to sign it, and most of the communist bloc countries sent very high-level ministers. As one British diplomat observed, "this is not surprising since it was the Soviet Union which first proposed a treaty on this subject and Mr. Brezhnev's personal prestige, we have been assured by Soviet colleagues, is bound up with it." Thirteen of the signers were NATO countries, and the Americans sent the highest-ranking diplomat, Secretary of State Cyrus Vance. Along with Gromyko, Vance used the signing ceremony in Geneva as a highly publicized springboard to resume talks on the Strategic Arms Limitation Treaty (SALT). Only 10 of the initial signatories were among the "non-aligned" nations.[46]

The debate over the ENMOD treaty highlights a consolidation of two contradicting views. One was that global catastrophic environmental change had become possible, and it needed to be stopped. The other, which became evident in the long efforts to define what "environmental warfare" actually meant, was that human actions were insignificant compared to the forces of nature. The Nixon administration, and later the Ford and Carter administrations, willingly conceded the environmentalists' argument that large-scale and long-term harm to the environment was a bad outcome—and in fact they made a grandiose gesture of banning weapons that might accomplish such harm. But in the end, most forms of warfare were left out, and only the most imaginary ones stayed in. In the process, negotiators simply reclassified existing ways of war as temporary. Even looking at what happened in Vietnam—which had kick-started the issue in the first place—the Department of Defense argued vehemently that scientists had gotten it wrong. It insisted that in the end, the mangrove trees would grow back, the chemical wasteland created by Agent Orange ultimately would succumb to the sheer power of nature, and plants would grow again. To them, that meant a temporary modification of nature. The same reasoning applied to rainmaking: yes, it was a modification, but it did not make a difference in the great scheme of things— certainly it did not make a permanent alteration to the climate.

The main effect of the ENMOD Treaty was not to ban anything real. After all, nuclear weapons remained untouched, and the language of "widespread, long-lasting, and severe" kept almost everything out of the treaty. *The Times* of London correspondent Alan McGregor called it "a substitute for real achievement in curbing the present arms race."[47] The main effect was to reinforce the impression that global catastrophic environmental change was quite possible, and that the Cold War superpowers already possessed knowledge of how to accomplish it. These were not warnings coming from the margins of society—from a few academic scientists or the tree-hugging fringe—but from the heads of state of the United States and the Soviet Union. The superpowers legitimized global environmental catastrophe as a potential future. In their zeal to sign a treaty banning essentially nothing, they cavalierly had employed extremely dire language. Embracing such images brought environmental change on par with nuclear weapons as a harbinger of global cataclysm.

10

Adjustment or Extinction

We expect temperatures to continue their rise in the grain area because of worldwide increases in atmospheric carbon dioxide.
—Central Intelligence Agency, *Soviet Climate Change: Implications for Grain Production*, 1985

During the 1980s Africa endured and continues to experience wars, insurgencies, drought, desertification, insect plagues, famines, undernourishment, diseases, dysfunctional economic policies—and now the AIDS pandemic.
—Central Intelligence Agency, 1987

ON THE STREETS of Dakar in the early 1970s, the people talked of rain. It seemed to have gone for good. In just a few years, a dry year had turned into two, then three—and soon farmers began to wonder whether something long-term, or even permanent, might be under way. Visually the drought seemed especially meaningful in Dakar. Until quite recently the administrative seat of French West Africa, it had become the capital of the much smaller nation of Senegal. The drought simply made the city, with its oversized, French-inspired architecture, seem too grand for such a poor country. All around were the signs of new climates, both political and natural.

In economic terms, the drought afflicting the northern fringe of sub-Saharan Africa—the Sahel Region—already had taken a massive toll. Dubbed by the *Times* of London a "catastrophic harvest," the groundnut crop in 1972–73 plummeted by a quarter. The Senegalese attempted to turn to the sea, to fish their way out of the disaster. Despite potential bright spots in the economy—phosphate exports, marine repair and maintenance—everyone knew that prospects for future prosperity boiled down to a single variable: rainfall.[1] There were glimmers of hope—a storm here, a rainier season there—but the water table kept falling, year after year. By 1974 the initial dry year had become a drought, and the drought had lasted for six years. The Senegalese government began to reevaluate the definition of a normal crop and to persuade farmers that the poor rain-fall had come to stay. That meant they would have to plant lower-yielding, drought resistant nuts and more grains to feed themselves—a course of action few farmers wished for. The government turned out to be right. The truth was that a much longer-term problem had arrived in the Sahel, as it already had arrived in Ethiopia, introducing a headline in newspapers around the world that would become so commonplace in the decades to come that it would cease to be news: "Famine in Africa."[2]

The Sahel drought was the centerpiece for discussions about the earth's vulnerability in the 1970s. Had humans done it? A decade or so earlier, few would have entertained the notion. But now human action topped all the lists of potential reasons for the drought. Human economic decisions had not helped: Sahelian states had long focused on cash crops, making them less able to feed themselves in times of crisis. But had humans *caused* the drought? Some blamed European aid, funneled through Christian relief organizations, government "development" funds, or even the United Nations. Large-scale well-digging programs had boosted the numbers of people and livestock living in the region, and humans would pay the price. As English journalist Martin Walker described it in the *New York Times*:

> These lands of the Sahel . . . are among the poorest in the world and when this longest of recorded droughts began in 1966, the region was also trying to cope with the problem of over-population. The good intentions of aid organizations in providing pump-driven wells removed a vital natural restraint upon the cattle herds. . . . With unlimited well water, with vaccination programs and even minimal health care, the numbers of cattle and people probably doubled between 1959 and 1966.

In this telling of events, overgrazing of sparse desert grass caused the Sahara itself to move southward. For the nomadic and peasant people, cash crop economies already had disrupted their ancient ways of living. Now, the drought had dealt the fatal blow. It had produced "such a calamity," Walker wrote, that scientists' statistical machinery was not able to measure it meaningfully. The culprit seemed clear in the headline:

"Drought: Nature and Well-meaning Men Have Combined to Produce a Catastrophe Imperiling Many Millions."[3]

Yet there seemed to be something much bigger under way. With famine in Africa constantly in the news, British observers were disturbed to note that the British Isles were experiencing the least rainy years in living memory. It was easy to make the connection to the disaster in the Sahel. In the summer of 1976, Ugandan President Idi Amin gloated that God was punishing Britain for a host of sins, ranging from imperialism in Africa to the support of Israel. In fact, the drought hit most of Europe, though it did not cut Europeans as deeply as it had Africans.[4]

How much of these changes could be attributed to men, and how much to the normal fluctuations of nature? Had humans finally tinkered too much with the natural world? Some climatologists believed that despite centuries-old patterns of rainfall in Africa, there was something rather different and long-lasting happening there. Polar air masses were not receding northward as much in the summer, meaning that monsoon rains could not move northward either. "No one knows for sure why this has happened," Walker wrote, "although some scientists believe it has to do with the recently observed fact that the temperature of the earth has dropped gradually over the past few decades." The globe was cooling. If true, this would have dire implications for not only the Sahel, but for the world.[5]

Did scientists take human-induced climate change seriously in the 1970s? The answer to this question cannot be separated from the discussions about purposeful environmental modification for military purposes. Scientists weighed in on both questions simultaneously, and the answer to one depended on their views about the other. John Sawyer was publishing influential work on the Greenhouse Effect in the United Kingdom, while American and Soviet scientists alike were deeply concerned with modeling environmental change, continuing the computer work that had inspired the Club of Rome study, *The Limits to Growth*.

The foundational work on anthropogenic climate change asked the same question that military scientists asked: did humans have the ability to make environmental changes on a "synoptic scale" (to use NATO's term)? What kinds of activities would produce "widespread, long-lasting, and severe" effects (to use the criteria of disarmament specialists)? In fact, several of the ENMOD delegates were deeply troubled that the American and Soviet proposals only addressed military manipulations of the environment. There was no meaningful distinction between the scientific work on one or the other. If catastrophic scenarios rang true, what difference did it make whether they took place in peace or war? For a brief moment, negotiators entertained the idea of including peacetime catastrophic environmental change in the treaty. But they hesitated. As British delegate Mark Allen insisted, "intention, not accidental result, must surely be the criterion for establishing a treaty banning environmental modification for military purposes, although there will inevitably be a grey area between the two." Disarmament specialists were not in a position to judge how far the geophysicists and meteorologists should go in experimenting with the natural world, nor how much industrial output could be tolerated, even if changes wrought by scientists and industry in peacetime could have enormous consequences for other nations.[6]

Even if they could not be included in the ENMOD negotiations, peacetime environmental changes could still have genuine strategic significance in the Cold War. The US Central Intelligence Agency followed the science of climate change and population pressures quite closely. In 1974, it projected that population trends, food production, and climate change all were going to make the world a colder place. Using MIT-inspired system dynamics to predict the future, it issued a report that echoed Gordon MacDonald's earlier expressed fear of global cooling. The scientific consensus appeared to be that the future promised shorter growing seasons and broad areas of deficit rainfall. Such changes could produce disparities of production quite rapidly, deepening geopolitical tensions.[7]

The CIA also kept a particularly close eye on the Sahel drought, to track the impacts on the Soviet Union and China. The Soviet Union had managed, in the 1960s, to increase agricultural production. This had provided the Soviet Union—and the Soviet economic system—with a boost of credibility in the Cold War's diplomatic front. Soviet economists had interpreted this as the beginning of an upward trend. However, using climate data, American intelligence analysts believed otherwise. The CIA argued that enhancements in Soviet agricultural production in the 1960s and early 1970s were not to be credited to government policies but rather to a major climate fluctuation that took place between 1960 and 1974. The evidence of that change was all over sub-Saharan Africa. The flow of air from the North Atlantic tended to dip farther south than usual, bringing more rain, mild winters, and cool summers. That pattern pushed the Sahara desert southward, but it also doubled grain production in the Soviet republic of Kazakhstan. While the Soviet government hoped that grain production would continue to increase, climate modeling led the CIA to doubt it.

The dry spell that devastated the Sahel and worried Britain also had sent record rains to central Asia. When the Sahel drought finally ended, the CIA believed that the Soviet boom years were over. A new period of dryness was about to begin in central Asia, the agency believed, and Soviet agriculture was destined for a drawdown.[8]

Although the American intelligence agency had pointed out the global "cooling" trend in 1974, it reversed its position by 1976:

> During the 1960s the Northern Hemisphere was cooling. This period was marked by hemispheric changes such as the Sahelian drought, failures of the Indian monsoon, increasing polar ice, and increased rainfall in the Soviet grain belt. Recently, the cooling trend has reversed, and the Northern Hemisphere now is warming. Rains have returned to the Sahel and India, and rainfall has decreased in the Soviet grain belt. Changes of this magnitude involve the exchange of large amounts of energy affecting climate over many years.[9]

The Sahel drought had been the proverbial weather bell. Now that the rains had returned, a new era seemed to have begun. More important for the United States, the Soviet economy likely would be harmed by further warming.

The change in opinion about global warming versus global cooling sharpened climate scientists' views on the mechanism for altering climate, leading them to believe it could be done—indeed it already was happening. Conventional wisdom since the early twentieth century held that increases in carbon dioxide *should* make the earth warm up. And yet since 1945 there appeared to be a decrease in global temperatures. Some scientists had said that increased chemical aerosols from pollution in the atmosphere sent more incoming solar radiation back into space, making the earth cooler than it otherwise would have been. Other scientists suggested that this atmospheric pollution should have the opposite effect, warming the earth because it prevented the escape of heat from the surface. American scientist Marshall Atwater pointed out in 1970 that there was a germ of agreement here, namely, that reflectivity was of prime importance. The lower cloud layers had a certain albedo—the scientific term for this reflectivity—that was subject to change based on the composition of the atmosphere itself. Therefore adding pollutants could contribute to climate change, because the albedo determined how much heat was scattered back into space and how much was trapped underneath the clouds. Very small changes in the ratio of absorption to scattering would determine whether the atmosphere was heating or cooling.[10]

Rather than deny the possibility of changes, military and intelligence analysts tried to imagine how they would work to America's advantage or disadvantage. For example, just as the CIA wondered about the effects of albedo on Soviet wheat, military analysts warned that it might be possible to punch a hole in the ozone layer, exposing Americans or Russians to fatal amounts of radiation. Such concerns in turn heightened anxiety about non-military alterations of the ozone layer, such as what might occur due to the emissions from supersonic airplanes. In 1970, the president's Council on Environmental Quality warned that the vapor from supersonic transportation might destroy parts of the ozone layer and allow in excessive amounts of deadly ultraviolet radiation. One commentator wrote in the *New York Times*, "it would be mad to proceed with a project that might warp the climate of the world."[11]

In the late 1970s, the United States government took the earth's vulnerability to climate change more seriously than it ever had before. By then it had spent years negotiating with the Soviet Union in summit meetings to broker nuclear arms limitations and to hammer out the ENMOD Treaty. President Jimmy Carter tried to follow through with the process begun under Nixon and Ford to deal with potentially catastrophic change in military contexts. But scientists' focus on albedo and carbon dioxide unexpectedly brought these discussions into arenas not confined to arms control. The United States found itself on unfamiliar ground, and President Carter was ill-equipped to answer tough questions on climate change. In 1977, the year the ENMOD Treaty was signed, Carter directed his Council for Environmental Quality to work with the State Department to make projections for the future even in the case of peace. That collaboration led to the *Global 2000 Report to the President*, which tried to assess the scientific evidence for a range of environmental issues.[12]

Politically, the Carter administration had laid an albatross around the United States' neck. When Carter requested the study, he said that it would "serve as the foundation of our longer-term planning." What he received was an unequivocal prediction of dire consequences and a call for international cooperation. It went far beyond climate change. It presented in the clearest terms a consensus view within government, based on the advice of environment experts and professional diplomats, that global trends were degrading the earth's natural resources, endangering entire species, and contaminating its oceans and air. It urged an unprecedented effort at global cooperation and commitment. Although the *Global 2000 Report* avoided the word *catastrophe*, its language pulled few punches: "Vigorous, determined new initiatives are needed if worsening poverty and human suffering, environmental degradation, and international tension and conflicts are to be prevented." The report established a government-sanctioned mandate—one that the subsequent market-oriented Reagan administration would resent—that highlighted international problems such as acid rain from pollution, ozone depletion from the emissions of aerosol cans and refrigerators, ocean and river contamination, and of course climate change due to the burning of fossil fuels.[13]

Meanwhile, rather than take this controversial kitchen-sink approach, other government bodies had begun to assess climate change by itself. One of the first to do so was the JASON group, a body of university scientists who for many years had advised American government and military organizations on an ad hoc basis but now turned its attention to the problem of carbon dioxide. It was the perfect opportunity for JASON member Gordon MacDonald to convene the best minds in the country on his personal obsession—global catastrophic change. He was the geophysicist who in the late 1960s had predicted catastrophic weapons designed to "wreck the environment," had served on President Nixon's Council on Environmental Quality, and had called for openness about weather modification in Vietnam. Under his guidance, the JASON group pointed out the global consequences of climate warming, predicting crop vulnerabilities in many parts of the world.[14]

With these bleak views emanating from within government, the Carter administration soon found itself in need of a more comprehensive view specifically on carbon dioxide, because the question kept coming up in international discussions. For example, in advance of the 1980 meeting of leading industrialized democracies (the G7 summit) in Venice, the West German government submitted the "carbon dioxide problem" to the agenda. American diplomats needed reliable information. Also, Carter was confronted with a major fuel crisis as countries of the Middle East banded together to limit supplies to the United States. One of the proposed solutions was a major crash program in developing synthetic fuels. These, however, would entail serious carbon emissions. So President Carter asked the National Academy of Sciences—not a government agency—to prepare some recommendations about carbon dioxide. They made short work of it, confirming that continued increases in carbon dioxide would result in substantial global climate changes. Congress then appropriated some more money and the academy undertook a long, detailed study of carbon dioxide and climate change. It was known as the Carbon Dioxide Assessment Committee, and it would leave a deep footprint upon the debates about catastrophic environmental change—particularly about global warming.[15]

The academy's long report was as much a document on Cold War geopolitics as it was an environmental assessment. Although it was unambiguous in its scientific conclusions, it framed its recommendations in terms of global strategy and economic choices. Based on climate model simulations of increased carbon dioxide, it stated, "we conclude with considerable confidence that there would be global mean temperature increase."[16] As culprits, the report pointed not only to fossil fuel emissions but also to the loss of forests, as well as the combined effects of other greenhouse gases. And yet the academy did not jump to catastrophic conclusions about the effects of climate change in the short term. The effects on plants of increased levels of carbon dioxide, along with changes in temperature and weather, could not be generalized—some positive and negative impacts would result by the year 2000, most of them modest. Farmers likely would adapt to changes, these scientists said. In the long term, however, the academy projected an increased melting rate of glaciers and ice caps, which would likely raise the sea level by some 70 centimeters in the next century. One particular concern was the disintegration of the West Antarctic Ice Sheet, a process that the committee guessed would take at least three to five centuries, raising the sea level about five or six meters. But the changes would be gradual enough, the committee supposed, for people to adjust.[17]

Looking back at this committee—the first major US effort at a comprehensive view of climate change—it is easy to forget how inseparable it was from military discussions about altering the climate and how informed it was by defense and geopolitical perspectives. It was commissioned just two years after the ENMOD Treaty went into force—a treaty that explicitly banned climate modification for military purposes, on the grounds that tampering with climate would have catastrophic consequences for the entire world. To lead the study, the academy invited physicist William Nierenberg, a long-standing veteran of the JASON group and co-author of its report on climate. He also was a member of the National Academy's Climate Research Board. Having joined JASON in 1962, Nierenberg had led the group that developed the idea of the electronic sensor network to be used in the jungles of Vietnam, a project that had made JASON infamous when revealed in the Pentagon Papers. He also was a longtime scientific advisor to NATO, which had considered the ramifications of environmental warfare at length in the 1960s. By the time he took the helm of the academy's climate change panel, he was director of the Scripps Institution of Oceanography, one of the world's most important centers of research on the ocean sciences. In many ways Nierenberg was the perfect person to evaluate climate, because he had been in contact with both the civilian and military sides of geophysics during his career and had considerable experience confronting the possibilities of global environmental catastrophe.[18]

The hostile reaction by economists to the 1972 Club of Rome–sponsored *World Dynamics* and *The Limits to Growth* made the inclusion of economists' voices on the academy panel seem particularly important to ensure that it would be taken seriously across all academic disciplines. Harvard economist Thomas C. Schelling filled this role, convening his own subpanel of experts to comment on the economic and social consequences of climate change. Like Kenneth Boulding, Schelling was a conflict resolution specialist who would see striking parallels between Cold War strategy and environmental issues. As he later put it, "I confessed I knew virtually nothing of the subject and was told I could learn most of what was known in the four weeks before the committee would meet." In fact he assembled a team of economists who already were skeptical of environmental doomsaying. One of the most vocal critics of Jay Forrester's work on environmental modeling, William Nordhaus, was an influential participant in Schelling's group.[19]

Schelling was no expert on climate, but like Nierenberg he was deeply interested in world affairs and defense issues. He had helped administer the Marshall Plan in the late 1940s and spent much of his career trying to apply game theory to the Cold War conflict. He spent a year at the RAND Corporation in the late 1950s, and a 1958 issue of the *Journal of Conflict Resolution* was devoted entirely to his ideas. He published a book, *The Strategy of Conflict* in 1960—the same year that Herman Kahn unveiled strategic thinking at RAND with his *On Thermonuclear War*. In his book Schelling introduced a remarkable aspect of bargaining strategy—that one could win a game by persuading the opponent that one's hands were tied, forcing an advantageous settlement. Rather than react to the opponent's move, one could point out the danger of letting matters slip beyond anyone's control. That uncertainty might force the opponent to reconsider what, under traditional game theory, might be considered a rational decision. Schelling emphasized how much the "players" had become dependent upon each other and how talk of catastrophe could give one side an advantage over the other.[20]

Schelling's perspectives on decision theory set the tone of the academy's report, *Changing Climate*. The authors explicitly distanced themselves from earlier environmental predictions and avoided talk of catastrophe. Describing most carbon dioxide projections as "primitive," they wrote that few of them drew upon statistics, econometrics, or decision theory. Statisticians, game theorists, and economists had invested considerable energy in analyzing complex dynamics, and yet few environmental models took account of feedbacks between climate change, carbon dioxide control strategies, and the economy. Certainly none of them were robust enough to take into account the likely responses of particular nations, or even groups of nations. To be taken seriously, global environmental modeling had to be brought into line with the techniques developed over nearly four decades of Cold War conflict.[21]

The academy's skepticism about the ability to address the carbon dioxide problem reflected everything Schelling knew about the perils of cooperation in gaming. Individuals had little incentive to cooperate (limit their emissions), since their utility for doing so was spread out among all individuals and was dissipated further when some individuals defected from the rules. This was classic game theory, lifted from Schelling's expertise about US-Soviet relations and applied to the global environment. A carbon dioxide control strategy could only work, he maintained, if all major nations took part, yet there seemed to be few examples of a multinational environmental pact succeeding.

The Soviet Union was the major reason these scientists, and particularly Schelling and Nordhaus, were suspicious of international agreements. For one, global regulations appeared to deny the power of market-oriented economics and even smacked of socialism. These economists viewed climate change through the same lens they used for every environmental issue from population growth to ocean pollution—and they treated climate change with the same skepticism they harbored against *The Limits to Growth*. Because Forrester and Meadows had played fast and loose with the numbers in order to point out flaws in the global economic system, Schelling believed more restrained analysis was in order. It may be that to him, Nordhaus, and many others, predictions of catastrophe lacked credibility. Environmentalism seemed all of a piece—global doomsaying that recommended regulated markets. As some authors have argued, environmentalists may have been dismissed as watermelons—green on the outside, red on the inside.[22]

In addition to that, there were more specific reasons to be skeptical of cooperation across Cold War lines. The Soviet Union had leverage, Schelling believed. It was one of the few countries that probably would *benefit* from a rise in global temperatures, because higher temperatures might improve its grain production. More important than that, the Soviet Union and its allies burned a large percentage of the world's coal and possessed large stocks of it in the ground. Acknowledging an imminent catastrophe, rather than a long-term challenge, would empower the Soviet Union more than the United States, because treaty signatories would have to find ways of convincing the Soviets to stop burning coal. "Given the unlikelihood that the United States or other western nations will compensate the Soviet Union for participating," the academy argued, "it is hard to see why the Soviets would participate." Without them, developing countries would balk at making sacrifices themselves, and the whole project would fail. The West would have drowned itself in its own catastrophic rhetoric, regulating itself while the Soviet bloc and the developing world continued on as usual. So Schelling did not recommend regulations or immediate action of any kind. The way to start the process of addressing climate change would be through continued global monitoring, sophisticated economic approaches, and more international dialogue.[23]

Some historians have attempted to reevaluate William Nierenberg's role in framing scientific discussions about climate change. They criticize Nierenberg for downplaying the scientific facts of climate change and playing up the social and economic factors that put climate change in a larger context of humans adapting to their environment. They also criticize Schelling for recommending against national decisions to limit emissions, saying that he underestimated the possibility of negotiating successful global agreements. Nierenberg's subsequent actions highlighted his political preferences, particularly by co-founding the George Marshall Institute, a conservative think tank that played down environmental dangers and extolled the virtues of market mechanisms rather than regulations.[24]

It is true that Nierenberg tended to favor conservative policies. In fact, his response to environmental challenges followed the contours of his Cold War worldview. Like many others, he distrusted the doomsaying environmental modeling from the early 1970s that had glossed over price fluctuations and the fluidity of markets. He also shared the belief of many of his fellow NATO scientific advisors that humans' ability to have an impact on natural processes was probably overstated. Further, he recoiled from environmentalists' radical solutions, which seemed to undermine the American economic system by saddling it with tight environmental rules and regulated markets.[25]

However, Nierenberg did not deny global warming, nor did Schelling or any of the other authors. *Changing Climate* was not a nay-saying document. It clearly identified the problem as global warming and it pointed to burning fossil fuels as the culprit. Even Schelling's section of the report expressed deep concern, promising a warming of unusual dimensions on a global climate that already was unusually warm, given the past cycles of climate fluctuation. Schelling worried that the changes brought about by climate change would fall on the peoples of the world unequally, leading to further divisive geopolitics in an already fractured world. In fact, despite being a complete newcomer to environmental issues when first asked to join the environmental committee, Schelling would spend the next decades writing about the economic problems associated with global warming.[26] What he and his fellow economists focused on in the early 1980s was the importance of gradual economic adjustment. He did not deny climate change but instead argued that the people of the world likely would be able to adapt.

Such adaptability turned out to be a persuasive reason to be complacent about climate change—and about a range of environmental challenges. That was America's strength: conventional wisdom had it that market economies adjusted well to change, whereas socialist economies controlled by centralized states did not. Although the academy had stated that the Soviets would benefit from global warming, others believed the opposite to be true. The Soviets might have diplomatic leverage if American scientists acknowledged catastrophic change, but they would be at a distinct disadvantage if the issue were ignored. Flexibility and capacity to respond to environmental pressures might be the Soviets' Achilles heel. A centralized state was sluggish whereas a market-driven economy could adjust more quickly. At least, this is what some intelligence analysts believed.

The Central Intelligence Agency used *Changing Climate* to project the future of the Soviet economy and took it as a harbinger of future troubles. Earlier computer models had faltered somewhat—Soviet grain production had not fallen nearly as much as the CIA expected a decade earlier, when the global cooling trend first appeared to reverse itself. By the 1980s, rainfall had decreased slightly in the Soviet Union, but not on a drastic scale, and it remained well above averages prior to 1970. On the other hand, the CIA fully took in the lesson about global warming coming from *Changing Climate*, namely, that its effects would depend on a country's ability to respond. Temperatures would rise in critical agricultural areas in the Soviet Union. Warming trends would lengthen the growing season in northern areas where hardy crops such as rye were grown, but they also would worsen the dry conditions in traditional grain-producing areas. Would the Soviet government be able to compensate for these changes? That was the crucial question, and the CIA did not believe the Soviets could do it. Because of global warming, and because of the inability of the Soviet economy to compensate adequately with fertilizer, grain production from 1986 to 1990 would—according to CIA estimates—fall well below annual targets, by about 25 percent,[27] an extraordinary shortfall for any country. If true, it would mean that the Soviet Union would fail to meet its goals of self-sufficiency and would continue to rely on Western agriculture. Not only that, Soviet wheat would be more vulnerable than ever to disease. Would this end up being the kind of "inevitable vassalage" envisioned by NATO in the early 1960s? It seemed as if climate change was working against the Soviet Union already.

There also was a lesson to learn from the CIA's earlier projections, since they had not come true. The impact of climate change had been less than expected, partly because the Soviet Union was able to adjust its economy to a surprising degree, by increasing fertilizer output and deliveries. This reinforced the view that, as devastating as environmental change could be, other kinds of human action would either mitigate or worsen any given crisis. Political, social, and economic responses to fluctuations in climate could be, on balance, far more significant than the climate fluctuation itself. If true, the West's robust, market-based, diversified economy was well positioned to make adjustments.

Ongoing studies of the causes of the 1972 Sahel drought reinforced these tendencies to emphasize society's capacity to adjust to environmental stresses. In a series of books, interdisciplinary and international panels of experts challenged the conventional wisdom that climate change alone could have catastrophic effects. They distrusted terms like "desertification," which implied that changes in the earth were the principal causes of droughts and famines. These books—*Nature Pleads Not Guilty* (1981), *The Constant Catastrophe* (1982), and *The Roots of Catastrophe* (1986)—found fragility not in nature but in unhealthy and vastly unequal social and economic systems, in which the pressures of climate fluctuations simply gave more power to those already in charge, leaving most people to languish. Inflexible market structures and totalitarian regimes fared the worst. These books questioned the notion that natural disasters were the main source of affliction, even claiming that the low rainfall was within the normal range over the long term. The roots of catastrophe, the authors claimed, were in how societies organized themselves.[28]

In the United States, these studies echoed what many analysts already were saying. Robert Schware and William Kellogg, researchers at the National Center for Atmospheric Research, had emphasized sociopolitical responses to climate change on the pages of the influential international policy journal Foreign Affairs. There they quoted the noted historian Arnold Toynbee, who had claimed that societies flourished most when subjected to prolonged healthy doses of environmental challenges.[29] Schware gushed in praise of the Sahel studies, saying that climate scientists needed to move beyond climate forces and Malthusian population doomsaying. Too often, he said, governments concluded that the solution was to find ways of producing more food or of decreasing population. The massive study of the Sahel, he believed, had "torn to shreds" such easy answers.[30] It was naïve, Schware believed, to treat climate alterations as the single most important cause of future catastrophe, ignoring the ability (or inability) of society to adjust.

A real world test of this premise already was occurring in Africa. The Sahel tale was repeating itself in the most outlandish ways, giving Africans cataclysmic events on multiple fronts: climatic changes, insect hordes, and devastating disease—with war as their constant companion. Scientists, journalists, and intelligence analysts watched and learned. Again in sub-Saharan Africa the rain had ceased to fall, leading to a truly disastrous drought and famine in Ethiopia in 1984–85. Hundreds of thousands—perhaps as many as a million—died in the famine. It had been caused in part by the lack of rain, but also because of diminished access to food and health care amid major military insurgencies. Humanitarian relief organizations broadcast pleas for help on Western television networks, showing images of shockingly emaciated children covered in flies. Popular musicians recorded songs designed to funnel profits from record sales to help the starving people of Africa. In the United Kingdom, for example, they organized concerts to raise money and recorded "Do They Know It's Christmas?" The short-lived American group USA for Africa gathered dozens of popular musicians to record "We Are the

World," urging listeners with the line "We are the ones who make a brighter day, so let's start giving."

Most of the money raised in this way went to the various military groups who controlled Ethiopia or was requisitioned by the central government. The US government was aware of this. Secret CIA documents (now partially declassified) reported that Ethiopian president Mengistu Haile Mariam, backed by the Soviet Union, was deeply suspicious of Western help and maintained strict control over incoming aid. He knew that his predecessor, Emperor Haile Selassie, had been deposed in 1974 during a similar famine, and he tried to shield powerful groups (especially the army) from the full effects of it. He also used food aid to implement a major resettlement program—luring hundreds of thousands of people away from areas dominated by insurgent groups. He resisted any comprehensive feeding effort and explicitly withheld food from reaching areas controlled by his enemies. Because feeding people became a form of political legitimization, both the government and the insurgents used military force to control the flow of food. The famine—which had the appearance of being Mother Nature's wrath—had been caused by various power plays in the country, to the detriment of the vast majority of people.[31] Efforts to ameliorate the disaster from outside could have helped, but in the wrong hands, the aid made matters worse. As the CIA interpreted it, in the case of Ethiopia, a Soviet-backed regime had turned an environmental challenge into a regional catastrophe.

As if the famine were not enough of a calamity for the region, the long-awaited rains that finally came in 1985 and 1986 created ideal breeding grounds for locusts. Devastating crop-devouring migratory locusts appeared not only in Ethiopia but also Uganda, Kenya, and all the way down to South Africa. Favorable rains only made matters worse. But by this time such disasters had become practically banal, at least from the point of view of Westerners. The *Washington Post* called the locust swarms, which could stretch for miles, "Africa's Latest Plague." By the summer of 1986, four major species of African locusts and Senegalese grasshoppers had struck the continent, threatening to invade across the Suez Canal into the Middle East. The UN's Food and Agriculture Organization warned that a single swarm of locusts could consume in one day what 40,000 humans could eat in a year. According to the US Agency for International Development, Africa was on the brink of the worst locust infestation in 60 years.[32]

Western newspapers found catastrophic language irresistible—"of biblical proportions" was a popular phrase. At first, an international effort seemed to control the locusts. A massive insecticide spraying campaign, helped from above by the watchful eyes of American and European satellites, eliminated the threat in eastern and western Africa. UN Food and Agriculture Organization director Edouard Saouma declared, "We waged war on the farmer's oldest enemy and we won."[33] But soon the insects were back, this time north of the Sahara desert, threatening Tunisia, Algeria, and Morocco in 1988—in numbers that dwarfed the crisis just two years before. "Millions, sometimes billions of locusts take to the air, usually in the morning, forming what resemble storm clouds that can blacken the sky," warned the *New York Times*.[34] And they turned up in sub-Saharan Africa again in the spring. Reporters offered more biblical imagery, quoting references to locusts in the Old Testament book of Exodus.

On top of this enormous calamity loomed the onset of an unknown epidemic disease many Africans eventually called SIDA—or as was known in English-speaking countries, AIDS (acquired immune deficiency syndrome). This disease appeared almost simultaneously in the United States, Haiti, and parts of Africa, though it gained widespread attention first in the United States. There it began to take on all the characteristics of the disease long feared, and long planned for, in defense establishments in the United States and Soviet Union. It was widespread and even seemed to discriminate—apparently killing disproportionate numbers of homosexuals and black people. But soon its true indiscriminate nature became clear, and it took on the form of a catastrophic disease sweeping across the globe.

What made AIDS so destructive was that it broke down the immune system, leaving human life vulnerable to even the most trivial kinds of infections. By the spring of 1981, doctors in the United States were seeing extremely puzzling hospital cases. Rare diseases, typically quashed by the immune system, began to appear—such as *Pneumocystis* pneumonia and Kaposi's sarcoma, a cancer that left purplish lesions all over the body before finally killing the person. National Institutes of Health scientist Abe M. Macher marveled at AIDS. "If Alfred Hitchcock were alive, he'd have his next movie," he said. "When people discuss this syndrome at scientific meetings, it sounds like something out of 'The Andromeda Strain.'"[35]

Had humanity somehow caused the emergence of AIDS? From the outset, the AIDS epidemic took on an air of natural or divine retribution for something humans had done. As one author put it, from its earliest stages the AIDS epidemic "has been viewed through profoundly powerful

metaphors."[36] Its associations with drug use, homosexuality, sexual pro-
miscuity, and people of African descent may explain the slow public health
response to it in many countries. Perceptions that AIDS was the "gay
plague" encouraged some to see the disease as God's punishment. It was
particularly rife in major cities and among homosexuals with multiple
partners. As novelist Larry Kramer told the *New York Times*, "It's like being
in wartime. We don't know when the bomb is going to fall." Some of the
earliest bits of evidence that it struck heterosexuals were the cases coming
from Africa and Haiti—in the latter case, doctors wondered if there was a
link to voodoo practices.[37]

By 1986 AIDS seemed to put the world on the verge of a major cataclysmic event. MIT scientist David Baltimore, chairing a special committee of the US National Academy of Sciences, believed that combating
the disease would require the most intensive effort in history. Baltimore
said he was frightened of the consequences, and that the present epidemic
could become a worldwide catastrophe. In the United States alone, more
than 25,000 people had contracted AIDS, and about half thus far had
died. Academy president Frank Press noted that if trends continued, in
1990 the annual number of Americans dying of AIDS would equal the
total number of Americans killed in the entire Vietnam War—about
58,000.[38]

Suspicion that humans had sown the seeds of their own destruction
gave way to numerous explanations of these calamitous events. Astute
observers noticed that the rise of AIDS was occurring around the same
time that smallpox was dying out, due to a massive vaccination campaign
sponsored by the World Health Organization in the 1970s. That campaign
ended in 1980, and WHO was able to announce that smallpox had been
eradicated. But the threat of smallpox as a biological weapon continued,
and vaccinations continued on a smaller scale in the United States and
Soviet Union. Scientists at the Walter Reed Army Medical Hospital produced evidence in 1987 that smallpox vaccination of a young soldier had
induced a dormant HIV virus to develop into AIDS. *The Times* of London
announced "Smallpox Vaccine 'Triggered Aids Virus.'" It pointed out that
tying the origins of AIDS to the eradication of smallpox could explain
many of the demographic oddities of AIDS—its inexplicable simulta-
neous appearances, as well as its concentration in areas such as central
Africa, Haiti, and Brazil, areas of intensive smallpox vaccinations.[39]

Unlike the recurrent scourges such as smallpox or bubonic plague,
AIDS was entirely new. Questions of responsibility ran rampant, and

soon tracing the disease's origins became a source of international tension. The French were the first to ban imports of blood from the United
States, though the Americans were reluctant to see themselves as a source
of infection. Other than blaming homosexuals, many Americans blamed
Haiti. When evidence emerged that AIDS may have existed in central and
west Africa in the 1960s, Africans scrambled to point their fingers. Rwan-
dans and Zambians blamed neighboring Zaire; Ugandans faulted Tanza-
nia. But most felt that AIDS had come to Africa from Europe or the
United States. The Zambian president's press secretary called the attempt to locate the disease in Africa a "propaganda campaign" by the
West. Kenyan president Daniel arap Moi called it "a new form of hate
campaign." Despite widespread reports by doctors and scientists of an
epidemic in Zaire, government officials denied its existence. In fact, in
1985 the World Health Organization had received no reported cases of
AIDS from the countries in west, central, and east Africa.[40] The Soviet
government's attitude ran parallel to the African ones. Despite numerous
cases of Kaposi's sarcoma, government officials refused to acknowledge
more than a handful of AIDS victims. They characterized it as a Western
problem, recommending that Soviet people cease all contacts with
foreigners.

Such responses to AIDS reinforced Western views that the Soviet
Union was ill-equipped to deal with genuine natural challenges, from climate change to public health. In a repeat of its behavior in the Korean War
more than 30 years earlier, the Soviet government began in 1985 to blame
the AIDS epidemic on the Americans. In October 1985, Soviet official Val-
entin Zapevalov claimed that AIDS had come from American biological
warfare laboratories, specifically those at Fort Detrick and at the Centers
for Disease Control in Atlanta. He did so in an article called "Panic in the
West: or What Hides Behind the Sensationalism of AIDS." Zapevalov
soon followed this with an interview with Soviet virologist S. Drozdov,
who implied that its origins in central Africa may have been by design,
perhaps by the CIA.[41]

The mysterious origins of AIDS reinforced fears that it was a scientist's
concoction. Writing in Britain's *Journal of the Royal Society of Medicine*,
medical researcher John Seale concluded that it was feasible, even "quite
likely," that AIDS was man-made, since its transmission was through
blood transfusions and sharing needles. The disease virus could have been
transferred in vitro from an animal into human tissue culture, then transferred in vivo "through humans used as guinea pigs." The new virus would

be spread most easily with the aid of hypodermic needles—especially improperly sterilized ones, common not only among drug users but throughout the health care facilities in Africa and the Caribbean. He wrote:

> The Soviet Government's hypothesis seems to be that the AIDS virus was developed by the Pentagon which, through incompetence, scored a cold war version of an "own goal" by infecting their own population and their NATO allies. On the other hand, an alternative hypothesis might be that the virus was developed in the Ivanovsky Institute in Moscow, or in laboratories in Novosibirsk, and released in the USA in the mid-1970s. This does not imply an updated, biological war version of Pearl Harbor. Suffice to say that any determined person, with access to the AIDS virus in any laboratory, could start an epidemic in any country, which thereafter would inevitably spread to every country.[42]

Seale reminded readers of a myxomatosis pandemic that had killed millions of rabbits in Europe—all of these deaths could be traced back to a mere two rabbits infected with the disease that were released into the wild in 1952.

Soviet newspapers spread the idea that Americans were capable of unleashing this deadly scourge across the globe and may have done so unintentionally. One 1987 *Izvestia* article about these alleged laboratory origins was called "AIDS: The American Gift." But after the fall of the Berlin Wall, the plot thickened. In September 1990, the Soviet weekly magazine *Literaturnaya Gazeta* revealed that the scenario imagined by Zapevalov was rooted in Soviet experience. It provided details about a mysterious 1979 anthrax epidemic that had struck the town of Sverdlovsk. Previously, the Soviet government had claimed that contaminated meat had caused it. Now the magazine reported that human casualties had preceded those in the livestock. The anthrax must have come from the nearby biological weapons facility. The US Central Intelligence Agency began to suspect other accidents within the Soviet Union as well, including a 1990 outbreak of plague in Aralsk, Kazakhstan. As in the case of the Sverdlovsk incident, the Soviet government had blamed tainted meat.[43]

The US government viewed the AIDS epidemic outside the United States through a Cold War lens and tried to avoid letting Soviet disinformation turn Africa away from the United States. The CIA warned internally of a determined Soviet campaign to blame AIDS on American biological weapons research. Because Africa was especially hard-hit by AIDS, it would be particularly vulnerable to propaganda, and susceptible to suggestions that Americans had used Africa as an experimental zone for biological weapons. "Exploiting black African sensitivities to racism and so-called Western imperialism," one CIA report claimed, "Moscow has taken full advantage of regional fears, ignorance, and some careless Western statements in its efforts to provoke anti-US sentiment." The CIA document cited several examples of Soviet influence. One was a 1986 "letter to the editor" that appeared in newspapers in Kenya, Senegal, and Uganda, pointing to Fort Detrick as the source for AIDS, timed to precede a summit of the continent-wide Organization for African Unity, a meeting of African leaders.

Apparently, Soviet bloc intelligence agencies had orchestrated a series of well-timed releases of disinformation. Another of these, this time preceding the meeting of the Non-Aligned Movement in Harare, Zimbabwe, was the 1986 publication of a scientific study in Zimbabwe also tracing the disease to Fort Detrick. The study was written by East German scientists Jakob and Lilli Segal and Ronald Demhlow. It had been circulated widely among representatives from all over the world, not just Africa. "Made available to a large Third World audience in Harare," the CIA lamented, "this lengthy creation has since appeared in dozens of countries worldwide and been serialized for weeks in Tanzanian, Ghanian, and other African newspapers despite frequent and repeated US denials of the Segal allegations." Other newspapers suggested that the Americans were using Africans as guinea pigs to test a vaccine.[44] East German Stasi (secret police) officers later recalled explicitly spreading this story that AIDS "was allegedly communicated to the public through test subjects in an entirely uncontrolled fashion and thus triggered this deadly catastrophe. The United States was pictured as the origin of all threats—the classic image the East had of its enemy."[45]

What happened to Africans in the 1980s was a perfect storm of environmental cataclysm. In a secret 1987 assessment, the CIA marveled at it: "During the 1980s Africa endured and continues to experience wars, insurgencies, drought, desertification, insect plagues, famines, undernourishment, diseases, dysfunctional economic policies—and now the AIDS pandemic." Despite African governments' early denials, the CIA believed that about 50,000 Africans already had died from the disease, and that two out of five Africans were infected with the virus. It was becoming hard for politicians to ignore. Indeed the Zambian president's son died of it.

Given its apparently universal mortality rate, the CIA projected annual African deaths from AIDS after 1992 to climb into the millions. With governments' inability to enact strong control measures, analysts could only guess at the social upheavals and conflicts destined to rock the continent.[46] The lesson drawn by the CIA was that, like the Soviet Union, these governments were unable to adjust quickly to natural challenges.

Within the US government, policy analysts' views were further tempered by the Soviet Union's routine efforts to play up the catastrophic consequences in the most cynical ways, for obvious propaganda purposes. This is not to say that Americans did not have propaganda, or to cast stones at the Soviet Union's foreign policy. After all, Nixon also had emphasized the risks of man-made catastrophes. Nonetheless, the Soviet government's narrative about disasters such as AIDS and climate change—which the Soviet government maintained despite its apathy toward its own serious public health and environmental problems— undermined the credibility of environmental catastrophic thinking among many Westerners who worked in the scientific, defense, and intelligence communities.

In the United States, the sharpest dispute about climate change in the 1980s was not about carbon dioxide but rather about the possibility of "Nuclear Winter." A number of American scientists, including Carl Sagan, the host of the television science series *Cosmos*, had used computer models to project the future of the earth's atmosphere in the aftermath of a nuclear war. They argued that the smoke and dust from the explosions would block out the sun for an extended period, limiting the amount of solar radiation reaching the earth. This in turn would alter the climate seriously, making it much colder—a nuclear winter, as the concept became known. In the Sunday newspaper magazine *Parade*, in 1983 Sagan unveiled the basic idea of nuclear winter and tried to use it to argue for a greater effort at arms control.

The most strident opposition to Sagan's climate models came from within the defense establishment. Why should this be so? For starters, many of them did not consider it an important finding. They already knew nuclear war would be devastating. After all, that was the point of deterrence. The Reagan administration eventually acknowledged that nuclear winter might be an outcome of a successful nuclear strike and argued that it was one more reason to invest in missile defenses. Others attacked the science, arguing that Sagan's models were too simplistic. Still others believed that Sagan's political agenda compromised nuclear winter's credibility.[47] In addition to these factors, the Soviet Union's immediate approval and outspoken support for the concept of nuclear winter proved to be the kiss of death for it in the West. Nearly simultaneously with Sagan's work, Soviet climate scientists claimed to have verified it independently. US defense and intelligence insiders were convinced not only that Sagan was wrong—and politically motivated—but that he and other climate modelers had become Soviet pawns. Further, Sagan explicitly aligned himself with Paul Ehrlich, who was not a climate scientist but who was very well known for his catastrophic doomsaying about over-population. This served to associate climate science even further with other environmental issues such as population growth.

It also created the same enemies. These included the economists and scientists who believed environmentalists and anti-nuclear activists were strengthening the Soviet Union and weakening the United States. These skeptics believed that environmental ideas, including nuclear winter, were not rooted in reliable science. Several of these, including physicists Edward Teller, Fred Seitz, Robert Jastrow, and William Nierenberg founded in 1984 the George C. Marshall Institute as a center for science and public policy. It advised on a range of issues, including not only nuclear winter but also the Strategic Defensive Initiative and climate change, and was named for President Truman's secretary of state, the architect of the "Marshall Plan" to aid European recovery. The institute claimed that its goal was to counter scientific appraisals that had been misused by interest groups. They did so in the name of national security.[48]

Behind closed doors, the intelligence community had even more reason to be skeptical of climate science because all the evidence pointed to a massive effort by the Soviets to use catastrophic doomsaying against the United States. "We believe that there is a wide difference," CIA analysts guessed in 1984, "in what Soviet officials say publicly and what they believe privately." Officially, the Soviet party line appeared to be that nuclear winter was real and its effects both certain and severe. Soviet scientists claimed to have made an independent confirmation of the hypothesis, and typically they reported even worse climatic changes than Westerners did. By the CIA's estimation, the Soviets were rather quick to point out that nuclear war *of any dimension* would spell the end of the human race, or its degradation to such a degree that prehistoric man would seem advanced by comparison. "Western scientists," said one CIA report, "have been amazed at this kind of intellectual dishonesty."[49]

Although the Soviets clearly were interested in understanding the effects of nuclear war, anything they might have said about climate had to be taken with a grain of salt. At least, that is what US defense analysts had concluded by 1986. This was based not only on habitual skepticism but also on huge disparities in computing technology. The Soviet government had not sufficiently invested in computers, and therefore scientists lacked the capacity to produce the complex projections required for even minimally credible climate modeling. Based on the availability of high-performance computers used for scientific calculations—mainframes, robust minicomputers, even personal computers—the US capability dwarfed the Soviet one by 700 to 1. And the Soviets (according to CIA estimates) had none of the new supercomputers, such as the Cray-1, with which defense scientists gamed out the weather patterns, nuclear effects, and battlefield contingency plans. Thus to defense scientists, Soviet claims about nuclear winter—and climate generally—seemed purely derivative, and hardly the "independent confirmation" that Soviet leaders claimed.[50]

Ironically, Soviet scientists' only real access to such supercomputers came when they visited the United States. In the 1970s, US-USSR scientific exchange agreements brought Soviet computer modelers into contact with American colleagues and their powerful hardware. One of them, Vladimir Aleksandrov, worked on a Cray-1 supercomputer at the US National Center for Atmospheric Research in 1978, 1980, and 1982. One of his tasks was to design a software program on weather circulation that might work on relatively slow Soviet computers. In 1983 he was back in the USSR working on nuclear winter. With what computing capability they had, he and other scientists attempted to project not only climate change but also space militarization, ballistic missile defense, and many other global strategic issues requiring the creation of future scenarios. Despite their rapid confirmation of nuclear winter—"a highly unusual accomplishment in Soviet science," the CIA reported—their computers were not up to the task of producing original work. To compare: Aleksandrov described a single 40-hour modeling calculation on the Soviet BESM-6 computer, based on a simplified general circulation model. On a Cray-1 computer, this would have taken about eight minutes. The sophisticated calculations done by the Americans were taking hours of time on Crays.[51] Even leaving aside the controversy about nuclear winter in the United States, defense analysts felt that it was safe to dismiss whatever the Soviets said and treat it as mere propaganda—the research itself was sloppy and inaccurate, and any legitimate findings typically were based on American ideas, data, and models.

These clear limitations had not stopped Aleksandrov from arriving at the most dramatic conclusions, emphasizing the catastrophic climate changes from any nuclear war scenario:

The impenetrable black cover would spread from the northern hemisphere to the southern, and eventually enclose the entire planet. All sources of fresh water would freeze over, all ecological balances would be upset, and all harvests would fail. The total terrestrial biota, that is, the total population of various species of animals, plants, and microorganisms, would completely perish. . . . Conclusions drawn from our calculations indicated that if 100 or 150 megatons of nuclear fuel (that is, 50 times less than in the Sagan scenario) were used in a nuclear exchange, the major cities of Europe, Asia, and North America would be destroyed, and the Nuclear Winter would begin unabated.[52]

Aleksandrov's dire warnings mirrored Sagan's, except he applied it to much less destructive nuclear conflicts, suggesting that the earth was even more vulnerable than the American nuclear winter advocates had suspected.

Even within the Soviet Union, climate researchers were embarrassed by the far-reaching conclusions Aleksandrov had made, based as they were on crude computer models. Mikhail Budyko, probably the Soviet climatologist best known outside the Soviet Union, urged a little more caution. After all, even slight differences in the parameters of these models could create large differences in outcomes. Noting how much Aleksandrov had simply duplicated the American work, he argued for more genuinely independent studies.[53]

The Reagan administration treated nuclear winter as part of a well-coordinated Soviet propaganda campaign to blame the United States for the dangers of the arms race. Scientists involved in classified research were even less receptive than usual to catastrophic claims made by climate modelers. "Catastrophe" seemed to be the bread and butter of Cold War rhetoric. Soviet scientists appeared at international scientific conferences to raise consciousness about nuclear winter and encouraged the World Health Organization to publicize it. Aleksandrov traveled to international meetings, spoke about scientists' social responsibility, met with American political leaders, and even appeared before a US congressional subcommittee. That kind of access to the American political system had been a veritable coup for Moscow. It may have persuaded some congressmen that nuclear winter was real, but it had little impact upon the defense establishment. American intelligence analysts concluded: "Clearly, Soviet leaders want US leaders to believe the nuclear winter hypothesis."[54]

Such cavalier use of climate models in the nuclear winter debate, perhaps by Sagan but definitely by Soviet scientists, reinforced existing skepticism about climate change predictions and propped up the long-standing view that human impacts on climate were unlikely to have catastrophic effects on the earth's large-scale systems. Especially within the defense establishment, where scientifically oriented people had been assessing the effects of nuclear war for decades and where planners already were well versed in the limitations of manipulating the environment even when that was the goal, skepticism about climate modeling ran high. Sagan's ill-fated effort with nuclear winter, and its near-universal dismissal within defense circles, reinforced the notion that predictions of environmental doom were based on flawed science. This worldview of scientists working for the armed services meshed perfectly with those of economists who already were deeply critical of the catastrophic narrative emerging from the environmental movement.

Aside from its scientific merits, nuclear winter was an end-of-the-world story that fit the times. Sagan had presented a scenario that was total in scope, enveloping quite literally the entire earth. As an idea, it spoke directly to fears—not merely of widespread damage but of wholesale annihilation. Some would say he exploited those fears; others would say he gave voice to them. Either way, nuclear winter was part of a pattern of projecting wholesale destruction in a time of enormous geopolitical, national, and often personal stress for people facing the prospect of nuclear war. Sagan was trying to point out the insanity of nuclear weapons. What he got instead was bickering about the science of climate.

Had they occurred earlier, the nuclear winter controversy and the African calamities would have made ideal "wildcat" ideas in NATO's early 1960s attempts to evaluate environmental warfare. But in the 1980s, after the abandonment of offensive biological weapons, ratification of the Geneva Protocol, and the signing of the ENMOD Treaty, American and allied scientists were less interested in finding new methods of maximizing human death through nature and much more concerned about avoiding inadvertent destruction. The disasters of the 1980s, especially the droughts in Africa and the global AIDS epidemic, cast long shadows over any attempts to assess the effects of environmental change. Scientists and military planners took very seriously the notion that humans were a cause, for better or for worse. Yet they often approached the problem as part of the Cold War conflict with the Soviet Union, and their solutions (or lack thereof) derived from their perceptions of the strengths and weaknesses of the superpowers. The US defense and intelligence establishment attempted to understand whether humans had become the instruments of their own extinction or if they could adjust to changes. Often they concluded that because Western market economies were capable of swift adjustment, and Communist centralized economies were sluggish, complacency about environmental change favored the West over the East. Given two paths, the West appeared more capable of avoiding extinction.

Conclusion

THE MIRACLE OF SURVIVAL

I want to say, and this is very important. At the end, we lucked out. It was luck that prevented a nuclear war. We came that close to a nuclear war at the end. . . . Rational individuals came that close to total destruction of their societies.

—ROBERT MCNAMARA, former US Secretary of Defense,
The Fog of War (film, 2003)

FOR THOSE WHO believe the book of Genesis, the evils of humans once grew so intense that God regretted creating them at all. So God sent a great flood to destroy all living things (not just humankind) sparing only a select few. At the end of the story, a rainbow appeared as a message that never again would a worldwide flood come to make all the earth pay for humanity's sins. It is a tale of bad men and women, divine retribution, and immense collateral damage—a catastrophe, one might say today, of biblical proportions.

Imagery from the Bible is often sprinkled over predictions of the earth's future. After the Second World War, that future rarely seemed bright. With the advent of nuclear weapons and intercontinental ballistic missiles, all the peoples of the earth seemed just moments from their end. In one 1984 study, 39 percent of the Americans surveyed agreed, "When the Bible predicts that the earth will be destroyed by fire, it's telling us about nuclear war."[1] In another study, many nuclear *scientists* believed that nuclear weapons would be God's mechanism for destroying the world in preparation for Judgment Day and the Second Coming of Christ.[2]

Nuclear weapons were just one part of how scientists imagined fighting the clash of civilizations between East and West. Without question, the Cold War gave the world a disturbing array of futures to fear, many of them derived from the real or perceived powers of scientists to impart enormous destruction upon mankind. A war could have broken out among the Soviet Union, the United States, and all their allies in any of the Cold War's nearly five decades. The wars that did occur—in Korea, Vietnam, Afghanistan, Central America, and so many corners of the world—invariably were perceived by the superpowers through the lens of the Cold War struggle. Had those wars widened into a third world war, it likely would have been nuclear and might have been biological as well. It could have involved weather modification, as occurred in Vietnam, and one can only imagine which of the other "wildcat" ideas for manipulating nature might have been employed. One thing is certain: soldiers and armies would not have been the most important targets. A total war would have meant the deaths of millions of men, women, and children of all ages, all races, all creeds. Some would have been killed quickly, others would have died slowly, and still others would have lived in a completely transformed world.

This vision of the future, routinely used in fiction, was not really fiction at all. Scientists and the military cooperated to make it possible. As historians pore over formerly declassified documents, they see desperate men and women planning a third world war and arming nature in the most hideous ways, not to win battles but to maximize human death. Even those charged with protecting their countries had to make bizarre choices—such as preserving frozen bull semen—about what to carry into a desolated, post-apocalypse world. They learned to appreciate biological diversity as a strategy of survival and began to stockpile seeds to keep under shelter during the coming holocaust. By any calculation, a third world war would have been a global catastrophe. As Defense Secretary Robert McNamara later recalled, rational individuals came extraordinarily close to destroying their whole societies. How easy it is to forget what a miracle it was to survive the Cold War.

The release of some formerly "black" scientific data about the environment, along with the declassification of government documents by the United Kingdom, NATO, and the United States, has helped to clarify the symbiotic relationship between scientists and military partners throughout the Cold War. In the United States, there was a fleeting period of historical openness and government candor between the end of the Cold War in 1991 and subsequent developments such as a Chinese espionage scandal in 1999 and the Al-Qaeda attacks on the Pentagon and World Trade Center in 2001. In 1995, President Bill Clinton ordered the declassification of most documents more than a quarter-century old. This gave researchers access to an unprecedented amount of formerly classified information, some of which was later re-classified (both the Clinton administration and subsequent George W. Bush administration had second thoughts about revealing so much about the past).[3] That brief opening sparked several studies of the interdependent relationships among scientific, military, intelligence, and diplomatic issues, agendas, and people.[4] Although these perspectives were not entirely new, the documentation often was. It became quite clear that scientists offered their services not only to develop ideas but also to gather intelligence, to act as diplomats, and to find myriad ways to serve US interests vis-à-vis the Soviet Union. One historian, who tracked American efforts to build dual-use technologies to collect scientific data while capturing Soviet radio signals, described it simply: "the worlds of basic, academic-type research co-existed with highly classified research and development tied to military systems."[5] Rather than merely courting patronage from the military, and inventing ways to make their research seem useful, scientists often had to invent ways to make their research seem disinterested.[6]

The Clinton declassification included historical images from the first spy satellite systems dating back to the 1960s—CORONA, ARGON, and LANYARD. These satellite programs had provided the first windfall dataset about the lay of the land in the Soviet Union and China.[7] For historians, their declassification provided insight not only into American reconnaissance activities but also into a much broader phenomenon—what one scholar called "the shaping and reordering of the postwar earth sciences" due to the priorities of the Department of Defense (DOD), creating a new earth-imaging system upon which even civilian scientists relied heavily. That reliance increased yearly, leading the Office of Management and Budget in 1973 to acknowledge that systems developed exclusively for civilian use "cannot compete in any meaningful way with DOD-developed techniques."[8]

The collaboration between scientists and the military continued to shape environmental thought and the environmental sciences after the Cold War. Stimulated by Vice-President Al Gore and other politicians, a group of scientists called the MEDEA Committee began in the 1990s to salvage classified data from the Cold War era that might help track changes in climate, assess deforestation, and shed light on other environmental developments. Doing so made perfect sense: the military had all the best information, collected over five decades. The treasure trove identified by the MEDEA Committee included far-ranging material, from the glacier-fed lakes of Antarctica to the deserts of Sudan, just a small reflection of what the magazine *Science* called "billions of dollars worth of intelligence assets" including satellites, planes, ships, and other sources.[9] All of these now would serve the interests of scientists who might lack classified security clearance but were willing to pay attention to changes in the earth, its biota, its oceans, and its atmosphere. Even with the fear of a third world war receding into the past, scientists could continue to keep the earth under surveillance, with help from the relics of the Cold War. Those billions of dollars worth of intelligence assets had created the modern environmental sciences, now cleansed of their provenance—their origins and development in the collaboration between scientists and the military as they imagined and planned to fight a third world war.

Even in the new post–Cold War context of openness, these environmental data were deemed applicable not only to purely scientific work on the environment. The MEDEA committee became an advisory arm of the Central Intelligence Agency, and environmental data continued to shape security policies as it had before. The name "MEDEA" was no coincidence; a sorceress in ancient Greek mythology, she helped, and later married, the hero Jason as he completed his tasks. Similarly, the MEDEA group was closely identified with the JASON group, the elite coterie of scientists who for decades had been advising the US government on matters ranging from battlefield tactics to global climate change. One of the "Jasons," Gordon MacDonald, had been deeply involved in explaining how environmental warfare might lead to catastrophic consequences, advised the government during the ENMOD negotiations, participated in the first government reports on global warming, and chaired the MEDEA committee. Even with the Cold War over, MacDonald believed that environmental issues stood at the center of American national security. These Cold War–era intelligence assets would continue to be used to understand the earth's vulnerability, its manipulability, and the national security consequences for the United States.[10]

Arming Mother Nature has explored how modern science and the Cold War together gave birth to ideas about the catastrophic consequences of human-induced changes in the natural environment. There is an extraordinary irony in it. The conflict that created this awareness also conspired to defeat efforts to address global environmental problems. The Cold War sent scientists to learn how to exploit the natural world and to protect humans in the event of worldwide conflagration. It created anxiety and nursed a catastrophic worldview among environmentalists and scientists alike, suggesting that humans already were toying with "synoptic scale" forces that might have long-term effects. Yet the Cold War also created skepticism about the notion of catastrophe, as politicians on both sides of the global conflict played up the dangers for political purposes, and as scientists interpreted even the most massive geophysical convulsions as temporary, ephemeral changes in the sweep of natural history. Even when scientists agreed that serious, long-term changes were under way, many intelligence analysts and other commentators believed that these would harm the Soviet Union more than the United States—because the flexible, adaptable West could adjust well to change, whereas the sluggish, centrally planned East could not. Disagreements about how to address changes of a global nature—global regulatory agreements or reliance on market mechanisms—simply deepened because of apparent similarities between what environmentalists wanted and what the Soviet Union claimed to want. Prescriptions for global intervention struck some economists not just as sloppy science but also as indictments of Western-style capitalism.

After the fall of the Soviet Union in 1991, those who concerned themselves with global environmental problems adhered to patterns established in the preceding decades. They repeated the anxieties of the Cold War, stepped along well-trod paths of argument and counterargument about global markets and price adjustments, and imagined their world collapsing around them. They often approached environmental issues with the tools developed to face down the Soviet Union. Even as late as 2005, Nobel Prize–winning economist Thomas Schelling reflected that doing something about climate change "is what I expect to be, during this century, what nuclear arms control was during the century just past, namely an immense challenge to 'cooperation amid conflict.'"[11]

What happened to the catastrophic style of environmental thought after the demise of the Soviet Union? During his four years in office, President George H. W. Bush seemed to preside over a series of momentous world events, including the dismantling of the Berlin Wall in 1989 and the dissolution of the Soviet Union in 1991. With no "total war" on the horizon, Bush's biggest diplomatic challenge may have been to avoid seeming too triumphant. When he came to the UN Earth Summit in Rio de Janeiro in 1992 to discuss the need for joint global action to address environmental issues, it seemed for the first time that the Soviets could not be used as an excuse for doing nothing about worldwide environmental problems. But it also was a time of vindication for the flexible, market-driven Western system. Bush used the summit as an opportunity to praise his country's track record on environmental issues and to insist that protecting the environment did not signal a concession to the kitchen-sink environmental approach that had characterized *The Limits to Growth* some two decades before. He said that "growth is the engine of change, the friend of the environment." The treaty that emerged from the summit encouraged signatories to work together, but it did not bind them by international law. Later, when negotiators returned to put some teeth into it with the Kyoto Protocol, the United States balked.[12]

In environmental debates in the 1990s, the imagery of such a colossal and powerful enemy as the Soviet Union proved impossible to resist. Market-oriented economists and scientists routinely called environmentalists socialists. They could cast the debate as vindicated free market capitalism versus discredited socialism, just as it had been between the United States and Soviet Union. One was good, and the other had proven itself a monumental failure. In this interpretation, environmentalism was anti-progress, even anti-freedom. Limiting freedom of action seemed to be the road to totalitarianism.[13]

But that was just one way to spin the legacy of the Cold War. Environmentalists did it too, using time-honored catastrophic rhetoric to justify dramatic changes to the world economic system. Al Gore did this explicitly in his agenda-setting 1992 book, *Earth in the Balance*. Gore's father had suggested that Harry Truman should dump radioactive waste on Korea. The son now attempted to fill the void left by the fall of the Soviet Union by replacing it with the global environmental crisis. The American edition of his book carried the vague subtitle "Ecology and the Human Spirit," whereas the British edition was more explicit: "Forging a New Common Purpose." This was a deliberate redirection of the Cold War struggle against the Soviet Union. Not facing up to global environmental challenges was much like being "soft" on communism.[14]

When in 1992 Gore was selected as Bill Clinton's presidential running mate—and when Clinton won the election—suddenly the vice-president of the United States also was the leading voice in presenting the environmental crisis as the central problem facing the world. Not since Richard Nixon had the White House played such a strong role in emphasizing the fragility of man in the face of his own manipulations of nature. Whereas market-oriented economists saw environmentalists as green on the outside and red on the inside, Gore painted the unbridled global capitalist economic system as the new behemoth, a post–Cold War Soviet Union. "The long struggle between democracy and communism," he wrote, "is in many ways the clearest example of how free societies can sustain a shared commitment to a single overarching goal over a long period of time and in the face of daunting obstacles."[15]

Gore proposed a holistic approach of vast proportions—what he called a "Global Marshall Plan." It would use the same tools the United States had employed throughout the Cold War to win the hearts and minds of the world: a massive education and propaganda campaign to bring attention to environmental problems, financial aid for countries in the developing world, and scientific training and technological donations. Instead of a Strategic Defense Initiative, he wrote, the world needed a Strategic Environment Initiative. Gore's book fully embraced catastrophic environmentalism, abandoning any doubt that humans could cause global cataclysm—man had acquired godlike powers, he wrote, but still lacked godlike wisdom.

In the eyes of his critics, Gore's book was a re-hash of the global catastrophic predictions being made since the first computer simulations in the early 1970s. As before, much of the anti-Gore critique came from market-oriented politicians or academic scholars who dreaded the planetary-scale government interventionism that Gore implied. Robert W. Hahn, a scholar from the conservative think tank, the American Enterprise Institute, wrote a 40-page response to the book in the *Yale Law Journal*, deriding "Mr. Gore's Fantasy World" and comparing it with the "Real World." He wrote mockingly that Gore wanted to save the planet: "Nothing short of a complete overhaul of the world economic system and a redefinition of our relationship to nature will satisfy him." Hahn disliked how Gore presented the alternative as "global environmental holocaust."[16] Alex Kozinski, a Reagan-appointed federal judge, called Gore's book a "Jedi mind trick." It was not a new common purpose for the post–Cold War era but just the same doomsday approach that had characterized the movement since the late 1960s. He later wrote: "With the benefit of hindsight, we know that *The Limits to Growth* was a bunch of hooey; virtually nothing the Club of Rome predicted with such alarm has come to pass. Of course, its members did not then come out with a big press release: 'Oh what fools we were! We apologize for worrying the world unnecessarily.'"[17]

Debates over global warming in the 1990s and 2000s inherited this political dynamic. This was partly Al Gore's doing, when he focused on climate change with his later book and film *An Inconvenient Truth* (2006). Just as Carl Sagan once thought it prudent to partner up with Paul Ehrlich, Gore thought that his Global Marshall Plan to address a range of issues fit well with climate change—called a "planetary emergency" in the subtitle—and many climate scientists adopted Gore as a key ally. The political dynamic also was reinforced by conservative think tanks, such as the George C. Marshall Institute, which cast doubt upon climate change just as it had for nuclear winter many years before. These battle lines were drawn long before and had very little to do with the specific issue of climate change. Instead they hinged upon what to do about the human ability to alter the natural environment beyond national borders, on a global scale. Despite its roots in military research and its early acceptance by scientists and military and intelligence analysts, the climate change issue often wore the false appearance of a scientific dispute—one that also happened to be a political battle between liberals and conservatives, regulators and free marketeers. The truth was that the politics of climate change conformed to the same mold established in the early 1970s when environmentalists and economists clashed over different issues.

Public discussions of environmental problems have been locked into a "catastrophic" groove for decades, leaving little middle ground. In the early twenty-first century, "climate dissidents," as one scholar has called them, encouraged the perception that scientists remained torn about whether introducing carbon dioxide into the atmosphere caused global warming.[18] On the other side of the coin, politically naïve scientists played directly into these "dissident" hands. In defending the findings of groups such as the United Nations Intergovernmental Panel on Climate Change (IPCC), scientists found the rhetoric of environmental catastrophe irresistible. By employing it, they merely reinforced skepticism among those who had ridiculed such rhetoric for decades, across a host of environmental issues. In her sociological analysis of political tactics in the climate change debate, Myanna Lahsen emphasized this point. "Scientists working with environmental activist groups," she wrote, "typically invoke scientific evidence and the authority of the IPCC only when it reinforces the case that humans' actions are leading to catastrophe."[19]

The unlearned lesson, evident since the late 1960s, was that cataclysmic predictions were easy to dismantle and ridicule. When Danish political scientist Bjørn Lomborg published a book listing the litany of environmentalists' dire predictions that never came to pass, dating from the first computer simulations in *The Limits to Growth*, environmentalists treated it as heresy, or at least as a right-wing hatchet job. But the 2001 book, called *The Skeptical Environmentalist*, held a potent message: when every problem is treated as a global crisis, real global crises are easily ignored. Lomborg showed how environmental organizations such as the World Wide Fund for Nature, Greenpeace, and the Worldwatch Institute made claims that contradicted their data. Using the same data, Lomborg was able to suggest entirely opposite conclusions on issues ranging from population growth, infectious disease, air pollution, and global warming.[20]

These latter observations are merely food for thought. It is not the main purpose of this book to demonstrate that catastrophic rhetoric serves to undermine the credibility of climate science or environmentalists' goals. Nor do I wish to lampoon those who, against scientific consensus backed up by decades of evidence, have insisted that human actions cannot have devastating consequences for the earth and its inhabitants. My interest in writing this book began with a less polemical notion, that if we wish to understand how humans came to believe they were capable of changing the natural environment on a vast scale, with catastrophic results, we first should look at those people who tried to accomplish it. There was no small number of people attempting to do so, for good or for ill. Locating the roots of catastrophic environmental thinking in those scientists, military leaders, and politicians who believed they would have to manipulate and exploit nature in a global war against the Soviet Union offers a complementary perspective to the copious work on environmentalism that emerged from other sources. Scientists working with the military extended "total war" thinking to the natural environment, to maximize the catastrophic consequences of war. In the process, they fostered a profound belief in the manipulability of the natural world and the susceptibility of humans to dangers on an enormous scale. Politicians, diplomats, and intelligence analysts maneuvered to respond to the opportunities and challenges presented by this scientific work on human-induced change. For decades, military establishments in the Cold War funded research on environmental warfare, maintained global surveillance of the atmosphere and oceans, and tried to understand the vulnerabilities of the nation and the earth. Explorations in the environmental sciences probed the darker side of human nature. Through science, humans tried to harness the power of nature against their foes. Perhaps in the process, they discovered they were arming nature against themselves.

Notes

INTRODUCTION

1. Technical information is taken from the United States Geological Survey website. http://earthquake.usgs.gov/earthquakes/world/events/1960_05_22.php. Accessed on September 1, 2010.
2. "Chile Ravaged by New Earthquake," *The Times* (May 24, 1960), 12.
3. These statements are made by former Secretary of Defense Robert McNamara in the 2003 film, *The Fog of War: Eleven Lessons from the Life of Robert S. McNamara*, directed by Errol Morris.
4. "Estimate of the Effect on the Nature of War of Future Technical Developments in Weapons." No author or date, attached to Fleet Admiral William D. Leahy, memorandum to the Secretary of War and Secretary of the Navy, June 14, 1947, NARA RG 218, Central Decimal File 1948–50, Box 207, Folder "Future Technical Development of New Weapons."
5. Von Neumann's views are discussed in James Rodger Fleming, *Fixing the Sky: The Checkered History of Weather and Climate Control* (New York: Columbia University Press, 2010), ch. 7.
6. Richard Rhodes, *Dark Sun: The Making of the Hydrogen Bomb* (New York: Simon & Schuster, 1996).
7. McGeorge Bundy, *Danger and Survival: Choices about the Bomb in the First Fifty Years* (New York: Random House, 1988), 249.
8. John McCormick, *Reclaiming Paradise: The Global Environmental Movement* (Bloomington: Indiana University Press, 1989).
9. The rise in environmental consciousness was surely multicausal. The seminal work on the role of American affluence is Samuel P. Hays, *Beauty, Health, and Permanence: Environmental Politics in the United States, 1955–1985* (New York: Cambridge University Press, 1987). For a discussion of other causes, including countercultural protest, women's activism, and changing politics among liberals,

see Adam Rome, "'Give Earth a Chance': The Environmental Movement and the Sixties," *Journal of American History* 90:2 (2003), 525–54.

10. Joseph Masco, "Bad Weather: On Planetary Crisis," *Social Studies of Science* 40:1 (2010), 7–40. Stephen Bocking and Donald Worster, among others, have pointed to the nuclear fallout crisis as a key episode in the rise of environmental consciousness. See Stephen Bocking, *Ecologists and Environmental Politics: A History of Contemporary Ecology* (New Haven: Yale University Press, 1997); Donald Worster, *Nature's Economy: A History of Ecological Ideas* (New York: Cambridge University Press, 1990). The role of fallout in sparking consciousness receives substantial attention in John McCormick, *Reclaiming Paradise*. On the role of fallout in shaping notions of environmental risk, see Toshihiro Higuchi, "Atmospheric Nuclear Weapons Testing and the Debate on Risk Knowledge in Cold War America, 1945–1963," in J. R. McNeill and Corinna Unger, eds., *Environmental Histories of the Cold War* (New York: Cambridge, 2010), 301–22.

11. For example, today scientists stand in consensus that global climate change is real and that humans are a cause, principally through the introduction of carbon dioxide into the atmosphere. Contribution of Working Group I to the Fourth Assessment Report of the Intergovernmental Panel on Climate Change, 2007. See especially chapter 9. Available at www.ipcc.ch/publications_and_data/ar4/wg1/en/contents.html. Accessed September 14, 2010.

12. See Spencer R. Weart, *The Discovery of Global Warming* (Cambridge: Harvard University Press, 2003).

13. Ronald E. Doel, "Constituting the Postwar Earth Sciences: The Military's Influence on the Environmental Sciences in the USA after 1945," *Social Studies of Science* 33:5 (October 2003), 635–66; Allan Needell, *Science, Cold War and the American State: Lloyd V. Berkner and the Balance of Professional Ideals* (Amsterdam: Harwood Academic, 2000).

14. NATO report VKC-EX3-PH1/GP2 (Von Kármán Committee), November 1962, NATO Archives, Brussels, Belgium, p. 61.

CHAPTER 1

1. "German Professors Denounced," *The Times* (July 2, 1945), 2.

2. For a discussion of war casualties, see Gerhard L. Weinberg, *A World at Arms: A Global History of World War II* (New York: Cambridge University Press, 1994), 894.

3. Gerard Daniel Cohen, *In War's Wake: Europe's Displaced Persons in the Postwar Order* (New York: Oxford University Press, 2011); Petra Goedde, *GIs and Germans: Culture, Gender, and Foreign Relations, 1945–1949* (New Haven: Yale University Press, 2002); Norman Naimark, *The Russians in Germany: A History of the Soviet Zone of Occupation, 1945–1949* (Cambridge: Belknap Press, 1995).

4. Clara E. Councell, "War and Infectious Disease," *Public Health Reports* 56:12 (1941), 547–43.

5. "Public Health in India," *The Times* (September 14, 1945), 5. On the continuing struggle against smallpox in the postwar era, see Erez Manela, "A Pox on Your Narrative: Writing Disease Control into Cold War History," *Diplomatic History* 34:2 (2010), 299–23.

6. W. K., "Epidemics Are Feared after the War," *New York Times* (April 1, 1945), E9.

7. "Imported Smallpox," *The Times* (March 13, 1946), 2.

8. "Europe's Epidemics Are Held in Check," *New York Times* (November 27, 1945), 7. On DDT's use, see David Kinkela, *DDT and the American Century: Global Health, Environmental Politics, and the Pesticide that Changed the World* (Chapel Hill: University of North Carolina Press, 2011).

9. "Cholera Increasing in India," *The Times* (October 11, 1947), 4.

10. Thomas Parran, "Charter for World Health," *Public Health Reports* 61:35 (1946), 1265–68, quote on p. 1267.

11. WHO.IC.EQ/20, "Information Regarding the 1946 (Hegira 1365) Pilgrimage," August 18, 1947, folder "WHO-1, 452-1-2," World Health Organization Archives, Geneva, Switzerland.

12. Committee on Quarantine, illegible title (on epidemic of cholera in Egypt), October 16, 1947, folder "WHO-1, 452-11-1," World Health Organization Archives, Geneva, Switzerland.

13. "Cholera in Egypt Unabated," *The Times* (October 8, 1947), 3; "Cairo Sprayed against Cholera," *The Times* (October 7, 1947), 3; "Cholera Still Raging in Egypt," *The Times* (October 31, 1947), 3.

14. "Cholera in Egypt Unabated," *The Times* (October 8, 1947), 3; "Liberation Battalions for Egypt: Muslim Brotherhood Plan," *The Times* (September 26, 1947), 3; "Egyptian Cholera Outbreak," *The Times* (October 20, 1947), 4.

15. "Japanese on Trial in Russia," *The Times* (December 28, 1949), 5; "Soviet War Crimes Charges," *The Times* (December 29, 1949), 3.

16. "Soviet Demand for Trial of Hirohito," *The Times* (February 3, 1950), 3.

17. "Soviet Said to Lack Right to Ask Trial," *New York Times* (February 3, 1950), 8.

18. For a detailed discussion of the Japanese work and the American decision to grant immunity to Unit 731 participants, see Sheldon H. Harris, *Factories of Death: Japanese Biological Warfare, 1932–1945, and the American Cover-Up* (New York: Routledge, 2002).

19. Chuck Yeager and Leo Janos, *Yeager: An Autobiography* (New York: Bantam, 1985). Errol Morris (director), *The Fog of War: Eleven Lessons from the Life of Robert S. McNamara* (Sony, 2003). The process of selecting cities on which to drop atomic bombs has been discussed by many authors, including Gar Alperovitz, *The Decision to Use the Atomic Bomb* (New York: Vintage, 1995), ch. 43.

20. George W. Merck, "Report to the Secretary of War on Biological Warfare," *Bulletin of the Atomic Scientists* 2:16 (1946); T. Rosebury, E. A. Kabat, and M. H. Boldt, "Bacterial Warfare," *Journal of Immunology* 56:7 (1947); Theodor Rosebury, *Peace or Pestilence: Biological Warfare and How to Avoid It* (New York: McGraw-Hill, 1949).

21. H. R. Hulme to D. W. Henderson, November 27, 1946, UK National Archives, WO 188/704.

22. Gerard Piel, "BW," *Life* (November 18, 1946), 118–30. Quote on p. 130.

23. Alden Waitt to Gerard Piel, November 6, 1946, UK National Archives, WO 188/703.

24. Alden H. Waitt to Colonel Graydon C. Essman, November 14, 1946, UK National Archives, WO 188/703.

25. "Estimate of the Effect on the Nature of War of Future Technical Developments in Weapons." This document, although classified "restricted," was a version of another higher-classification paper with more sensitive information deleted. No author or date, attached to (and explained in) Fleet Admiral William D. Leahy, memorandum to the Secretary of War and Secretary of the Navy, June 14, 1947, NARA RG 218, Central Decimal File 1948–50, Box 207, Folder "Future Technical Development of New Weapons."

26. There is considerable literature on the concept of total war; some see origins in the wars of the French Revolution, but others have analyzed it in particular regard to the American Civil War and the world wars. See Peter Paret, ed., *Makers of Modern Strategy: From Machiavelli to the Nuclear Age* (Princeton: Princeton University Press, 1986).

27. Edmund Russell, *War and Nature: Fighting Humans and Insects with Chemicals from World War I to Silent Spring* (New York: Cambridge University Press, 2001).

28. "Estimate of the Effect on the Nature of War of Future Technical Developments in Weapons." No author or date, attached to Fleet Admiral William D. Leahy, memorandum to the Secretary of War and Secretary of the Navy, June 14, 1947, NARA RG 218, Central Decimal File 1948–50, Box 207, Folder "Future Technical Development of New Weapons."

29. "Estimate of the Effect on the Nature of War of Future Technical Developments in Weapons." No author or date, attached to Fleet Admiral William D. Leahy, memorandum to the Secretary of War and Secretary of the Navy, June 14, 1947, NARA RG 218, Central Decimal File 1948–50, Box 207, Folder "Future Technical Development of New Weapons."

30. See Rosebury, *Peace or Pestilence*, ch. 2.

31. Robert W. Berry to the Joint Chiefs of Staff, March 1, 1948, NARA RG 218, Central Decimal File, 1948–1950, Box 206, Folder 5A.

32. Rear Admiral Ellis M. Zacharias, "Absolute Weapons . . . More Deadly than the Atom," *United Nations World* (November 1947), 13–15.

33. Zacharias, "Absolute Weapons."

34. George Brock Chisholm, "Social Responsibility," *Science* 109:2820 (1949), 27–30, 43.

35. James Conant to Vannevar Bush, April 29, 1948, NARA RG 218, Central Decimal File, 1948–1950, Box 206, Folder 6.

36. James Conant to Vannevar Bush, April 29, 1948, NARA RG 218, Central Decimal File, 1948–1950, Box 206, Folder 6.

37. W. G. Lalor to Chairman, Research and Development Board, July 6, 1948, NARA RG 218, Central Decimal File, 1948–1950, Box 206, Folder 6.

38. William D. Leahy to Secretary of Defense, July 7, 1948, NARA RG 218, Central Decimal File, 1948–1950, Box 206, Folder 6.

39. James Forrestal to the President, March 16, 1948, NARA RG 218, Central Decimal File, 1948–1950, Box 206, Folder 6.

40. Vannevar Bush, *Modern Arms and Free Men: A Discussion of the Role of Science in Preserving Democracy* (New York: Simon & Schuster, 1949), 147.

41. These studies initially were conducted on rats. The human work continued after the war, and Hamilton requested further supplies of plutonium to be used in human studies. Only in December 1946, just prior to turning over its activities to the newly created Atomic Energy Commission, did the District call a halt to these experiments. Colonel Kenneth D. Nichols said as much in a memorandum, pointing out that human experimentation was neither to be recommended nor interpreted as within the bounds of contract 48-A. However, the studies would be resumed under the AEC in 1947. United States Department of Energy, Advisory Committee on Human Radiation Experiments, Final Report, available at www.eh.doe.gov/ohre/roadmap/achre/report.html. See chapter 5.

42. R. Overstreet and L. Jacobson to Joseph G. Hamilton, November 11, 1946, NARA RG 218, Central Decimal File, 1948–1950, Box 206, Folder 5.

43. Overstreet and Jacobson to Hamilton, November 11, 1946.

44. Overstreet and Jacobson to Hamilton, November 11, 1946.

45. Joseph G. Hamilton to Colonel K. D. Nichols, December 31, 1946, NARA RG 218, Central Decimal File, 1948–1950, Box 206, Folder 5.

46. Hamilton to Nichols, December 31, 1946.

47. Hamilton to Nichols, December 31, 1946.

48. Hamilton to Nichols, December 31, 1946.

49. Alden H. Waitt to Director, Research and Development Division, War Department General Staff, February 7, 1947, NARA RG 218, Central Decimal File, 1948–1950, Box 206, Folder 5.

50. War Department, Office of the Chief, Chemical Corps, "Project: Radioactive Materials for Military Purposes," n.d. [forwarded with letter dated February 7, 1947], NARA RG 218, Central Decimal File, 1948–1950, Box 206, Folder 5.

51. Von Neumann is quoted in "Background History," February 15, 1948, attached to L. R. Groves to Joint Chiefs of Staff, February 15, 1948, NARA RG 218, Central Decimal File, 1948–1950, Box 206, Folder 5.

52. Rainbow Team to Major General Alfred M. Gruenther, January 7, 1949, NARA RG 218, Central Decimal File, 1948–1950, Box 206, Folder 7.

53. National Military Establishment, Office of the Secretary of Defense, "Secretary Forrestal Issues Statement on Biological Warfare Capabilities," press release, March 12, 1949, NARA RG 218, Central Decimal File, 1948–1950, Box 206, Folder 8.

54. On the impacts of these events, see Melvyn P. Leffler, *A Preponderance of Power: National Security, the Truman Administration, and the Cold War* (Stanford: Stanford University Press, 1992).

CHAPTER 2

1. Department of Defense Directive, "Policy on Chemical, Biological and Radiological Warfare," November 28, 1951, NARA RG 218, Central Decimal File, 1951–1953, Box 152, Folder CCS 385.2 (12-17-43) Sec. 13.
2. Philipp Gerhardt, "Brucella Suis in Aerated Broth Culture: III. Continuous Culture Studies," *Journal of Bacteriology* 52 (1946), 283–92.
3. Cora M. Downs, Lewis L. Coriell, S. S. Chapman, and Alice Klauber, "The Cultivation of *Bacterium tularense* in Embryonated Eggs," *Journal of Bacteriology* 53 (1947), 89–100.
4. Winston R. Miller, Lolita Pannell, Leo Cravitz, William A. Tanner, and Mabel S. Ingalls, "Studies on Certain Biological Characteristics of *Malleomyces mallei* and *Malleomyces pseudomallei*: I. Morphology, Cultivation, Viability, and Isolation from Contaminated Specimens," *Journal of Bacteriology* 55 (1948), 115–26.
5. Secretary of Defense to Caryl Haskins, March 16, 1949, NARA RG 218, Central Decimal File, 1948–1950, Box 206, Folder 8.
6. Ad Hoc Committee on Biological Warfare of the Department of Defense, report, July 11, 1949, NARA RG 218, Central Decimal File, 1948–1950, Box 206, Folder 8.
7. Ad Hoc Committee on Biological Warfare, July 11, 1949.
8. Ad Hoc Committee on Biological Warfare, July 11, 1949.
9. The Haskins report alludes to the communist satellite question briefly and refers to a document furnished to the committee by the CIA entitled "Report on Possible Recent Uses of BW within Yugoslavia," dated November 23, 1948. See Ad Hoc Committee on Biological Warfare, July 11, 1949.
10. Ad Hoc Committee on Biological Warfare, July 11, 1949.
11. A. M. Prentiss Jr., Colonel (USAF), memorandum of conversation to Colonel Bayer, June 23, 1950, NARA RG 218, Central Decimal File, 1948–1950, Box 206, Folder 9.
12. Prentiss, memorandum of conversation to Colonel Bayer, June 23, 1950.
13. Joint Strategic Plans Committee, report to the Joint Chiefs of Staff, on "Chemical, Biological, and Radiological Warfare," August 7, 1950. The Army view is contained in J. E. Hull to Secretary of Defense, August 22, 1950. Both documents are in NARA RG 218, Central Decimal File, 1948–1950, Box 206, Folder 9.
14. The disparity in Army and Navy views is evident in early drafts of Joint Strategic Plans Committee, report to the Joint Chiefs of Staff, on "Chemical, Biological, and Radiological Warfare." NARA RG 218, Central Decimal File, 1948–1950, Box 206, Folder 9.

15. Memorandum by the Chief of Naval Operations for the Joint Chiefs of Staff on "Chemical, Biological, and Radiological Warfare," September 6, 1950, NARA RG 218, Central Decimal File, 1948–1950, Box 206, Folder 9.

16. Omar N. Bradley (Chairman, Joint Chiefs of Staff) to Secretary of Defense, September 8, 1950, NARA RG 218, Central Decimal File, 1948–1950, Box 206, Folder 9. See also G. Marshall to Secretary of the Army, Secretary of the Navy, and additional recipients, October 27, 1950, NARA RG 218, Central Decimal File, 1948–1950, Box 207, Folder "Chemical, Biological, and Radiological Warfare."

17. W. G. Lalor, Memorandum for Chief of Staff, U.S. Army; Chief of Naval Operations; Chief of Staff, U.S. Air Force, February 21, 1951, NARA RG 218, Central Decimal File, 1948–1950, Box 207, Folder "Chemical, Biological, and Radiological Warfare." See also Report by the Joint Strategic Plans Committee to the Joint Chiefs of Staff on Chemical, Biological and Radiological Warfare, p. 216 of JCS 1837/18, February 12, 1951, NARA RG 218, Central Decimal File, 1948–1950, Box 207, Folder "Chemical, Biological, and Radiological Warfare."

18. Biological Department, Chemical Corps, SO and C Divisions, Special Report No. 138, "Feathers as Carriers of Biological Warfare Agents," December 15, 1950, NARA RG 218, Central Decimal File, 1948–50, Box 207, Folder CCS 385.2 (12-17-43) B. P. Part I.

19. Biological Department, Chemical Corps, SO and C Divisions, "Feathers as Carriers of Biological Warfare Agents," December 15, 1950.

20. William Webster, Memorandum for the Joint Chiefs of Staff, February 14, 1951, NARA RG 218, Central Decimal File, 1948–1950, Box 207, Folder "Chemical, Biological, and Radiological Warfare."

21. W. G. Lalor, Memorandum for the Chairman, Research and Development Board, September 13, 1951, NARA RG 218, Central Decimal File, 1951–53, Box 152, Folder CCS 385.2 (12-17-43) Sec. 12. See appendix for discussion of the reasons for the ranking.

22. "United Nations Facing an 'Entirely New War,'" *The Times* (November 29, 1950), 4.

23. Roger Dingman, "Atomic Diplomacy during the Korean War," *International Security* 13:3 (1988–1989), 50–91.

24. "Atomic Belt Urged for Korea," *New York Times* (April 17, 1951), 3.

25. "Atomic Belt Plan Held Not Feasible," *New York Times* (April 18, 1951), 16.

26. "Atomic Belt Urged for Korea," *New York Times* (April 17, 1951), 3.

27. "Bacteriological Warfare in Korea," March 1952, UK National Archives, FO 1110/494. See also T. S. Tull to John Raynor, March 17, 1952, UK National Archives, FO 1110/494.

28. Overseas Press Services, "Far Eastern Commentary: Germs and Propaganda," by Guy Wint, March 22, 1952, UK National Archives, FO 1110/494.

29. Overseas Press Services, "Insulated Insects," by J. M. Spey, March 4, 1952, UK National Archives, FO 1110/494.

30. "Bacteriological Warfare in Korea," March 1952, UK National Archives, FO 1110/494.

31. Overseas Press Services, no title, March 1, 1952, UK National Archives, FO 1110/494.

32. "World Opinion Rises in Protest against the Use of Bacteriological Warfare in Korea and China," *Bulletin of the World Council of Peace* 22 (March 25, 1952), held in UK National Archives, FO 1110/494.

33. He received copies of handwritten confessions of captured American airmen, along with photographs of the Chinese scientists who had identified the infected animals and insects. He also received several photographs of flies, spiders, beetles, fungi, and other alleged carriers of pathogens. Archives, Institut Curie, Fonds Joliot-Curie, box F-130.

34. Archives, Institut Curie, Fonds Joliot-Curie, box F-130.

35. Jeffrey Lockwood, *Six-legged Soldiers: Using Insects as Weapons of War* (New York: Oxford University Press, 2009).

36. "Report of the International Scientific Commission for the Investigation of the Facts Concerning Bacterial Warfare in Korea and China," 1952, Archives, Institut Curie, Fonds Joliot-Curie, box F-130.

37. "Virus Culture," *The Times* (October 30, 1953), Archives, Institut Curie, Fonds Joliot-Curie, folder "Correspondence Jean Malterre."

38. American Committee for Cultural Freedom to Frédéric Joliot-Curie, May 2, 1952, and Frédéric Joliot-Curie to Warren Austin, May 3, 1952, Archives, Institut Curie, Fonds Joliot-Curie, Box F-129.

39. T. S. Tull to B. A. B. Burrows, July 8, 1952, UK National Archives, FO 1110/494.

40. Tom Buchanan, "The Courage of Galileo: Joseph Needham and the 'Germ Warfare' Allegations in the Korean War," *History* 86: 284 (2001), 503–22.

41. These letters are contained in Archives, Institut Curie, Fonds Joliot-Curie, folder "Correspondence Jean Malterre." Other participants included Andrea Andreen (Sweden), Oliviero Olivo (Italy), Franco Graziosi (Italy), Samuel P. Bessoa (Brazil), N. N. Zhukov-Verezhnikov (USSR), and Jean Malterre (France).

42. Franco Graziosi to Jean Malterre, November 25, 1953, Archives, Institut Curie, Fonds Joliot-Curie, folder "Correspondence Jean Malterre."

43. Archives, Institut Curie, Fonds Joliot-Curie, F-130, Folder "Rapport Needham."

44. Memo to J. W. Nicholls [author not clear], n.d., UK National Archives, FO 1110/494.

45. T. S. Tull to J. W. Nicholls, August 22, 1952, UK National Archives, FO 1110/494.

46. Henry H. Dale and Robert Robinson, "Report on Germ Warfare," *The Times* (October 17, 1952), 7.

47. F. G. Gregory, J. B. S. Haldane, S. M. Manton, and A. C. Offord, "Germ Warfare Report," *The Times* (October 29, 1952), 7.

48. Frank Darvall (director-general of the English-Speaking Union) and Charles Judd (director-general of the United Nations Association) met privately with members of the Royal Society, trying without success to push them to denounce

the Needham report. They then turned to Member of Parliament Anthony Nutting, pressing him to instigate a government-sponsored refutation. But without being allowed into allegedly affected area, this would have proven impossible. "I replied that I could not see what action the Government could take beyond showing all the umpteen flaws in the Needham report and thus pouring as much ridicule upon it as possible." Anthony Nutting, note, December 5, 1952, UK National Archives, FO 1110/494.

49. British Embassy, Washington, to Foreign Office (departmental distribution), March 25, 1952, UK National Archives, FO 1110/494.

50. Foreign Office to British Embassy, Washington, n.d., UK National Archives, FO 1110/494.

51. P. Dixon, record of conversation with Dean Acheson, May 27, 1952 (conversation May 26, 1952), UK National Archives, FO 1110/494.

52. Frédérique Matonti, "La colombe et les mouches. Frédéric Joliot-Curie et le pacifisme des savants," *Politix* 15:58 (2002), 109–40.

CHAPTER 3

1. V. E. Wilkins [Chairman of the International Committee] to His Excellency the Minister of Agriculture, Prague, April 27, 1950. See also V. E. Wilkins to His Excellency the British Ambassador, British Embassy, Prague, July 22, 1950, UK National Archives, FO 371/86298.

2. British Embassy, Prague, to Foreign Office, No. 427, June 30, 1950, UK National Archives, FO 371/86298.

3. British Embassy, Prague, to Foreign Office, No. 450, July 8, 1950, UK National Archives, FO 371/86298.

4. British Embassy, Prague, to Foreign Office, No. 458 and No. 459, July 11, 1950, UK National Archives, FO 371/86298.

5. British Embassy, Prague, to Foreign Office, No. 464, July 13, 1950, UK National Archives, FO 371/86298.

6. "The Colorado Beetle," *The Times* (September 4, 1901), 7; "The Beetle that Went on its Travels," *The Times* (June 19, 1947), 5.

7. "Contamination of Crops," Porton report No. 2178, Serial No. 3, February 27, 1941, UK National Archives WO 189/2114.

8. Ministry of Supply, Advisory Council on Scientific Research and Technical Development, Crop Committee, notes of a meeting held on November 29, 1949, received January 11, 1950, UK National Archives, WO 195/10738.

9. Quoted in Charles S. Elton, *The Ecology of Invasions by Plants and Animals* (London: Chapman and Hall, 1958), 93.

10. "Entomological Aspects of B.W.," note of discussion, August 9, 1951, UK National Archives, WO 188/2122.

11. Extract from P. A. Buxton, "The Use of Insects in Biological Warfare," September 1951, UK National Archives, WO 188/2122.

12. Extract from P. A. Buxton, "The Use of Insects in Biological Warfare," September 1951.

13. Extract from P. A. Buxton, "The Use of Insects in Biological Warfare," September 1951.

14. J. R. McNeill, *Mosquito Empires: Ecology and War in the Greater Caribbean, 1620–1914* (New York: Cambridge University Press, 2010).

15. Extract from P. A. Buxton, "The Use of Insects in Biological Warfare," September 1951.

16. "Bertie Blount," Obituary, *The Times* (July 27, 1999), 21.

17. Ministry of Supply, Advisory Council on Scientific Research and Technical Development, Crop Committee, "The Dangers of Clandestine Communist Attack on Crops," August 25, 1950, UK National Archives, WO 195/11082.

18. Ministry of Supply, Advisory Council on Scientific Research and Technical Development, Crop Committee, "The Dangers of Clandestine Communist Attack on Crops," August 25, 1950.

19. Warren Dean, *Brazil and the Struggle for Rubber: A Study in Environmental History* (New York: Cambridge University Press, 2002).

20. Ministry of Supply, Advisory Council on Scientific Research and Technical Development, Crop Committee, "The Dangers of Clandestine Communist Attack on Crops," August 25, 1950.

21. "Collyer Raps Plans for Rubber Control," *New York Times* (May 24, 1949), p. 45.

22. Ministry of Supply, Advisory Council on Scientific Research and Technical Development, Crop Committee, "The Dangers of Clandestine Communist Attack on Crops," August 25, 1950.

23. Ministry of Supply, Advisory Council on Scientific Research and Technical Development, Crop Committee, "The Dangers of Clandestine Communist Attack on Crops," August 25, 1950.

24. Thomas R. Mockaitis, *British Counterinsurgency, 1919–1960* (New York: St. Martin's Press, 1990), 119.

25. Quoted in John A. Nagl, *Counterinsurgency Lessons from Malaya and Vietnam* (Westport, CT: Praeger, 2002), 74–75.

26. See Michael E. Latham, *Modernization as Ideology: American Social Science and "Nation-Building in the Kennedy Era* (Chapel Hill: University of North Carolina Press, 2000), 176–77.

27. Ministry of Supply to Technical Services, Washington, May 7, 1952; Technical Services, Washington to Ministry of Supply, May 6, 1952, UK National Archives, AIR 20/8729.

28. G. M. Wyatt, handwritten note, May 8, 1952, UK National Archives, AIR 20/8729.

29. T. C. Jerrom to Mr. Childs, May 13, 1952, UK National Archives, AIR 20/8729.

30. These deliberations are recorded in UK National Archives, AIR 20/8729.

31. The author of this particular handwritten passage is unclear. See UK National Archives, AIR 20/8729.

32. Ministry of Supply, Advisory Council on Scientific Research and Technical Development, Crop Committee, "Investigations at Porton—Progress Report September 1952" by Professor G. E. Blackman, September 10, 1952, UK National Archives, WO 195/11991.

33. Advanced Air Headquarters Malaya to Air Headquarters Malaya, February 9, 1953, "Destruction of Communist Terrorist Crops," UK National Archives, AIR 20/8735.

34. A. S. Crafts, "Herbicides," *Annual Review of Plant Physiology* 4 (1953), 253–82.

35. "SA/AC Letter on Crop Destruction Trials," February 1953, UK National Archives, AIR 20/8735.

36. F. H. P. Austin to Under-Secretary of State, "Reports from Army Chemical Center," October 5, 1955, UK National Archives, AIR 20/8729.

37. Minutes of Meeting of Specialists on Infestation Control in Stored Foods, Station of Agricultural Entomology, Florence, Italy, September 6–18, 1948, Food and Agriculture Organization Archives, Box 10AGP154, Folder "Infestation Meetings." BELIT 1744.

38. Summary of Proceedings, International Meeting on Infestation of Foodstuffs, London, England, August 5–12, 1947, Food and Agriculture Organization Archives, Box 10AGP154, Folder "Infestation Meetings."

39. Summary of Proceedings, International Meeting on Infestation of Foodstuffs, London, England, August 5–12, 1947.

40. Minutes of Meeting of Specialists on Infestation Control in Stored Foods, Station of Agricultural Entomology, Florence, Italy, September 6–18, 1948, Food and Agriculture Organization Archives, Box 10AGP154, Folder "Infestation Meetings."

41. Summary of Proceedings, International Meeting on Infestation of Foodstuffs, London, England, August 5–12, 1947.

42. Questions of this nature, based on American studies of spraying techniques from the air, are recorded in the UK National Archives, AIR 20/8729.

43. Brief for Director General of Armament for Meeting of the Chiefs of Staff Chemical Warfare Sub-Committee, August 10, 1949 (dated August 4, 1949), UK National Archives, AIR 20/8729.

44. Brief for Director General of Armament for Meeting of the Chiefs of Staff Chemical Warfare Sub-Committee, August 10, 1949.

45. Note by Air Ministry, "Revision of 1947 Report on Crop Destruction," November 22, 1949, UK National Archives, AIR 20/8729.

46. Peter Crowcroft, *Elton's Ecologists: A History of the Bureau of Animal Population* (Chicago: University of Chicago Press, 1991).

47. Elton, *The Ecology of Invasions by Plants and Animals*, 142.

48. Elton, *The Ecology of Invasions by Plants and Animals*, 142.

49. Elton, *The Ecology of Invasions by Plants and Animals*, 115.

50. This interpretation of Elton's scientific pedigree appears in Peder Anker, *Imperial Ecology: Environmental Order in the British Empire, 1895–1945* (Cambridge: Harvard University Press, 2001).

51. Elton, *The Ecology of Invasions by Plants and Animals,*109. These military terms are emphasized in Matthew K. Chew, "Ending with Elton: Preludes to Invasion Biology," Ph.D. dissertation, Arizona State University, 2006.

52. Quoted in Elton, *The Ecology of Invasions by Plants and Animals,* 125.

53. United States Army Chemical Corps, *Summary of Major Events and Problems* (Army Chemical Center, Maryland: U.S. Army Chemical Corps Historical Office, 1960). For an excellent discussion of entomological warfare at Camp/ Fort Detrick, See Jeffrey A. Lockwood, *Six-Legged Soldiers: Using Insects as Weapons War* (New York: Oxford University Press, 2009), ch. 17.

54. United States Army Chemical Corps, *Summary of Major Events and Problems.*

55. LeRoy D. Fothergill, "Biological Warfare and Its Defense," delivered before the Nevada State Medical Association, Reno, Nevada, August 23, 1956, UK National Archives, WO 188/709.

56. Fothergill, "Biological Warfare and Its Defense."

57. Letter No. 24, March 1957, UK National Archives, WO 188/709.

58. "Food Economy of the Sino-Soviet Bloc," report by the Joint Intelligence Committee to the Joint Chiefs of Staff, JCS 1924/100, November 13, 1957, NARA RG 218, Central Decimal Files, 1958, Box 77, folder CCS 385.2 (12-17-43) Sec. 24.

59. "Food Economy of the Sino-Soviet Bloc," November 13, 1957.

60. "Food Economy of the Sino-Soviet Bloc," November 13, 1957.

61. J. H. Rothschild, "Germs and Gas: The Weapons Nobody Dares Talk About," *Harper's Magazine,* cutting in UK National Archives, WO 188/709.

62. "Study 'Ishmael' Summary of Proceedings," January 30, 1957, UK National Archives, MAF 357/42.

63. Joseph Edwards to J. G. Carnochan, March 19, 1959, UK National Archives, MAF 355/68.

64. R. Scarisbrick to G. Wortley, April 14, 1959, UK National Archives, MAF 355/68.

65. G. Wortley, Report of a Visit to the Milk Marketing Board, Thames Ditton, May 4, 1959, UK National Archives, MAF 355/68. For the Arctic suggestion, see G. Wortley to J. Edwards, July 29, 1959, UK National Archives, MAF 355/68.

66. G. Wortley to J. Edwards, Milk Marketing Board, July 29, 1959, UK National Archives, MAF 355/68.

67. G. F. Smith, "Artificial Insemination with Frozen Semen, Cost Must Be Kept Down," *Times Supplement on Agriculture,* July 2, 1963, UK National Archives, MAF 355/68. A. W. Stableforth to C. H. A. Duke, June 29, 1962, UK National Archives, MAF 355/68. On Wortley's view, see G. Wortley, "Protection of Semen Banks," June 22, 1962, and T. Hetherington to E. S. Virgo, September 18, 1963, UK National Archives, MAF 355/68.

68. For correspondence with Dadd, see T. Hetherington to C. V. Dadd, August 29, 1960, P 1890; and C. V. Dadd to T. Hetherington, September 6, 1960, UK National Archives, MAF 355/66.

69. T. Hetherington to B. D. Hayes, August 26, 1960, UK National Archives, MAF 355/66. See also T. Hetherington to I. P. M. Macdonald, August 31, 1960, UK National Archives, MAF 355/66.

70. T. Hetherington to W. T. Barker, February 15, 1961, UK National Archives, MAF 355/66.

71. R. J. E. Taylor to Leslie W. Osborne, Agricultural and Food Attaché, British Embassy in Washington, September 4, 1963; Leslie Osborne to R. J. E. Taylor, September 6, 1963, UK National Archives, MAF 355/66.

72. Ministry of Agriculture, Fisheries and Food, South Eastern Region, "Problems of Agricultural Requisites under Nuclear Warfare Conditions," n. d., UK National Archives, MAF 355/66.

CHAPTER 4

1. Leopold is discussed, and quoted, in Roderick Frazier Nash, *Wilderness and the American Mind* (New Haven: Yale University Press, 2001), 259.

2. See Marc Trachtenberg, "A 'Wasting Asset': American Strategy and the Shifting Nuclear Balance, 1949–1954," *International Security* 13:3 (1988–1989), 5–49.

3. David A. Hounshell, "The Cold War, RAND, and the Generation of Knowledge, 1946–1962," *Historical Studies in the Physical Sciences* 27:2 (1997), 237–67.

4. On the detection of Joe-1, see Michael D. Gordin, *Red Cloud at Dawn: Truman, Stalin, and the End of the Atomic Monopoly* (New York: Farrar, Straus and Giroux, 2009), ch. 5. Also see Doyle L. Northrup and Donald H. Rock, "The Detection of Joe 1," *Studies in Intelligence* 10 (1966), 23–33. Available at www.foia.cia.gov. Accessed on June 28, 2010.

5. On Krypton-85, see Gordin, *Red Cloud at Dawn*, ch. 7.

6. Numerous scholars have noted the connections between geophysical data and military planning during the Cold War. A good introduction to the topic is Ronald E. Doel, "Constituting the Postwar Earth Sciences: The Military's Influence on the Environmental Sciences in the USA after 1945," *Social Studies of Science* 33:5 (2003), 635–66.

7. Jeffrey G. Barlow, *The Revolt of the Admirals: The Fight for Naval Aviation, 1945–1950* (Washington: Naval Historical Center, 1994). On scientists' advice for the Navy and other armed services, see Jack S. Goldstein, *A Different Sort of Time: The Life of Jerrold R. Zacharias, Scientist, Engineer, and Educator* (Cambridge: MIT Press, 1992).

8. Much of the older literature on the International Geophysical Year emphasizes the diplomatic benefits of cooperation and usefulness of science to ease international tensions. See Walter Sullivan, *Assault on the Unknown: The International Geophysical Year* (New York: McGraw-Hill, 1961); Sydney Chapman, *IGY: Year of Discovery* (Ann Arbor: University of Michigan Press, 1959); and Harold Bullis, *The Political Legacy of the International Geophysical Year* (Washington: Government Printing Office, 1973). By contrast, more recent literature highlights

the collaboration with military partners in the years surrounding the IGY. See, for examples, Dian Olson Belanger, *Deep Freeze: The United States, the International Geophysical Year, and the Origins of Antarctica's Age of Science* (Boulder: University Press of Colorado, 2006); Jacob Darwin Hamblin, *Oceanographers and the Cold War: Disciples of Marine Science* (Seattle: University of Washington Press, 2005).

9. On the budget impacts of the IGY, see J. Merton England, *A Patron for Pure Science: The National Science Foundation's Formative Years, 1945–1957* (Washington: National Science Foundation, 1982); and Roger L. Geiger, "What Happened after Sputnik? Shaping University Research in the United States," *Minerva* 35:4 (1997), 349–67.

10. The role of the IGY in extending the postwar scientific boom to the earth sciences is emphasized in Roger D. Launius, James Rodger Fleming, and David H. DeVorking, eds., *Globalizing Polar Science: Reconsidering the International Polar and Geophysical Years* (New York: Palgrave Macmillan, 2010).

11. Allan A. Needell, *Science, Cold War, and the American State: Lloyd V. Berkner and the Balance of Professional Ideals* (Amsterdam: Harwood, 2000).

12. Central Intelligence Agency, "Recent Developments in the Soviet Arctic," October 13, 1954, available at www.foia.cia.gov. Accessed on June 28, 2010.

13. Central Intelligence Agency, "Geophysical Research in the USSR," CIA/RR-G/I-157, August 1955, available at www.foia.cia.gov. Accessed on June 28, 2010.

14. J. J. Bagnall, "The Exploitation of Russian Scientific Literature for Intelligence Purposes," *Studies in Intelligence* 2 (1958), 45–49, available at www.foia.cia.gov. Accessed on June 28, 2010.

15. For example, American oceanographer Henry Stommel had predicted the existence of a deep current flowing south in the western boundary of the North Atlantic, and this was confirmed during the IGY. Other major deep currents, such as the Cromwell Current (Pacific Equatorial Undercurrent), were found to extend farther than previously believed. See J. W. Chamberlain, Charles R. Bentley, John C. Behrendt, Morton J. Rubin, and John A. Knauss, "Results of the IGY: Aeronomy, Glaciology, Meteorology, and Oceanography," *Science* 142:3590 (1963), 414–16, 418, 421.

16. Kenneth L. Hunkins, Maurice Ewing, Bruce C. Heezen, and Robert J. Menzies, "Biological and Geological Observations on the First Photographs of the Arctic Ocean Deep-sea Floor," *Limnology and Oceanography* 5:2 (1960), 154–61.

17. R. Revelle and H. Suess, "Carbon Dioxide Exchange between Atmosphere and Ocean and the Question of an Increase of Atmospheric CO_2 during the Past Decades." *Tellus* 9, 18–27 (1957).

18. Spencer R. Weart, "Money for Keeling: Monitoring CO_2 Levels," *Historical Studies in the Physical and Biological Sciences* 37:2 (2007), 435–52.

19. The point is made succinctly in Spencer R. Weart, "The Discovery of the Risk of Global Warming," *Physics Today* 50:1 (1997), 34–40. See also Spencer R. Weart, *The Discovery of Global Warming* (Cambridge: Harvard University Press, 2003);

and also Weart's much more extensive analysis, available at www.aip.org/history/climate/.

20. The importance to the atmospheric sciences of establishing this global observational infrastructure, ultimately creating global institutions for data collection, is emphasized in Paul N. Edwards, *A Vast Machine: Computer Models, Climate Data, and the Politics of Global Warming* (Cambridge: MIT Press, 2010).

21. The role of the fallout controversy in sewing distrust among scientists and laypersons alike is discussed in Robert Divine, *Blowing on the Wind: The Nuclear Test Ban Debate, 1954–1960* (New York: Oxford University Press, 1978); Carolyn Kopp, "The Origins of the American Scientific Debate over Fallout Hazards," *Social Studies of Science* 9:4 (1979), 403; Donald Worster, *Nature's Economy: A History of Ecological Ideas* (New York: Cambridge University Press, 1990); Stephen Bocking, *Ecologists and Environmental politics: A History of Contemporary Ecology* (New Haven: Yale University Press, 1997).

22. Lindesay Parrott, "Case of Bikini Fishermen Causes a Furor in Japan," *New York Times* (March 28, 1954), E5.

23. "Japanese Geneticists on Radiation," *Science* 126:3263 (1957), 68–69.

24. Jacob Darwin Hamblin, *Poison in the Well: Radioactive Waste in the Oceans at the Dawn of the Nuclear Age* (New Brunswick: Rutgers University Press, 2008), 108–108.

25. The author has written about this particular episode in much greater detail in Jacob Darwin Hamblin, "'A Dispassionate and Objective Effort': Negotiating the First Study on the Biological Effects of Atomic Radiation," *Journal of the History of Biology* 40:1 (2007), 147–77.

26. See Hamblin, "'A Dispassionate and Objective Effort.'"

27. "1955 Von Neumann Memo to Strauss," *New York Times* (August 11, 1958), 7.

28. Note of Meeting held in Sir George Dunnett's Room on November 18, 1955, to consider Defence Planning for the Fishing Industry, November 25, 1955. Present: Sir George Dunnett, H., Gardner, R. G. R. Wall, C. F. Huntley. UK National Archives, MAF 355/31.

29. Note of Meeting held in Sir George Dunnett's Room, November 18, 1955.

30. Michael Graham to C. F. Huntley, February 16, 1955, UK National Archives, MAF 355/31.

31. Hugh Gardner to C. F. Huntley, November 29, 1955, UK National Archives, MAF 355/31.

32. Preliminary Note on the Major Fisheries Considerations Following Megaton Bombs on Glasgow and Edinburgh, May 1962, UK National Archives, MAF 355/31.

33. Preliminary Note on the Major Fisheries Considerations, May 1962.

34. Handwritten comments, unsigned and undated, adjacent to T. Hetherington to J. Cruickshank, November 22, 1963, UK National Archives, MAF 355/31.

35. T. Hetherington to J. Cruickshank, November 22, 1963, UK National Archives, MAF 355/31.

36. Handwritten comments, unsigned and undated, adjacent to T. Hetherington to J. Cruickshank, November 22, 1963.

37. A. Preston to L. G. Hanson, November 2, 1964, UK National Archives, MAF 355/31.

38. Charles L. Dunham, memorandum for Mr. Murray, February 19, 1957, NARA RG 326, Entry 67B1, Box 47, Folder "Medicine, Health, & Safety, Vol. 3."

39. On Projects Gabriel and Sunshine, see Barton Hacker, *Elements of Controversy: The Atomic Energy Commission and Radiation Safety in Nuclear Weapons Testing, 1947–1974* (Berkeley: University of California Press, 1994), 181–83.

40. "RAND Sunshine Project," June 1, 1954, RM-1280-AEC, Los Alamos National Laboratory, HSPT-REL-94–443.

41. Hacker, *Elements of Controversy*, 183.

42. Hal Hollister to various, February 27, 1958, NARA RG 326, DBM, Box 3369, folder 1.

43. Hal Hollister to various, January 22, 1958, NARA RG 326, DBM, box 3369, folder 1.

44. Committee on the Effects of Atomic Radiation on Agriculture and Food Supplies, "Agriculture, Food Supplies, and Atomic Radiation," *Science* 124:3211 (1956), 63–66.

45. CO-ORDINATION/AE/SR.2, February 10, 1956, Food and Agriculture Organization Archives, Box 10TAC344, Folder "ACC Subcommittee on Atomic Energy."

46. R. A. Silow to F. T. Wahlen, March 25, 1957, Food and Agriculture Organization Archives, Box 10TAC344, Folder "Radiation Committee."

47. FAO Nutrition Division, "Note on Principal Calcium Contributors in National Diets in Relation to Strontium 90," Food and Agriculture Organization Archives, Box 10TAC344, Folder "Radiation Committee."

48. FAO Nutrition Division, "Note on Principal Calcium Contributors in National Diets in Relation to Strontium 90."

49. R. A. Silow to D. L. Bramao, November 15, 1957, Food and Agriculture Organization Archives, Box 10TAC344, Folder "Radiation Committee."

50. CO-ORDINATION/AE/SR.2, February 10, 1956.

CHAPTER 5

1. Emphasis in original. Athelstan F. Spilhaus, "Sea and Air Resources," *Geographical Review* 44:3 (1954), 346–51.

2. Athelstan Spilhaus, "Control of the World Environment," *Geographical Review* 46:4 (1956), 451–59. Quote on p. 459.

3. On pre-IGY scientific theories about climate change, see James Rodger Fleming, *Historical Perspectives on Climate Change* (New York: Oxford University Press, 2005).

4. Some of these efforts at cloud seeding are discussed in Ted Steinberg, *Acts of God: The Unnatural History of Natural Disaster in America* (New York: Oxford University Press, 2000), 127–30.

5. "Snow for Weather Control," *Science News-Letter* (February 22, 1947), 127.

6. "Artificial Weather Made," *Science News-Letter* (November 1, 1947), 277.

7. James Rodger Fleming, *Fixing the Sky: The Checkered History of Weather and Climate Control* (New York: Columbia University Press, 2010), ch.5.

8. Irving Langmuir, "Control of Precipitation from Cumulous Clouds by Various Seeding Techniques," *Science* 112:2898 (July 14, 1950), 35–41.

9. Langmuir, "Control of Precipitation from Cumulous Clouds."

10. Bernhard Haurwitz, Gardner Emmons, George P. Wadsworth, and Hurd C. Willett to Brig. General D. N. Yates, August 16, 1950, reprinted in *Bulletin of the American Meteorological Society* 31:9 (1950), 346–47.

11. Ferguson Hall, Gardner Emmons, Bernhard Haurwitz, George P. Wadsworth, Hurd C. Willett, "Dr. Langmuir's Article on Precipitation Control," *Science* 113:2929 (February 16, 1951), 189–92.

12. Bernhard Haurwitz, Gardner Emmons, George P. Wadsworth, and Hurd C. Willett to Brig. General D. N. Yates, August 16, 1950.

13. B. Haurwitz and Gardner Emmons to J. L. Orr, January 12, 1951, UK National Archives, CAB 124/2711.

14. J. L. Orr, "Statement of the Extent of Cloud Seeding Effects with Respect to the Winnipeg Floods of 1950," February 22, 1951, UK National Archives, CAB 124/2711.

15. Henry G. Houghton, "An Appraisal of Cloud Seeding as a Means of Increased Precipitation," *Bulletin of the American Meteorological Society* 32:2 (February 1951), 39.

16. Bullard is quoted in Solly Zuckerman to E. D. T. Jourdain, June 29, 1951, UK National Archives, CAB 124/2711

17. D. A. Davies, D. Hepburn, and H. W. Sansom, "Report on Experiments at Kongwa on Aritificial Control of Rainfall, January–April 1952," *East African Meteorological Department Memoirs* II:10 (1952), in UK National Archives, CAB 124/2712.

18. Extract from the House of Commons Report vol. 516, no. 120, col. 716, June 16, 1953, UK National Archives, CAB 124/2712.

19. "Dr. Krick Thinks We Should Have Much More Rain," *Daily Mail* (March 1, 1954), cutting in UK National Archives, CAB 124/2712.

20. Draft brief from Meteorological Office, "Adjournment Debate on Weather Modification," February 20, 1954, UK National Archives, CAB 124/2712.

21. See Fleming, *Fixing the Sky*, ch. 5.

22. Minutes of House of Commons debate on weather modification, February 23, 1954, UK National Archives, CAB 124/2712.

23. Minutes of House of Commons debate on weather modification, February 23, 1954.

24. Dudley Pope, "Tornado," *Evening News* (December 9, 1954), held in UK National Archives, CAB 124/2712.

25. Alan Dick, "This!*!*! Weather," *Daily Herald* (December 21, 1954), cutting in UK National Archives, CAB 124/2712.

26. Beverley James, "And What a Year for Weather!" *Express* (date unclear), cutting in UK National Archives, CAB 124/2712.

27. Nona Brown, "Northeast Hurricanes: Freaks or Portents?" *New York Times* (October 24, 1954), E4.

28. "Tornadoes not Linked to Atom," *New York Times* (November 18, 1954), 37; "A-Bomb Link to Tornadoes Is Discounted," *Washington Post and Times-Herald* (November 18, 1954), 13.

29. L. Machta and D. L. Harris, "Effects of Atomic Explosions on Weather," *Science* 121:3134 (1955), 75–81.

30. "A Stormy 1955?" *Financial Times* (January 1, 1955), cutting in UK National Archives, CAB 124/2712.

31. "Experts' Caution on Hydrogen Bomb and Weather," *The Times* (February 21, 1955), 5.

32. "Statement for the Joint Congressional Committee on Atomic Energy on April 15, 1955, by Dr. Harry Wexler, Chief, Scientific Services Division, U.S. Weather Bureau, Washington, D.C., Regarding Nuclear Explosions and Weather." UK National Archives, CAB 124/2712.

33. Committee on Meteorological Aspects of the Effects of Atomic Radiation, "Meteorological Aspects of Atomic Radiation," *Science* 124:3212 (1956), 105–12.

34. "Do H-Bomb Explosions Affect the Weather?" *The Times* (August 21, 1956), 11.

35. John Davy, "Weather Outlook—Uncertain," *Observer* (January 16, 1955), cutting in UK National Archives, CAB 124/2712.

36. "Do H-Bomb Explosions Affect the Weather?" *The Times* (August 21, 1956), 11.

37. R. N. Quirk to Mr. Jourdain and Professor Zuckerman, December 7, 1954, UK National Archives, CAB 124/2712; on sunspots, see R. N. Quirk to Mr. Jourdain and Mr. Lewin, May 17, 1955, UK National Archives, CAB 124/2712.

38. United States Nuclear Tests: July 1945 through September 1992 (United States Department of Energy, 1994), available electronically at www.nv.doe.gov/library/publications/. . ./DOENV_209_REV15.pdf.

39. Robert S. Norris and Thomas B. Cochran, *Nuclear Weapons Tests and Peaceful Nuclear Explosions by the Soviet Union: August 29, 1949 to October 24, 1990* (New York: Natural Resource Defense Council, 1996 draft available online at docs. nrdc.org/nuclear/nuc_10009601a_173.pdf).

40. Walter Sullivan, "U.S. Atom Blasts 300 Miles Up Mar Radar, Snag Missile Plan; Called 'Greatest Experiment,'" *New York Times* (March 19, 1959), 1.

41. "Science: Doughnut around Earth," *Time* (December 8, 1958), available online at www.time.com/time/magazine/article/0,9171,864535,00.html. Accessed September 3, 2009.

42. "Science: Reach into Space," *Time* (May 4, 1959), available online at www.time. com/time/magazine/article/0,9171,892531,00.html. Accessed September 3, 2009.

43. John C. Delvin, "Hurricane Daisy Moves out to Sea," *New York Times* (August 30, 1958), 32.

44. Kennett Love, "London Soaks up Weather Debate," *New York Times* (September 14, 1958), 26.
45. "Weather Quirks Puzzle Experts," *New York Times* (August 10, 1958), 96.
46. W. H. Parker, "Storms across the World," *The Times* (September 9, 1958), 9.
47. Gordon Manley, letter to the editor, *The Times* (September 12, 1958), 11.
48. Peter Ball, letter to the editor, *The Times* (September 12, 1958), 11.
49. Adrian C. Boult, letter to the editor, *The Times* (September 17, 1958), 11.
50. "It's Icy in West, Midwest, and East," *New York Times* (January 19, 1963), 14.
51. "Arctic Weather Grips Northern Hemisphere," *The Times* (January 25, 1963), 9; "Continent Still in Grip of Cold Weather," *The Times* (January 28, 1963), 7.
52. "800 Die in Europe as Cold Persists," *New York Times* (January 3, 1963), 1.
53. "A Winter for the Records," *New York Times* (February 1, 1963), 8.
54. "A Winter for the Records," *New York Times* (February 1, 1963), 8.
55. "Belt of Radiation from Atom Test Above Estimates," *New York Times* (September 2, 1962), 1.

CHAPTER 6

1. H. Wexler, "Modifying Weather on a Large Scale," *Science* 128:3331 (1958), 1059–63.
2. John W. Finney, "U.S. is Urged to Seek Methods to Control the World's Weather," *New York Times* (January 1, 1958), 1.
3. George H. T. Kimble, "Storm Clouds over Weather Control," *New York Times* (February 9, 1958), SM15.
4. E. V. Truefitt to George Deacon, February 6, 1958, GERD D5/1 Secret and Confidential files, 1950–58, George Edward Raven Deacon Papers, UK National Oceanographic Library.
5. Zuoyue Wang, *In Sputnik's Shadow* (New Brunswick: Rutgers University Press, 2008).
6. Ann Finkbeiner, *The Jasons: The Secret History of Science's Postwar Elite* (New York: Viking, 2006).
7. This study was conducted under the National Academy of Sciences at the request of the Air Research and Development Command of the US Air Force. See NAS-ARDC Committee on Weapons, "Long Range Scientific and Technical Trends of Interest to the United States Air Force," 1958, NARA RG 359, Subject Files, 1957–1962, Box 17, Folder "NAS ARDC Study Group."
8. NAS-ARDC Committee on Weapons, "Long Range Scientific and Technical Trends of Interest to the United States Air Force," 1958.
9. NAS-ARDC Committee on Weapons, "Long Range Scientific and Technical Trends of Interest to the United States Air Force," 1958.
10. NAS-ARDC Committee on Life Sciences, "Long Range Scientific and Technical Trends of Interest to the United States Air Force," 1958, NARA RG 359, Subject Files, 1957–1962, Box 17, Folder "NAS ARDC Study Group."

11. NAS-ARDC Committee on Life Sciences, "Long Range Scientific and Technical Trends of Interest to the United States Air Force," 1958.

12. Michael Gorn, *Harnessing the Genie: Science and Technology Forecasting for the Air Force, 1944–1986* (Washington: Office of Air Force History USA, 1988), 18.

13. Von Kármán's work typically was executed through NATO's Advisory Group for Aeronautical Research and Development (AGARD), though the group did not always limit itself to aeronautics. On aeronautical forecasting, see Gorn, *Harnessing the Genie*.

14. Although more than 200 scientists and military experts participated in the activities and reports under the Von Kármán committee, the original principal members were Von Kármán, G. S. Field (Defence Research Board, Canada), Karl Fischer (Ministry of Defense, Federal Republic of Germany), J. Guerin (Comité d'Action Scientifique de Défense Nationale, France), H. P. Robertson (Department of Defense, USA), Sir Solly Zuckerman (Ministry of Defence, UK), and as an ex-officio member, William A. Nierenberg (NATO Assistant Secretary General for Scientific Affairs). See Von Kármán Committee, "Long-Term Scientific Studies for the North Atlantic Treaty Organization: Final Report," September 1961, VKC-Final Report, NATO Archives, Brussels, Belgium.

15. NATO report VKC-EX1-GPIII on "Geophysics," March 1961, NATO Archives, Brussels, Belgium. P. 16. For a discussion of this military acclimatization, see Matthew Farish, "Creating Cold War Climates: The Laboratories of American Globalism," in J. R. McNeill and Corinna R. Unger, eds., *Environmental Histories of the Cold War* (New York: Cambridge University Press, 2010), 51–83.

16. NATO report VKC-EX1-GPIII on "Geophysics," March 1961, NATO Archives, Brussels, Belgium. P. 9.

17. NATO report VKC-EX1-GPIII on "Geophysics," March 1961, p. 23.

18. Part of this enthusiasm came from postwar confidence in weather prediction due the integration of meteorology with machine-based calculating power. See Kristine C. Harper, *Weather by the Numbers: The Genesis of Modern Meteorology* (Cambridge: MIT Press, 2008).

19. NATO report VKC-EX2-GP3&4 on "Weapons," June 1961, NATO Archives, Brussels, Belgium. P. 106.

20. NATO report VKC-EX1-GPIII on "Geophysics," March 1961, p. 30.

21. NATO report VKC-EX1-GPIII on "Geophysics," March 1961, Addendum i.

22. NATO report VKC-EX2-GP3&4 on "Weapons," June 1961, pp. 95–96.

23. On Plowshare, see Scott L. Kirsch, *Proving Grounds: Project Plowshare and the Unrealized Dream of Nuclear Earthmoving* (New Brunswick: Rutgers University Press, 2005). See also Daniel O'Neill, "Project Chariot: How Alaska Escaped Nuclear Excavation," *Bulletin of the Atomic Scientists* 45:10 (December 1989), 28–37.

24. NATO report VKC-EX2-GP3&4 on "Weapons," June 1961, p. 101.

25. NATO report VKC-EX2-GP3&4 on "Weapons," June 1961, p. 102.

26. The entire report, including the transcript of an address by Edward Teller to the participants, is NATO Report VKC-Ex3-PH1/GP2 on "Environmental Warfare," November 1962, NATO Archives, Brussels, Belgium.

27. "Wave Out of Chile," *New York Times* (May 29, 1960), E2.

28. William L. Laurence, "Tsunamis' Power," *New York Times* (May 29, 1960), E8.

29. NATO Report VKC-Ex3-PH1/GP2 on "Environmental Warfare," November 1962, NATO Archives, Brussels, Belgium. P. 9

30. NATO Report VKC-Ex3-PH1/GP2 on "Environmental Warfare," November 1962, p. 15.

31. An example of Pressman's work is J. Pressman, F. F. Marmo, and L. M. Aschenbrand, "Artificial Electron Clouds—VI: Low Altitude Study, Release of Cesium at 69, 82, and 91 km," *Planetary and Space Sciences* 2:4 (1960), 228–37.

32. NATO Report VKC-Ex3-PH1/GP2 on "Environmental Warfare," November 1962, p. 28.

33. NATO Report VKC-Ex3-PH1/GP2 on "Environmental Warfare," November 1962, pp. 59, 60.

34. NATO Report VKC-Ex3-PH1/GP2 on "Environmental Warfare," November 1962, p. 9.

35. Lynn Eden, *Whole World on Fire: Organizations, Knowledge, and Nuclear Weapons Devastation* (Ithaca: Cornell University Press, 2004).

36. NATO Report VKC-Ex3-PH1/GP2 on "Environmental Warfare," November 1962, p. 54.

37. NATO Report VKC-Ex3-PH1/GP2 on "Environmental Warfare," November 1962, p. 5.

38. NATO Report VKC-Ex3-PH1/GP2 on "Environmental Warfare," November 1962, p. 6.

39. NATO Report VKC-Ex3-PH1/GP2 on "Environmental Warfare," November 1962, pp. 19–24.

40. NATO Report VKC-Ex3-PH1/GP2 on "Environmental Warfare," November 1962, p. 25.

41. See J. Pressman and R. Casey, "A Heuristic Examination of the Kinematics of Simplified Rocket Trails," ARPA Order No. 258–61, Air Force Cambridge Research Laboratories, Bedford, Massachusetts, February 1962. This and other studies available at http://handle.dtic.mil/100.2/AD274153 Accessed December 16, 2010.

42. Peter Stubbs, "May Rockets Disturb the Weather?" *New Scientist* 350 (August 1, 1963), 230–33. Quote on p. 233.

43. NATO Report VKC-Ex3-PH1/GP2 on "Environmental Warfare," November 1962, p. 57.

44. Ronald E. Doel and Kristine C. Harper, "Prometheus Unleashed: Science as a Diplomatic Weapon in the Lyndon B. Johnson Administration," *Osiris* 21 (2006), 66–85, quote on p. 70.

45. "Text of Kennedy's Address to Academy of Sciences," *New York Times* (October 23, 1963), 24.

46. "Text of Kennedy's Address to Academy of Sciences," *New York Times* (October 23, 1963), 24.

CHAPTER 7

1. Zuoyue Wang, *In Sputnik's Shadow* (New Brunswick: Rutgers University Press, 2008), 174–75.

2. Herman Kahn, *On Thermonuclear War* (Princeton: Princeton University Press, 1960), 21.

3. Jerome Spingarn, "Picking Up the Pieces," *New York Times* (January 1, 1961), BR3.

4. Paul Deats Jr., review of Herman Kahn, *On Thermonuclear War*, *Journal of Bible and Religion* 30 (1962), 170–71. Donald N. Michael, review of Herman Kahn, *On Thermonuclear War*, *Science* 133:3453 (March 3, 1961), 635. Christopher Lasch, review of Herman Kahn, *On Thermonuclear War*, *The Massachusetts Review* 2 (1961), 574–80.

5. Peter Galison, "The Ontology of the Enemy: Norbert Wiener and the Cybernetic Vision," *Critical Inquiry* 21 (1994), 228–66.

6. Sharon Ghamari-Tabrizi, "Simulating the Unthinkable: Gaming Future War in the 1950s and 1960s," *Social Studies of Science* 30 (2000), 163–223.

7. NAS-ARDC Committee on Life Sciences, "Long Range Scientific and Technical Trends of Interest to the United States Air Force," 1958, NARA RG 359, Subject Files, 1957–1962, Box 17, Folder "NAS ARDC Study Group."

8. NAS-ARDC Committee on Life Sciences, "Long Range Scientific and Technical Trends of Interest to the United States Air Force," 1958.

9. Robert K. Plumb, "Science Group Maps Drive to Advise on Public Issues," *New York Times* (July 8, 1960), 1.

10. "Science Integrity Said to Be in Peril," *New York Times* (December 31, 1964), 21.

11. Michael Egan, *Barry Commoner and the Science of Survival: The Remaking of American Environmentalism* (Cambridge, MA: MIT Press, 2007), 47.

12. Nigel Calder, ed., *Unless Peace Comes: A Scientific Forecast of New Weapons* (New York: Viking, 1968), 14, 20.

13. Calder, *Unless Peace Comes*, quotes on p. 142 and p. 164.

14. Calder, *Unless Peace Comes*, 183.

15. Calder, *Unless Peace Comes*, 202.

16. James Rodger Fleming, *Historical Perspective on Climate Change* (New York: Oxford University Press, 1998).

17. Calder, *Unless Peace Comes*, 191.

18. Lewis Mumford, "History: Neglected Clue to Technology Change," *Technology and Culture* 2:3 (1961), 230–36. Quote on p. 234. Such ideas are more fully developed in Lewis Mumford, "Authoritarian and Democratic Technics," *Technology and Culture* 5:1 (1964), 1–8.

19. Jacques Ellul, "The Technological Order," *Technology and Culture* 3:4 (1962), 394–421. Quote on pp. 401–2.

20. Lynn White Jr., "The Historical Roots of Our Ecologic Crisis," *Science* 155:3767 (March 10, 1967), 1203–7. Quote on p. 1204.

21. Mark H. Lytle, *The Gentle Subversive: Rachel Carson, Silent Spring, and the Rise of the Environmental Movement* (New York: Oxford University Press, 2007).

22. Carson, *The Sea Around Us* (New York, Signet, 1961), ix.

23. Carson, *The Sea Around Us*, x.

24. Carson, *The Sea Around Us*, xii.

25. Carson, *The Sea Around Us*, xii.

26. Charles Elton, *The Ecology of Invasions by Animals and Plants* (London, 1958), 155.

27. Wang, *In Sputnik's Shadow*, 203–7, quote on p. 203.

28. These influences are traced in Thomas Robertson, *The Malthusian Moment: Global Population Growth and the Birth of American Environmentalism* (New Brunswick: Rutgers University Press, 2012).

29. Paul Ehrlich, "Eco-Catastrophe!," in Roger Revelle, Ashok Khosla, and Maris Vinovskis, eds., *The Survival Equation: Man, Resources, and His Environment* (Boston: Houghton Mifflin, 1971), 352–64. Quote on p. 358.

30. Ehrlich, *The Population Bomb*, ch. 5.

31. Ehrlich, *The Population Bomb*, 172.

32. Barry Commoner, "Response," *Bulletin of the Atomic Scientists* (May 1972), 17, 42–56.

33. Advertisement, *Bulletin of the Atomic Scientists* (May 1972), 47.

34. "Doomsday Gloom and Optimism," *The Times* (September 3, 1971), 5.

35. John Maddox, *The Doomsday Syndrome* (New York: McGraw-Hill, 1972), 158.

36. "Doomsday Gloom and Optimism," *The Times* (September 3, 1971), 5.

37. John Maddox, "False Prophets of Calamity," *The Times* (February 3, 1972), 14.

38. John Maddox, "False Prophets of Calamity," *The Times* (February 3, 1972), 14.

39. "The Observer," *The Times* (March 4, 1972), 5. Those who weighed in on the issues included plant pathologist Norman Borlaug, who had won the Nobel Peace Prize in 1970 for his efforts to stem the tide of famine in South Asia with hybrid strains of wheat. The introduction of such crops had been dubbed the Green Revolution. Others included Barry Commoner, American nuclear physicist (and director of the Oak Ridge National Laboratory), Alvin Weinberg, and Club of Rome founder Aurelio Peccei.

40. Aurelio Peccei, "The Threat to Man Is Man Himself," *New York Times* (February 18, 1971), 35.

41. M. Fortun and S. S. Schweber, "Scientists and the Legacy of World War II: The Case of Operations Research (OR)," *Social Studies of Science* 23:4 (1993), 595–642.

42. For more on the application of game and decision theory to social problems in the 1960s, see Jennifer S. Light, *From Warfare to Welfare: Defense Intellectuals and Urban Problems in Cold War America* (Baltimore: Johns Hopkins University Press, 2003).

43. Boulding is quoted in Harold E. Thomas, "Taking Arms against a Sea of Troubles," *Science* 156:3776 (May 12, 1967), 810–11. Quote on p. 810. On conflict resolution, see Kenneth E. Boulding, "My Life Philosophy," *The American Economist* 29:2 (1985), 5–14.

44. On Forrester's career, see Jay W. Forrester, "The Beginning of System Dynamics," Banquet Talk at the international meeting of the System Dynamics Society, Stuttgart, Germany, July 13, 1989, available at http://sysdyn.clexchange.org/sdep/papers/D-4165-1.pdf.

45. Paul N. Edwards, *The Closed World: Computers and the Politics of Discourse in Cold War America* (Cambridge: MIT Press, 1998), ch. 3.

46. The systems approach was rampant at the time among military analysts, particularly in operations research. See Ghamari-Tabrizi, "Simulating the Unthinkable."

47. Walter Sullivan, "Probing Questions Too Tough for a Mere Brain," *New York Times* (December 6, 1970), 254.

48. Walter Sullivan, "Probing Questions Too Tough for a Mere Brain," *New York Times* (December 6, 1970), 254.

49. Francis Arnold, "The Compassionate Computer," *The Times* (April 1, 1972), 14.

50. Claire Sterling, "A Computer Curve to Doomsday," *Washington Post Times-Herald* (January 5, 1972), A16.

51. Forrester, "The Beginning of System Dynamics." See Jay W. Forrester, *World Dynamics* (Cambridge, MA: Wright-Allen Press, 1971).

52. Forrester, "The Beginning of System Dynamics." See Donella H. Meadows, Dennis L. Meadows, Jørgen Randers, and William W. Behrens III, *The Limits to Growth* (New York: Universe Books, 1972).

53. Francis Arnold, "The Compassionate Computer," *The Times* (April 1, 1972), 14.

54. Kenneth E. Boulding, review of *World Economic Development*, by Herman Kahn, *Economic Development and Cultural Change* 29:3 (1981), 645–49.

55. Martin Shubik, "Modeling on a Grand Scale," *Science* 174 (December 3, 1971), 1014–15.

56. Pearce Wright, "Warning on Danger of 'Computer Fetish,'" *The Times* (March 8, 1973), 4.

57. Anthony Lewis, "To Grow and to Die," *New York Times* (January 29, 1972), 29.

58. Peter Jay, "Flaws in Ecodoomsters' Arguments," *The Times* (May 31, 1972), 14.

59. William D. Nordhaus, "World Dynamics: Measurement without Data," *The Economics Journal* 83:332 (1973), 1156–83.

CHAPTER 8

1. *The Germany and the Agricola of Tacitus* (Chicago: Barnes, 1897), 122.

2. Michael Latham, *Modernization as Ideology: American Social Science and "Nation Building" in the Kennedy Era* (Chapel Hill: University of North Carolina Press, 2000).

3. R. A. Titt, "Defoliant System," February 12, 1964, UK National Archives, WO 188/2752.

4. William Buckingham, *Operation Ranch Hand: The Air Force and Herbicides in Southeast Asia 1961–1971* (Washington: Office of Air Force History, United States Air Force, 1982).

5. Buckingham, *Operation Ranch Hand.*

6. A. W. H. Wardrop, "Informal Notes for Feasibility Study on Defoliation," May 25, 1964, UK National Archives, WO 188/2752.

7. On the American effort to court the British, see G. N. Gadsby to G. E. Blackman, February 2, 1965, UK National Archives, WO 188/2752. J. L. Harley, "Geoffrey Emett Blackman," *Biographical Memoirs of Fellows of the Royal Society* 27 (1981), 45–82.

8. See especially Stuart Leslie, *The Cold War and American Science: The Military-Industrial-Academic Complex at MIT and Stanford* (New York: Columbia University Press, 1993); Rebecca Lowen, *Creating the Cold War University the Transformation of Stanford* (Berkeley: University of California Press, 1997).

9. British intelligence on American practices circa 1964 can be found in "Anti-Crop Agents," UK National Archives, WO 188/2752.

10. "Feasibility Study of NGAST—A Defoliant," n.d., UK National Archives, WO 188/2752.

11. G. D. Heath, "Work on Defoliation at ABC Weed Research Organization, Kidlington, Oxen," December 23, 1968, and "Work on Defoliation under NGAST 3138," January 6, 1969, UK National Archives, WO 188/2193.

12. David Zierler, "Inventing Ecocide: Agent Orange, Antiwar Protest, and Environmental Destruction in Vietnam." Unpublished Ph.D. dissertation, Temple University, 2008.

13. Anthony Lewis, "Death in the Abstract," *New York Times* (January 4, 1971), 31.

14. Herbert Mitgang, "Defoliation: A Dying Land—Casualty of War," *New York Times* (October 10, 1971), E2; Walter Sullivan, "Sprays in Vietnam Said to Level Fifth of Mangrove Area," *New York Times* (December 30, 1970), 1.

15. Dana Adams Schmidt, "Pentagon Disputes Study of Spraying Devastation," *New York Times* (January 9, 1971), 3.

16. "Scientists Assail Vietnam Methods," *New York Times* (August 29, 1971), 8.

17. Victor Cohn, "Army Knew of Defoliation in '67 but Crop Spraying Continued," *Washington Post* (December 31, 1970), A1.

18. Walter Sullivan, "Catastrophic Effects Reported from Defoliants in Vietnam," *International Herald Tribune* (December 31, 1970).

19. Joyce Eggington, "US Spraying Devastates Vietnam," *The Observer* (January 3, 1971).

20. On the origins of this term, see Zierler, "Inventing Ecocide," ch. 2.

21. Jonathan Tucker and Erin Mahan, *President Nixon's Decision to Renounce the U.S. Offensive Biological Weapons Program* (Washington: National Defense University Press, 2009).

22. Joshua Lederberg, "A Treaty Proposal on Germ Warfare," *Washington Post, Times Herald* (September 24, 1966), A12.

23. James K. Batten, "Germ Warfare Brews behind the Ivy," *Washington Post, Times Herald* (September 4, 1966), E3.

24. Harnwell quoted in "U. of Penn Shuns Germ War Pact," *New York Times* (November 12, 1966), 6. See also "Penn Dropping 2 War Projects; Plans for Protest are Canceled," *New York Times* (May 7, 1967), 2.

25. Brian Balmer, *Britain and Biological Warfare: Expert Advice and Science Policy, 1930–1965* (London: Palgrave Macmillan, 2001).

26. "Germ Warfare Experiments Created 'Forbidden Island,'" *New York Times* (July 18, 1966), 16.

27. G. D. Heath, "Gruinard Island," April 17, 1967, UK National Archives, WO 188/2783.

28. Zierler, "Inventing Ecocide," 259.

29. J. Brooks Flippen, *Nixon and the Environment* (Albuquerque: University of New Mexico Press, 2000).

30. Fredrik Logevall, "The Swedish-American Conflict over Vietnam," *Diplomatic History* 17:3 (1993), 421–45.

31. "NATO Joins the Fight to Save the Environment," *New York Times* (November 7, 1969), 3. Anthony Lewis, "Not with a Bang but a Gasp," *New York Times* (December 15, 1969), 46.

32. On linkage, see Robert Dallek, *Nixon and Kissinger: Partners in Power* (New York: HarperCollins, 2007).

33. The French diplomat being quoted was M. Manet. R. M. Graham to M. Gowlland, October 5, 1971, UK National Archives, FCO 55/660.

34. Sophia Lambert to Mark Gowlland, October 21, 1971, UK National Archvies, FCO 55/660.

35. F. B. Wheeler, "The NATO and a European Security Conference," October 5, 1971, UK National Archives, FCO 55/667.

36. International Institute for Environmental Affairs, *The Human Environment: Science and International Decision-Making* (1971). See also Richard N. Gardner, "The Role of the UN in Environmental Problems," *International Organization* 26:2 (1972), 237–54.

37. M. I. Rothwell to Frank Wheeler, October 20, 1971, UK National Archives, FCO 55/673.

38. M. W. Holdgate, "International Organization for the Environment," November 2, 1971, UK National Archives, FCO 55/674.

39. Eldon Griffiths, note, April 20, 1971, UK National Archives, FCO 55/658.

40. K. G. MacInnes to Ronald Arculus, July 9, 1971, UK National Archives, FCO 55/655.

41. C. H. W. Hodges to Ronald Arculus, July 2, 1971, UK National Archives, FCO 55/655.

42. Ronald Arculus, "Brussels Group Meeting on 8 July about Rationalization of International Work on the Environment," July 9, 1971, UK National Archives, FCO 55/655.

43. Arculus, "Brussels Group Meeting on 8 July," July 9, 1971.

44. Arculus, "Brussels Group Meeting on 8 July," July 9, 1971.

45. Flippen, *Nixon and the Environment*.

46. F. B. Wheeler to M. E. Rothwell, July 20, 1971, UK National Archives, FCO 55/655.

CHAPTER 9

1. "Europe and the Environment," *The Times* (April 12, 1972), I, col C.

2. XXVI Session of the General Assembly, United Nations, 11 Committee, Statement of the Brazilian Delegate Ambassador Miguel Ozo Rio de Almeida, on Item 47 of the Agenda (United National Conference on the Human Environment), November 29, 1971, UK National Archives, FCO 55/674.

3. Claire Sterling, "The U.N. and World Pollution," *Washington Post, Times Herald* (July 28, 1970), A14.

4. Kathleen Teltsch, "U.N. Aide Lays Groundwork for 1972 Environmental Conference," *New York Times* (March 30, 1970), 34.

5. Bryce Nelson, "On the Planet Polluto," *New York Times* (April 25, 1971), BR56.

6. "Ecology, Survival and Society," *Science News* 101 (February 12, 1972), 100–101.

7. Stanley Johnson, "International Control of the Pollution Explosion," *The Times* (August 12, 1971), 12.

8. Walter Sullivan, "Struggling against the Doomsday Timetable," *New York Times* (June 11, 1972), E7.

9. Sterling, "The U.N. and World Pollution."

10. Walter Orr Roberts, "Atmospheric Research: A Powerful Concept Emerges," *Science* 147:3662 (March 5, 1965), 1093–98. On the development of computer techniques in meteorology, including the importance of weather control, see Kristine C. Harper, *Weather by the Numbers: The Genesis of Modern Meteorology* (Cambridge: MIT Press, 2008).

11. On Stormfury, see Chunglin Kwa, "The Rise and Fall of Weather Modification: Changes in American Attitudes toward Technology, Nature, and Society," in Clark A. Miller and Paul N. Edwards, eds., *Changing the Atmosphere: Expert Knowledge and Environmental Governance* (Cambridge: MIT Press, 2001), 135–65. H. E. Willoughby, D. P. Jorgensen, R. A. Black, and S. L. Rosenthal, "Project STORMFURY: A Scientific Chronicle, 1962–1983," *Bulletin of the American Meteorological Society* 66:5 (1985), 505–14. On the Florida cloud-seeding, see W. Henry Lambright and Stanley A. Changdon Jr., "Arresting Technology: Government, Scientists, and Weather Modification," *Science, Technology, and Human Values* 14:4 (1989), 340–59.

12. Kwa, "The Rise and Fall of Weather Modification," 162.

13. This was first revealed in Neil Sheehan, "Vietnam Archive: Pentagon Study Traces 3 Decades of Growing U.S. Involvement," *New York Times* (June 13, 1971), 1. Further information and details are in Neil Sheehan, E. W. Kenworthy, Fox Butterfield, and Hedrick Smith, *The Pentagon Papers* (Chicago: Quadrangle Books, 1971).

14. Ronald E. Doel and Kristine C. Harper, "Prometheus Unleashed: Science as a Diplomatic Weapon in the Lyndon B. Johnson Administration," *Osiris* 21 (2006), 66–85.

15. Marvin L. Goldberger to Richard M. Nixon, March 1, 1973, *Congressional Record—Senate*, March 8, 1973, S4129.

16. Goldberger to Nixon, March 1, 1973.

17. C. J. Makins to M. St. E. Burton, March 14, 1973, A678. The "non-subject" comment is in C. M. Mason to C. J. Makins, June 13, 1973, UK National Archives, DEFE 71/101.

18. I. C. Sloane to C. M. Mason, June 22, 1973, UK National Archives, DEFE 71/101.

19. Goldberger to Nixon, March 1, 1973.

20. J. S. Sawyer, "Man-made Carbon Dioxide and the 'Greenhouse' Effect," *Nature* 239 (September 1, 1972), 23–26. The quote is from Neville Nicholls, "Climate: Sawyer Predicted Rate of Warming in 1972," *Nature* 448 (August 30, 2007), 992.

21. J. S. Sawyer to M. St. E. Burton, March 28, 1973, UK National Archives, DEFE 71/101.

22. Sawyer to Burton, March 28, 1973.

23. C. M. Mason to C. J. Makins, June 13, 1973, UK National Archives, DEFE 71/101.

24. Inga Thorsson, "Disarmament Negotiations in Deep Crisis," *Bulletin of Peace Proposals* 13:2 (1982), 73–79.

25. Mrs. Thorsson (Sweden) on 7 May CCD/PV633, UK National Archives, DEFE 71/101.

26. D. E. S. Blatherwick to D. C. Kirk, July 19, 1974, UK National Archives, DEFE 71/101.

27. A sense of the definitional ambiguity among diplomats in the summer of 1974 can be found in C. J. Makins to D. M. Summerhayes, July 11, 1974, UK National Archives, DEFE 71/101; and C. J. Makins to D. E. S. Blatherwick, July 26, 1974, UK National Archives, DEFE 71/101.

28. These quotes, as well as reflections on American attitudes, are drawn from J. A. Thomas to Miss Richards, August 9, 1974; David Kirk to I. C. Orr, August 27, 1974; Miss M. Nutting, memo on "Environmental Warfare," August 7, 1974, UK National Archives, DEFE 71/101.

29. D. B. C. Logan to D. E. S. Blatherwick, August 8, 1974, UK National Archives, DEFE 71/101.

30. Draft passage for 1975 CCD brief, "Environmental Modification," n.d., UK National Archives, DEFE 71/101.

31. V. Israelyan, "New Soviet Initiative on Disarmament," translation in UK National Archives, FCO 66/824.

32. Israelyan, "New Soviet Initiative on Disarmament."

33. Israelyan, "New Soviet Initiative on Disarmament."

34. Israelyan, "New Soviet Initiative on Disarmament."

35. J. S. Sawyer, "Environmental Modification as a Weapon of War," March 12, 1975, UK National Archives, DEFE 71/101.

36. W. J. A. Wilberforce to J. C. Edwards, March 18, 1975, UK National Archives, FCO 66/824.

37. NATO Report AC/243-D355, received April 11, 1975, UK National Archives, FCO 66/824.

38. B. G. Cartledge, note, "Call by the Soviet Ambassador on the Prime Minister," June 16, 1975, UK National Archives, FCO 66/825.

39. "Ford Signs Ban on War Herbicides," *Washington Post* (April 9, 1975), A4.

40. "Move for Weather Warfare Ban," *The Guardian* (June 25, 1975).

41. "Diverting Soviet Rivers to Prevent Flooding Might Defrost the Arctic—but What About the Weather?" New Scientist (July 10, 1975), 61.

42. D. Costes to Miss B. Richards, "ENMOD Experts Group: First Day," August 5, 1975, UK National Archives, FCO 66/825.

43. Robert Hutchinson, "How to Make Weather a War Weapon," *Daily Telegraph* (August 6, 1975).

44. David Buchan, "Warfare Experts Try to Avoid Heavy Weather," *Financial Times* (August 7, 1975).

45. "Statement by the Secretary-General, Kurt Waldheim, at the Ceremony of Opening for Signature and Ratification of the Convention on the Prohibition of Military of Other Hostile Uses of Environmental Modification Techniques," May 18, 1977, UK National Archives, DEFE 24/1066

46. D. R. Ashe to David Own (MP), May 27, 1977, UK National Archives, DEFE 24/1066

47. "US-Soviet Negotiations on Arms Limitation Resume after 'Weather Warfare' Ban is Signed," *The Times*, clipping dated May 19, 1977, UK National Archives, DEFE 24/1066

CHAPTER 10

1. Godfrey Morrison, "Rainfall and Groundnuts Dominate an Economy Demanding Effort and Ingenuity," *The Times* (April 13, 1974), II.

2. G. M., "Hope Persists Though the Springs Stay Dry," *The Times* (April 13, 1974), II.

3. Martin Walker, "Famine South of Sahara," *New York Times* (February 24, 1974), 164; Martin Walker, "Drought," *New York Times* (June 9, 1974), 245.

4. "Amin View of Drought in Britain," *The Times* (August 27, 1976), 6.

5. Walker, "Drought."

6. Speech for Delivery by His Excellency Mr. Mark Allen at an Informal Meeting of Experts on Environmental Modification, August 7, 1975, UK National Archives, FCO 66/825.

7. The CIA report is cited in Carbon Dioxide Assessment Committee of the National Research Council, "On Changing Climate," *Population and Development Review* 10:1 (1984), 161–67.

8. "USSR: The Impact of Recent Climate Change on Grain Production," Central Intelligence Agency, October 1976, available through the Freedom of Information Act, www.foia.cia.gov. Accessed on June 10, 2010.

9. "USSR: The Impact of Recent Climate Change on Grain Production," Central Intelligence Agency, October 1976.

10. Marshall A. Atwater, "Planetary Albedo Changes due to Aerosols," *Science* 170:3953 (October 2, 1970), 64–66.

11. "Gamble with the Climate," *New York Times* (August 5, 1970), 34.

12. *Global 2000 Report to the President: Entering the Twenty-First Century. Vol. 1—The Summary Report* (Washington: Council on Environmental Quality, 1980).

13. *Global 2000 Report to the President*, quotation on p. 4.

14. G. F. MacDonald, H. Abarbanel, P. Carruthers, J. Chamberlain, H. Foley, W. Munk, W. Nierenberg, O. Rothaus, M. Ruderman, J. Vesecky, and F. Zachariasen (1979). *The Long Term Impact of Atmospheric Carbon Dioxide on Climate*, JASON Technical Report JSR- 78-07, SRI International, Arlington, Virginia.

15. The short study, sometimes referred to as the "Charney report," is *Carbon Dioxide and Climate: A Scientific Assessment* (Washington: National Academy of Sciences, 1979). The sequence of events is related in Thomas C. Schelling, "Autobiography," Nobelprize.org, available at http://nobelprize.org/nobel_prizes/economics/laureates/2005/schelling-autobio.html. Accessed June 16, 2010.

16. Carbon Dioxide Assessment Committee of the National Research Council, "On Changing Climate," *Population and Development Review* 10:1 (1984), 161–67.

17. *Changing Climate: Report of the Carbon Dioxide Assessment Committee* (Washington: National Academy Press, 1983).

18. Aside from Nierenberg, the committee consisted of Roger Revelle, Lester Machta, Peter G. Brewer, William D. Nordhaus, Thomas C. Schelling, Joseph Smagorinsky, Paul E. Waggoner, and George M. Woodwell. Other scientists were involved as well with the committee's working groups.

19. The sequence of events is related in Thomas C. Schelling, "Autobiography."

20. Thomas C. Schelling, "The Strategy of Conflict: Prospectus for a Reorientation of Game Theory," *Journal of Conflict Resolution* 2:3 (1958), 203–64. Thomas C. Schelling, *The Strategy of Conflict* (Cambridge: Harvard University Press, 1960).

21. *Changing Climate*, 72.

22. This point is made repeatedly in Naomi Oreskes and Erik M. Conway, *Merchants of Doubt: How a Handful of Scientists Obscured the Truth on Issues from Tobacco Smoke to Global Warming* (New York: Bloomsbury Press, 2010).

23. *Changing Climate*, 71.

24. Naomi Oreskes, Erik M. Conway, and Matthew Shindell, "From Chicken Little to Dr. Pangloss: William Nierenberg, Global Warming, and the Social Deconstruction of Scientific Knowledge," *Historical Studies in the Natural Sciences* 38:1 (2008), 109–52. A detailed critique of Oreskes et al. is Nicolas Nierenberg, Walter R. Tschinkel, and Victoria J. Tschinkel, "Early Climate Change Consensus at the National Academy: The Origins and Making of 'Changing Climate,'" *Historical Studies in the Natural Sciences* 40 (2010): 318–49.

25. Myanna Lahsen, "Experiences of Modernity in the Greenhouse: A Cultural Analysis of a Physicist 'Trio' Supporting the Backlash against Global Warming," *Global Environmental Change* 18:1 (2008), 204–19.

26. See for examples Thomas C. Schelling, *Incentives for Environmental Protection* (Cambridge: MIT Press, 1983); Thomas C. Schelling, "Some Economics of Global Warming," *The American Economic Review* 82:1 (March 1992), 1–14.

27. These CIA references to *Changing Climate* are in "Soviet Climate Change: Implications for Grain Production," Central Intelligence Agency, May 1985, available through the Freedom of Information Act, www.foia.cia.gov. Accessed on June 10, 2010.

28. The final volume summarizes these findings and offers an interpretation based on social structures rather than climate changes. See Rolando V. Garcia and Pierre Spitz, *The Roots of Catastrophe* (New York: Pergamon Press, 1986). See also Rolando V. Garcia, *Nature Pleads Not Guilty* (New York: Pergamon Press, 1981), and Rolando V. Garcia and Jose C. Escudero, *The Constant Catastrophe* (New York: Pergamon Press, 1982).

29. William W. Kellogg and Robert Schware, "Society, Science and Climate Change," *Foreign Affairs* 60:5 (1982), 1076–109. See p. 1097.

30. Robert Schware, "The Sahel Drought: The Poverty of the Official Version," *Africa Today* 30:1/2 (1983), 107–8.

31. Directorate of Intelligence, "Ethiopia: Interference in Relief Operations," July 15, 1985, Central Intelligence Agency, available through the Freedom of Information Act, www.foia.cia.gov. Accessed on May 24, 2010.

32. Keith B. Richburg, "Swarms of Voracious Locusts Are Africa's Latest Plague," *Washington Post* (July 24, 1986), A24.

33. Blaine Harden, "Africans Stop Locusts," *Washington Post* (October 31, 1986), A18.

34. Paul Delaney, "Billions of Locusts Pose Threat to North Africa," *New York Times* (April 20, 1988), A17.

35. Robert Marantz Henig, "AIDS: A New Disease's Deadly Odyssey," *New York Times* (February 6, 1983), SM28.

36. Gwyn Prins, "AIDS and Global Security," *International Affairs* 80:5 (2004), 931–52.

37. Henig, "AIDS."

38. Philip M. Boffey, "Federal Efforts on AIDS Criticized as Gravely Weak," *New York Times* (October 30, 1986), A1.

39. R. R. Redfield, D. C. Wright, W. D. James, T. S. Jones, C. Brown, and D. S. Burke, "Disseminated Vaccinia in a Military Recruit with Human Immunodeficiency Virus (HIV) Disease," *New England Journal of Medicine* 316:11 (March 12, 1987), 673–76. Pearce Wright, "Smallpox Vaccine 'Triggered Aids Virus,'" *The Times* (May 11, 1987). This claim was largely forgotten until 2010, when researchers made a related, but slightly different claim: that the smallpox vaccine actually had helped to suppress HIV, and the vaccine's absence after 1980 had paved a path for AIDS. See Steve Connor, "Smallpox Vaccine 'Helped Fight HIV,'" *The Independent* (London) (May 19, 2010), 16.

40. Lawrence K. Altman, "Linking AIDS to Africa Provokes Bitter Debate," *New York Times* (November 21, 1985), A1.

41. Zhores A. Medvedev, "AIDS Virus Infection: A Soviet View of Its Origin," *Journal of the Royal Society of Medicine* 79 (1986), 494.

42. John Seale, reply to Zhores A. Medvedev, *Journal of the Royal Society of Medicine* 79 (1986), 494–95.

43. "USSR: BW Accident Exposed," September 4, 1990, Central Intelligence Agency, available through the Freedom of Information Act, www.foia.cia.gov. Accessed on May 24, 2010. On the Aralsk plague, see "Possible BW Accident in USSR?" September 21, 1990, Central Intelligence Agency, available through the Freedom of Information Act, www.foia.cia.gov. Accessed on May 24, 2010.

44. "Sub-Saharan Africa: Implications of the AIDS Pandemic," SNIE 70/1-87, June 2, 1987, Central Intelligence Agency, available through the Freedom of Information Act, www.foia.cia.gov. Accessed on May 24, 2010.

45. Quoted in Herbert Romerstein, "Disinformation as a KGB Weapon in the Cold War," *Journal of Intelligence History* 1:1 (2001), 54–67, p. 60.

46. "Sub-Saharan Africa: Implications of the AIDS Pandemic," SNIE 70/1-87, June 2, 1987.

47. Lawrence Badash, *A Nuclear Winter's Tale: Science and Politics in the 1980s* (Cambridge: MIT Press, 2009).

48. See Oreskes and Conway, *Merchants of Doubt*, 54–59. See also www.marshall.org.

49. "The Soviet Approach to Nuclear Winter," NI IIA 84-10006, Director of Central Intelligence, December 1984, available at www.foia.cia.gov. Accessed May 24, 2010.

50. Directorate of Intelligence, "Total Soviet Computing Power," September 1986, Central Intelligence Agency, available at www.foia.cia.gov. Accessed on May 27, 2010.

51. "The Soviet Approach to Nuclear Winter," December 1984.

52. This quote is drawn from an April 27, 1984, issue of *Soviet Panorama* but is quoted here from "The Soviet Approach to Nuclear Winter," December 1984.

53. On Budyko's attitudes, see "The Soviet Approach to Nuclear Winter," December 1984. On Budyko's scientific ideas, see Mott T. Greene, "Arctic Sea Ice, Oceanography, and Climate Models," in Keith R. Benson and Helen

M. Rozwadowski, eds., *Extremes: Oceanography's Adventures at the Poles* (Saga-more Beach: Science History Publications, 2007), 303–29.
54. "The Soviet Approach to Nuclear Winter," December 1984.

CONCLUSION

1. Stephen Kierulff, "Belief in 'Armageddon Theory' and Willingness to Risk Nu-clear War," *Journal for the Scientific Study of Religion* 30:1 (1991), 84.
2. Hugh Gusterson, "Nuclear Weapons and the Other in the Western Imagina-tion," *Cultural Anthropology* 14:1 (1999), 111–43. See p. 128.
3. Matthew M. Aid, "Declassification in Reverse: the U.S. Intelligence Community's Secret Historical Document Reclassification Program," available online at The National Security Archive, www.gwu.edu/~nsarchiv/NSAEBB/NSAEBB179/. Accessed on December 1, 2010.
4. On the issues raised, see Ronald E. Doel, "Scientists as Policymakers, Advisors, and Intelligence Agents: Linking Contemporary Diplomatic History with the History of Contemporary Science," in Thomas Söderquist, ed., *The Historiog-raphy of Contemporary Science and Technology* (Amsterdam: Harwood, 1997), 215–44; and John Krige, "Atoms for Peace, Scientific Internationalism, and Sci-entific Intelligence," *Osiris* 21 (2006), 161–81.
5. David K. van Keuren, "Cold War Science in Black and White: U.S. Intelligence Gathering and its Scientific Cover at the Naval Research Laboratory, 1948–62," *Social Studies of Science* 31 (2001), 207–29.
6. Naomi Oreskes, "A Context of Motivation: U.S. Navy Oceanographic Research and the Discovery of Sea-Floor Hydrothermal Vents," *Social Studies of Science* 33:5 (2003), 697–742.
7. Kevin C. Ruffner, ed., *Corona: America's First Satellite Program* (Washington: CIA, 1995).
8. John Cloud, "Imaging the World in a Barrel: CORONA and the Clandestine Convergence of the Earth Sciences," *Social Studies of Science* 31:2 (2001), 231–51.
9. Jeffrey Mervis, "Panel of Scientists Helps Open Lid on Secret Images," *Science* 286:5437 (October 1, 1999), 34.
10. Walter Munk, Naomi Oreskes, and Richard Muller, "Gordon James Fraser Mac-donald, 1930–2002," in *Biographical Memoirs* (Washington: National Academies Press, 2004), 225–49.
11. Thomas C. Schelling, "Autobiography," Nobelprize.org. Available at http://nobelprize.org/nobel_prizes/economics/laureates/2005/schelling-autobio.html.
12. Fiona Godlee, "Rio Diary: A Fortnight at the Earth Summit," *British Medical Journal* 305: 6845 (1992), 102–5.
13. The strategy is pointed out in Oreskes and Conway, *Merchants of Doubt*, 251–55.
14. Albert Gore, *Earth in the Balance: Ecology and the Human Spirit* (Boston: Hough-ton Mifflin, 1992); Albert Gore, *Earth in the Balance: Forging a New Common Purpose* (London: Earthscan, 1992).

15. Gore, *Earth in the Balance*, 272.
16. Robert W. Hahn, "Toward a New Environmental Paradigm," *Yale Law Journal* 102:7 (1993), 1719–61. See p. 1720.
17. Alex Kozinski, "Gore Wars," *Michigan Law Review* 100:6 (2002), 1742–67.
18. Myanna Lahsen, "Technocracy, Democracy, and U.S. Climate Politics: The Need for Demarcations," *Science, Technology & Human Values* 30:1 (2005), 137–69.
19. Lahsen, "Technocracy, Democracy, and U.S. Climate Politics," quote on p. 146.
20. Bjørn Lomborg, The Skeptical Environmentalist: Measuring the Real State of the World (New York: Cambridge University Press, 2001).

Index